BLUE-CHIP BLACK

Title Withdrawn

JUL 26 2007

THE GEORGE GUND FOUNDATION
IMPRINT IN AFRICAN AMERICAN STUDIES

The George Gund Foundation has endowed
this imprint to advance understanding of
the history, culture, and current issues
of African Americans.

Blue-Chip Black

Race, Class, and Status in the New
Black Middle Class

KARYN R. LACY

UNIVERSITY OF CALIFORNIA PRESS   Berkeley   Los Angeles   London

University of California Press, one of the most distinguished university presses in the United States, enriches
lives around the world by advancing scholarship in the
humanities, social sciences, and natural sciences. Its activities are supported by the UC Press Foundation and
by philanthropic contributions from individuals and institutions. For more information, visit
www.ucpress.edu.

A portion of chapter 5 appeared previously in "Black
Spaces, Black Places: Strategic Assimilation and Identity Construction in Middle-Class Suburbia," *Ethnic
and Racial Studies* 27, no. 6 (2004): 908–30,
http://www.tandf.co.uk/journals. Portions of the book
also appeared earlier in " 'A Part of the Neighborhood?': Negotiating Race in American Suburbs," *International Journal of Sociology and Public Policy* 22
(2002): 39–74, http:/www.emeraldinsight.com/info/
journals/ijssp/notes.jsp.

University of California Press
Berkeley and Los Angeles, California

University of California Press, Ltd.
London, England

© 2007 by The Regents of the University of California

Library of Congress Cataloging-in-Publication Data

Lacy, Karyn, [date–].
    Blue-chip Black : race, class, and status in the new
Black middle class / Karyn Lacy.
        p.   cm.
    Includes bibliographical references and index.
    ISBN: 978-0-520-25115-1 (cloth : alk. paper)
    ISBN: 978-0-520-25116-8 (pbk. : alk. paper)
        1. African Americans—Social conditions—1975—
Case studies.   2. African Americans—Race identity—
Case studies.   3. Middle class—United States—Case
studies.   4. Social status—United States—Case studies.
5. United States—Race relations—Case studies.   6.
African Americans—Washington Region—Social con-
ditions.   7. African Americans—Race identity—
Washington Region.   8. Middle class—Washington
Region.   9. Social status—Washington Region.   10.
Washington Region—Race relations.   I. Title.

E185.86.L325   2007
305.896'0730722—dc22   2006025496

Manufactured in the United States of America

15   14   13   12   11   10   09   08   07
10   9   8   7   6   5   4   3   2   1

This book is printed on New Leaf EcoBook 50, a
100% recycled fiber of which 50% is de-inked post-
consumer waste, processed chlorine-free. EcoBook 50
is acid-free and meets the minimum requirements of
ANSI/ASTM D5634-01 (*Permanence of Paper*).

To Leanita McClain
May you find rest for your soul

Contents

Illustrations

Preface

When *The Cosby Show,* a sitcom featuring the Huxtables, a fictional upper-middle-class black family, was introduced by NBC, it was criticized by some despite its widespread popularity among both black and white viewers because, its detractors argued, it did not accurately depict America's black middle class. Cosby's television family did not at any time experience financial constraints, face racial discrimination, abuse drugs, experience teenage pregnancy, or negotiate neighborhood crime the way many blacks, even those who are middle class, do. Indeed, the Huxtables seemed to live a life more in sync with the white upper class than with other blacks. According to some, the show was valuable precisely because it "project[ed] universal values that both whites and blacks could identify with."[1]

To be sure, most black Americans do not live like the Huxtables. Most blacks are not affluent; they are not doctors and lawyers who occupy prime New York real estate and send their children to elite private colleges. Only 9 percent of the black population is made up people much like Cosby's fictional family—black professionals who earn more than fifty thousand dollars annually. The fact that this group represents a small segment of the black population, however, doesn't diminish the need for greater recognition of the conflicts and challenges associated with membership in the black middle class. Blacks who "make it" in this country do so against a backdrop of ongoing racial discrimination and persistent black poverty, coupled with the pervasive influence of hip-hop culture—a variant of "success" that circumvents the assimilationist path toward upward mobility. Often, discussions of these tensions end up as politicized debates about how blacks are treated by others, not how blacks treat those they encounter along the road to success. We know far more about the structural constraints facing middle-class blacks than we do about cultural conflicts and about how these blacks conceive of their own position in American society.

What it means to be middle class and black in a country obsessed with race, a country in which blackness is conflated with poverty and the public face of the middle class is a white face, is the focus of this book. More specifically, this study compares and contrasts the ways in which black residents of three middle-class suburbs in the Washington metropolitan area—one that is predominantly white, another that is predominantly black, and yet another that is predominantly black and upper middle class—think about and try to live out their identities as black people in America. This is yet another sense in which the blacks depicted in this study are atypical. Most middle-class blacks live in predominantly black suburbs that are not uniformly middle class; the majority do not live in predominantly white suburbs or distinctly middle-class black ones. Yet, as more blacks attain a middle-class status, there is reason to believe that the suburban communities I studied will become less and less exceptional over time.

When I began this study, I was interested in understanding how middle-class blacks, who presumably earn enough to live wherever they want, end up in either a predominantly white or a predominantly black neighborhood. Had middle-class blacks living in heavily black communities been "steered" there? Were middle-class blacks in majority white neighborhoods living among whites who shared their middle-class status? Encompassing the inner suburbs of Maryland and Virginia as well as "the District," the Washington, D.C., metropolitan area is an ideal place to explore questions about the housing decisions of middle-class blacks. On the one hand, like many urban centers on the East Coast, Washington, D.C., houses a largely black, racially isolated, poor population. The black poor are confined primarily to the southeast section of the city, notorious for its relentless support of four-term Washington mayor Marion Barry.[2] On the other hand, D.C. stands apart from most East Coast cities because those living in the counties surrounding the city are often middle-class and, at least on the Maryland side, distinctly black. As a result, middle-class blacks seeking a suburban home in the Washington area choose from a host of equally attractive suburbs that vary widely in terms of their racial composition. Moreover, suburban communities are enormously popular among black middle-class families. At the time of this study, the Washington metropolitan area boasted the highest rate of black suburbanization in the nation, just ahead of Atlanta.[3]

I learned quickly, however, that the process of finding housing was not what my subjects wanted most to talk about. They saw their housing decisions as relatively straightforward: find a place that you like, buy it, and move in. Instead, again and again, the same theme emerged: middle-class blacks on one side of the Potomac River were critical of blacks who lived on the other side. In Prince George's County, Maryland, where I began my data collection, I heard from some black residents, "You're going to interview blacks in Fairfax County? Black people don't live in Fairfax County!"—meaning that, in their opinion, *authentically* black people don't live in white neighborhoods. From some blacks in Fairfax County, Virginia, I heard, "You've been interviewing blacks in PG County? They don't know anything about the real world. Their neighborhoods are all black." Thus, early on in the study, I discovered that middle-class blacks were engaging in a practice that had been relatively neglected in the existing literature on identity construction: defining themselves by erecting distinctions not only against the black poor but also against other members of the black middle class. Intuitively, it makes sense that middle-class blacks would not all think the same way about their lives. Yet few studies have explored variation within the black middle class in their construction of racial identities or in other aspects of their identity.

For many years, sociologists concerned with the social construction of race argued that, unlike contemporary white ethnics who engage selectively in symbolic expressions of their ethnicity, blacks are not in a position to choose how and under what circumstances to identify racially. These studies suggested that black racial identities were fixed and invariant.[4] Subsequent studies outlined the identity options available to multiracial individuals and black immigrants to the United States;[5] however, few studies have explored the variety of identities available to native-born blacks. The ongoing assumption was that native-born blacks have undergone cultural assimilation or acculturation, but racial discrimination and labeling impedes their structural assimilation, that is, integration into mainstream institutions and social clubs. Many of the middle-class blacks in this study attended white colleges, some live in white neighborhoods, and others work in predominantly white environments. Their experiences suggest that even though structural assimilation has not occurred for the black masses, it has occurred for some subsets of the black population. Do their assimilation trajectories and class location allow middle-class blacks to decide when and where to identify racially?

In American society and in the sociological literature, there is now considerable debate over the ways that middle-class status does or does not facilitate the negotiation of black racial identities. Some sociological studies perceive race as a "master status," suggesting that a black racial identity often overshadows any potential alternative identities, even when an individual is middle class. According to this perspective, while many middle-class blacks can afford to eat in fine restaurants, vacation in luxury hotels, and buy homes in exclusive neighborhoods, there is still a high probability that they will experience racial discrimination and labeling. This kind of racial stigmatization is most likely to occur in public settings when middle-class blacks encounter whites who know little about them and assess black individuals on the basis of the characteristic that is most readily apparent—race.[6] From this perspective, race defines the black experience. Other studies suggest that some middle-class blacks are in a better position to manage their racial identities than others. One of these studies, conducted in a workplace environment, reports that black executives who deliberately assert a class-based identity are less likely to experience racial stigmatization than those who do not.[7] This perspective suggests that class may shape the lives of middle-class blacks more concretely than previous studies have acknowledged.

While both of these approaches have been useful in understanding the complexities of the black middle-class experience, not enough attention has been paid to variability in the construction of racial identities across a variety of contexts, ranging from public to private, and in other aspects of their identities. Too often, people forget that most middle-class blacks don't function exclusively in a racially distinct environment. Instead, they routinely move back and forth between the black world and the white world. Some of the time, these middle-class blacks find themselves in settings where they are compelled to self-identify as black. At other times, they find themselves in settings where race is less salient, settings where they push alternative identities to the foreground. Among the middle-class blacks in this study, race is not the master status that some scholars have made it out to be. Members of other racial groups may think of blacks as simply black, but some blacks—middle-class blacks in particular—conceive of a more nuanced social identity for themselves.

Blue-Chip Black examines how middle-class blacks construct and maintain five distinct social identities housed in a "tool kit" of social identities and chronicles their practices of choosing from this tool kit under different circumstances. I conducted in-depth interviews with thirty black middle-class couples and carried out ethnographic observation in three suburban communities in the Washington metropolitan area that vary in terms of their racial composition and socioeconomic status: a majority white middle-class suburb, which I call Lakeview; a predominantly black middle-class suburb known here as Riverton; and a majority black upper-middle-class suburb located within Riverton's borders, which I refer to as Sherwood Park. I found that middle-class black families in each of these communities make different choices about how and when to employ any one of the identities housed in the black middle-class tool kit. These choices vary according to the families' residential location, their economic stability, and their proximity to other racial groups.

By examining the identity construction processes of middle-class blacks in different residential locations, I draw attention to persistent divisions within the black middle class itself, an under-studied form of stratification that has significant implications for our understanding of racial and class-based inequality. Scholars have shown very effectively that the intersection of race and class matters in the accumulation of wealth, in the distribution of good jobs in the labor market, in the acquisition of desirable housing, and in the workplace. I argue that the race-class intersection also influences the identity options of individuals and is a key force in shaping how middle-class black people define themselves, who they identify with, and who they reject as unlike them. This book reveals how different groups of middle-class blacks make their identity choices.

Acknowledgments

Early on in this project, I learned that middle-class blacks think of their lives in terms of many social identities, and that race is not the most salient identity at all times, but it took me a long time to state this finding definitively. Mary Waters, one of my dissertation committee members, wrote a provocative book titled *Ethnic Options,* in which she argues that blacks don't have any choice but to identify as black. The narrow way that physical characteristics associated with blacks are socially defined and infused with meaning by the dominant group limits blacks to a black racial identity. Although I had come to a different conclusion, I worried that my disagreement would be offensive to her. So in my dissertation presentation, I tried to present my findings without saying that the data challenged her early work. During the question-and-answer period, Mary called me on my tactics, saying, "Karyn, just say I was wrong." This book is the result of Mary's willingness to have her students challenge and build on her work.

I am grateful too to Larry Bobo, Gwen Dordick, and Christopher Winship for their helpful advice and encouragement. Larry listened and offered guidance but left framing decisions up to me. Gwen taught me how to conduct ethnographic research and to trust my intuition about social behavior. As my advisor, Chris raised the "big picture" questions that helped me to iron out the wrinkles in this study. He also read and commented on my first manuscript draft. I benefited enormously from his willingness to delve into literature well beyond the boundaries of his own research interests.

I am also indebted to Katherine Newman and Michele Lamont, who, though they did not serve officially as committee members, contributed to the final product in innumerable ways. Michele read an early draft and commented with considerable enthusiasm. Kathy started me on my way with sound advice about my research design. Months later, she scrutinized my first draft of chapter 3. Kathy possesses an uncanny ability to comment with just the right amount of constructive criticism coupled with encouragement. I thank both Kathy and Michele for urging me on.

I was very fortunate to come across so many colleagues and friends who were willing to spend precious time reading early drafts of this book. I'm grateful to Xavier de Souza Briggs, Nancy DiTomaso, Timothy Dowd, Charles Gallagher, Brian Gratton, Alex Hicks, Pamela Smock, Sidney Tarrow, Mario Small, Karolyn Tyson, and George Wilson for detailed comments on one or more chapters. I owe an enormous debt to Annette Lareau. Annette read the entire manuscript at a critical moment, the point at which I believed I was done. She let me know that I was not and offered a mountain of feedback that helped me to reach the end of this impossibly long process. Just as important, Annette is a dedicated mentor, generous with her time and advice about how to negotiate the academic world. For thought-provoking conversations about the book, I thank Robert Adelman, Dalton Conley, Mitch Duneier, Sam Fulwood, David Laitin, Ezell Lundy, Reuben May, Kim Williams, and Julia Wrigley. Thanks to Elijah Anderson for always making time for me, to Ingrid Banks for help with verifying references, and to Katherine Mooney for editorial assistance.

Scholars who attended the talks I gave at the following institutions provided critical feedback that helped to strengthen the book's argument: Brown University, CUNY Graduate Center, Duke University, Emory University, Northwestern University, New York University, Princeton University, the University of California at Berkeley, the University of Pennsylvania, and the University of Virginia. While I was inspired by these lively exchanges, I cannot claim that each one of the wrinkles raised by the members of these audiences has been ironed out; I assume full responsibility for any remaining conceptual lapses.

This book wouldn't have become a reality without help from some very generous people and funding institutions. I thank the men and women featured in this book for letting me into their homes and their lives. I wish that I could thank them here one by one, but my assurance that I would maintain their anonymity does not allow me to do so. My hope is that they know how much I appreciate their sacrifices of their time and privacy. Old and new friends in the Washington area made it possible for me to use my time productively. Sam Fulwood started me on my way by introducing me to the right people and helped me to reach the finish line: the book's title emerged from my conversations with him. Jena Roscoe shared her home and her social networks. She also provided sanity breaks from this project. Eric and Cecilia Williams took me out for pizza and, along with their daughter, Maya, provided a space to talk about something other than sociology. Lisa Cannon made collecting data in D.C. a lot of fun. She introduced me to Eric Shoaf, who took the beautiful black-and-white photos of the suburban communities. Roderick Harrison helped me to narrow down a suitable Fairfax County site using census data, offered an insider's perspective on life in the Washington metropolitan area, and didn't get upset when I kept calling him with more questions. The Harvard Graduate Society provided a research fellowship that covered a good chunk of the data collection. A postdoctoral fellowship from the Ford Foundation allowed me to transform the data into a book.

Working with the editors at the University of California Press has been an extraordinarily rewarding experience. As a first-time book author, I made many mistakes. To my great relief, they have not been fatal. Naomi Schneider believed in this project from the start and managed somehow to maintain her enthusiasm even though it took me a lot longer to complete this book than I thought it would. Thanks also to Valerie Witte and to Jacqueline Volin, who kept the book on track throughout the production process. My thanks to the press's anonymous reviewers, whose careful reading of the manuscript and instructive feedback led to many changes, all for the better. France Winddance Twine made her identity known to me as one of the University of California Press's reviewers. I'm indebted to her for her contributions to my work and for her unbridled support of the book.

I started writing this book when I was a faculty member at Emory University and completed it when I moved to the University of Michigan. I appreciate the support I received from my colleagues in the Sociology and African-American Studies Departments at Emory. The administrative staff in sociology—Cathy David, Daphne Outlaw, and Maggie Stephens—made almost everything about beginning a new faculty position effortless. Leslie Martin, a graduate student in sociology, collected the data on rates of black suburbanization using the census and the American Housing Survey. My colleagues in sociology and the Center for Afro-American and African Studies at the University of Michigan have made my new university home a wonderful place to be. I can only begin to thank my chairs, Howard Kimeldorf, James Jackson, and Kevin Gaines, for granting me the leave time necessary to finish this book. Alford Young and Karin Martin are spectacular mentors. I'm grateful to Angel Harris for all the long hours he logged working with the census to generate the data that appear in the tables of this book.

I dedicate this book to Leanita McClain, the first black person appointed to the editorial board of the *Chicago Tribune*. McClain never felt comfortable with her ascension from the Ida B. Wells housing project to the ranks of the solidly upper-middle class. In a moving collection of her newspaper columns, *A Foot in Each World*, McClain's ex-husband, Clarence Page, suggests growing polarization between the black poor and middle class was more than mere theory to her. McClain worried that the poor black community of her youth—where many of her relatives still lived—resented her success. She worried, too, that many whites, for an altogether different set of reasons, would never fully accept her. Feeling alienated from poor blacks and upper-middle-class whites, McCain suggests in her columns that she didn't fit in anywhere. The enormous burden of having to constantly negotiate the demands of the black and white worlds exhausted her, and on a cold, rainy spring day in 1984, McClain took her own life. She was thirty-two.

My family believed this book would materialize even during the times when I doubted that it could actually happen. I thank my parents, Thomas and Janice Lacy, and my sister, Kim Lacy Johnson, for support that is unceasing. My grandmother, Phyllis Stallings, read this book way back when it existed only as a jargon-filled dissertation, calling me long distance each time she came across a quote that she especially liked. It was difficult to conduct this research on a graduate student's budget. Thanks to my uncle, Michael Lacy, and my aunt, Janet Gardner, for opening their homes to me when I really, really, really needed a place to stay. Kenneth Johnson Jr., my nephew, helps me to keep up with popular culture, lets me know when I'm out of style, and is simply a great kid.

Introduction

They're trying to be like the whites instead of being who they are," Andrea Creighton, a forty-three-year-old information analyst with the federal government, told me when I asked whether she believed blacks had made it in the United States or still had a long way to go. Andrea is black, and she perceives irrepressible distinctions between middle-class blacks and whites, even though many aspects of her life appear to reflect membership in the suburban middle-class mainstream. She and her husband, Greg, have two teenage children: a girl, age seventeen, and a boy, age fifteen. They have lived on a quiet street in Sherwood Park, an upper-middle-class suburb of Washington, D.C., for seven years. Their four-bedroom home is an imposing red-brick-front colonial with shiny black shutters, nestled on an acre of neatly manicured lawn. The children are active members of the local soccer team, and Greg is one of the team's coaches. Andrea and her husband each drive midsize cars and have provided their daughter, who is old enough to drive unaccompanied by an adult, with her own car. At first blush, they seem nearly identical to their white middle-class counterparts. But unlike the nearly all-white neighborhood that the average middle-class white family calls home, the Creightons' upscale subdivision is predominantly black. Andrea and Greg are pleased that their children are growing up in a community filled with black professionals. The Creightons' residence in Sherwood Park is one indication of the kind of social differentiation Andrea employs to define her identity as a member of the black middle class. Though she shares many lifestyle characteristics with mainstream whites, she feels that middle-class blacks are not mirror images of middle-class whites, nor should they aspire to be.

Middle-class, distinctly black suburban communities like Andrea's are rare in the United States, but Andrea's inclination to define middle-class blacks in relation to their white middle-class counterparts is not. Middle-class black and white families are assumed to be different, and an established body of evidence supports this perception, suggesting that racial disparities in key indicators of middle-class status—wealth, housing, and income—perpetuate glaring inequities between blacks and whites, even when the individuals occupy the same class.[1] But peering into Andrea's world reveals that some aspects of everyday life are similar for all middle-class people, regardless of race. That is, some middle-class blacks live in highly desirable neighborhoods, others have enrolled their children in exclusive private schools, still others work in predominantly white professional environments, and some have never had to endure economic hardship. The pool of class-based resources available to Andrea's family and others like hers suggest that there are two distinct groups of middle-class blacks in American society: the fragile black lower-middle class, a group that falls behind the white middle class on key measures of middle-class status; and the stable black middle class, a group that is virtually indistinguishable from its white counterpart on most standard economic indicators.[2]

Lower-middle-class blacks, the focus of most contemporary sociological studies on the black middle class, have very little in common with the white middle class. As a group, they typically earn less than fifty thousand dollars annually, do not hold college degrees, and are concentrated in sales or clerical positions rather than white-collar occupations. In this way, the black lower-middle class resembles the "blue-collar middle class" that emerged in Detroit as a direct result of the tremendous expansion of the auto industry.[3] Moreover, as recent ethnographies show, lower-middle-class blacks often live in racially segregated neighborhoods that are either inclusive of the black poor or contiguous with chronically poor black neighborhoods. Within these distressed black communities, lower-middle-class blacks typically live with high crime rates, poor municipal services, and underperforming schools. For these reasons, sociologist Mary Pattillo understandably characterizes the black lower-middle class in her book *Black Picket Fences* as separate from and unequal to the white middle class.[4]

Without a doubt, the black middle class is bottom-heavy, and lower-middle-class blacks concentrated at the bottom of this class structure may find themselves clinging by a frayed thread to a fledgling middle-class status. As the data in table 1 show, in 2000, lower-middle class blacks (those who earned between $30,000 and $49,999 annually) made up the majority (65 percent) of the black middle class. At the same time, a completely different group of middle-class blacks exists, one whose socioeconomic circumstances more closely resemble the white middle class. Members of this second group of middle-class blacks work as doctors, lawyers, accountants, engineers, and corporate managers, occupations that require at least a bachelor's degree. These blacks, who earned more than $50,000 annually, made up 35 percent of the black middle class in 2000, and they are the focus of this book. In terms of sheer numbers, this group, composed of high-earning middle-class blacks, mirrors its white counterpart in the same income category, which constituted 47 percent of the white middle class in 2000.

Middle-class blacks at the top of the black class structure do not experience a middle-class lifestyle in the same way that those at the bottom do. The middle-class black subdivisions in the suburbs of Washington, D.C., that I studied do not contain poor residents, nor do these communities suffer from the relentless social and economic maladies that plague poor communities. In terms of occupational status, educational attainment, income, and housing, the top segment of the black middle class is equal to the white middle class. The key distinction between the white and black middle classes is thus a matter of degree. Middle-class whites fit the public image of the middle class and may therefore take their middle-class status for granted, but blacks who have "made it" must work harder, more deliberately, and more consistently to make their middle-class status known to others.

This book explores how different groups of middle-class blacks go about doing this work of fitting in by examining the symbolic boundaries they erect between themselves and white strangers, the white middle class, and blacks from other classes to establish and sustain a black middle-class identity. The book addresses the following questions: What distinct identities are constructed and maintained by the black middle class? How do different groups of middle-class blacks vary in their use of these identities? In terms of their access to cultural and

TABLE 1. GRADATIONS OF MIDDLE-CLASS INCOMES, 2000

Annual Income	Whites				Blacks			
	Percentage of Men	Percentage of Women	Percentage of White Population	Percentage of White Middle-Class Population	Percentage of Men	Percentage of Women	Percentage of Black Population	Percentage of Black Middle-Class Population
Lower-Middle-Class Incomes								
$30,000–$49,999	24	16	20	53	20	15	17	65
Middle-Class Incomes								
$50,000–$99,999	19	8	14	37	12	6	8	31
Upper-Middle-Class Incomes								
$100,000 and above	6	1	4	10	1.5	0.5	1	4

SOURCE: U.S. Census Bureau, Current Population Survey (PINC-02, Part 25 and Part 49).

economic resources, are middle and upper-class blacks more like their white counterparts than they are like lower-class blacks?

To understand the different types of social identity that middle-class blacks construct and how they vary among individuals and across contexts, I conducted in-depth interviews with thirty black middle-class couples and complemented these interviews with participant observation in three different middle-class suburban communities. I spent time doing the things that residents of these communities do in their everyday lives: attending church, Parent-Teacher Association meetings, homeowner association meetings, block parties, and political meetings. The first community, Lakeview, is a majority-white middle-class suburban tract in predominantly white Fairfax County, Virginia. In 1990, Lakeview was 4 percent black, 31 percent of its residents were professionals, 44 percent had bachelor's or more advanced degrees, the median family income was $78,907, and the median monthly mortgage payment was $1,242. The second community, Riverton, is a predominantly black suburban tract in mostly black Prince George's County, Maryland. In 1990, Riverton was 65 percent black, 21 percent of its residents were professionals, 23 percent had bachelor's or more advanced degrees, the median family income was $66,144, and the median monthly mortgage payment was $1,212. The third community, Sherwood Park, is a majority-black upper-middle-class suburban community located within Riverton. This exclusive ten-year-old subdivision is 85 percent black, 90 percent of its residents are college-educated professionals, the median family income is $117,000, and the median monthly mortgage payment is $2,128. The mean individual income for the entire sample is $72,000. Riverton respondents separate Sherwood Park from the other Riverton subdivisions; therefore, I report my findings in the context of three suburban communities rather than two.

Most of *Blue-Chip Black* focuses on differences by residential location in how middle-class blacks think about and make use of their social identities. Whereas middle-class blacks from all three suburban communities characterize their encounters with white strangers in public settings and their strategies for managing these interactions similarly, in other contexts their conceptions of what it means to be black and middle class vary widely, from perceptions of economic stability, to the optimal way to prepare black children to traverse the color line, to attitudes about the collective interests of their respective communities.

STUDYING SOCIAL IDENTITIES IN BLACK COMMUNITIES

In recent years, scholars have published a number of informative community-based studies that examine the life experiences of the black middle class, marking the end of a long period of inattention to this group. However, this is the first study to focus specifically on the set of distinct identities that different groups of middle-class blacks construct and use in their everyday lives in both the public sphere and their suburban communities. Scholars who have conducted ethnographic studies of black communities have done a great deal to fill enormous gaps in our understanding of how middle-class blacks conceive of their place in American society since Frazier's scathing indictment of the group in the 1957 classic *Black Bourgeoisie* and Bart Landry's notable study of the growth and culture of the black middle class published in 1987. The ethnographers Stephen Gregory, Mary Pattillo, John Jackson, Monique Taylor, and Bruce Haynes have all focused attention on the complex ways in which middle-class blacks manage their lives in black neighborhoods. However, their studies present the black middle class as if the group is undifferentiated, that is to say, composed of people who think similarly about their place in American society relative to other groups above and below them on the class ladder.

One limitation of these existing ethnographic studies of the black middle class is that each focuses on a single black community, one that is not uniformly middle class but inclusive of the black working class and, in some cases, the black poor. These case studies are mainly concerned with how a distressed black community context shapes the lives of its middle-class residents. As the studies demonstrate, because their samples of middle-class blacks share community space with lower-class blacks, the middle-class population define their identities primarily in relation to the black lower classes. But a single-site research design does not shed light on how the identities constructed by different groups of middle-class blacks vary according to the specificities of their distinct community context. The present study's multi-site design contrasts three suburban communities that vary in terms of their racial and class composition. Indeed, by focusing on three middle-class communities where poor blacks are not present, I show that difference in residence has a significant effect on how middle-class blacks perceive themselves and others. This methodological contribution sets *Blue-Chip Black* apart from existing studies of the black middle class.

A second limitation of recent ethnographic studies of the black middle class is that not a single work focuses on a southern community. This is surprising given the growing economic and social importance of the South. Demographers note that "an unusually robust economy" in the Southeast accounts for a significant chunk of the country's economic growth during the 1990s. Industries such as manufacturing that experienced declines in the United States overall grew and in some cases expanded in the Southeast. Other industries that grew slowly in the United States overall, such as services, expanded rapidly in the Southeast. Strong economic growth in the region has contributed to a return migration already in progress. Both the white and black populations are increasing in the South.[5] The promise of steady employment has also lured Latino immigrants to the South in large numbers. Mary Waters and Tomas Jimenez refer to southern cities in states such as North Carolina and Georgia (in which the immigrant population has grown by 273.7 percent and 233.4 percent respectively) as "gateway cities," new ports of first-time entry for immigrants.[6] Defined for so long by the black-white boundary, the Southeast is well on its way to becoming one of the most multiracial regions of the country. Through its attention to the impact of a southern black community context on identity, this study provides a point of comparison for existing studies of northern black communities and contributes to the growing dialogue on the increasing importance of the South.

A third limitation of studies focused on the black middle class is that they fail to address variations among middle-class black *parents* in terms of how they socialize their children. Scholars have not paid sufficient attention to variations among middle-class black parents, who are concerned not only with negotiating their own social identities but also with nurturing a black middle class identity among their children. The ways in which parents accomplish this goal are conspicuously absent from the sociological literature. In their revealing glimpses into the lives of lower-middle-class and poor blacks, Mary Pattillo and Elijah Anderson document the grave concerns of black parents who face formidable obstacles in their efforts to raise upstanding citizens. Yet the parents' escalating fears are specific to the demands of their distressed urban neighborhoods; they do not reflect the concerns of more privileged, suburban, middle-class blacks.

Annette Lareau's sensitively rendered ethnographic exploration of how black and white parents from different class locations communicate class position to their children makes abundantly clear the hidden processes through which black children acquire a middle-class identity;

however, her study does not reveal significant differences in parenting ideologies across race. Lareau finds that black and white middle-class parents adopt the same type of cultural logic as a framework for raising their children. She writes of an upper-middle-class black child in her sample:

> The fact that Alexander is a young African American male also shaped various aspects of his life in important ways. He belonged to an all-Black church, and he had regular opportunities to form friendships with other Black children. His parents carefully scrutinized his social environment, always seeking, as [his mother] said, to keep him in the company of individuals who were also "cultured." . . . [His parents] were well aware of the potential for Alexander to be exposed to racial injustice, and they went to great lengths to protect their son from racial insults and other forms of discrimination. Nevertheless, race did not appear to shape the dominant cultural logic of child rearing in Alexander's family or in other families in the study.[7]

Because Lareau did not set out to investigate attitudes about racial identity or racial socialization (she was interested instead in the transmission and reproduction of class), it would be useful to explore whether a different sample of middle-class blacks shows patterns of class socialization that are racially coded.

These rich ethnographic studies depict the considerable challenges parents face while raising children, yet they fail to capture how much work it is for middle-class black parents to help their children remember that they are black, even as they seek to provide them with the advantages they would receive if they were white and middle-class. Researchers have not looked enough at the ways that mothers and fathers help to construct a black middle-class identity through deliberate work. This study explores parents' efforts and demonstrates that different groups of middle-class blacks may conceive of this process in different ways.

UNDERSTANDING BLACK IDENTITIES

Three theoretical concepts are central to understanding how middle-class blacks think about their identities: boundary-work, the tool kit model, and construction sites. Each of these concepts helps us to work through the confusion and conflict around the notions of "making it" and "being black."

BOUNDARY-WORK AND ASSIMILATION

It is now commonly understood that identities are socially constructed through groups' interactions with one another. The theoretical framework finds its intellectual antecedent in the work of anthropologist Fredrik Barth, who used the term *boundaries* rather than the more specialized term *boundary-work*. Barth laid the foundation for this type of sociological analysis in a stimulating volume titled *Ethnic Groups and Boundaries*.[8] Drawing on the experiences of European ethnic groups, Barth argued that ethnic groups define who they are by erecting and defending boundaries between themselves and outsiders.

According to Barth, a group's ethnic identity emerges not from the group's *isolation* from other cultures, as traditional anthropological models had claimed, but from ongoing *contact* with different cultures, interactions in which groups are motivated to define themselves in contradistinction to newcomers. "Boundaries persist," he wrote, "despite a flow of personnel between them. . . . Ethnic distinctions do not depend on the absence of social interaction and acceptance, but . . . do entail processes of exclusion and incorporation whereby discrete categories are maintained *despite* changing participation and membership in the course of individual life histories."[9] I argue that the ethnic boundaries model can be applied to middle-class blacks born in the United States. Whom middle-class blacks come into contact with informs the racial boundaries they construct and negotiate. In the post-segregation era, middle-class blacks interact routinely with whites—at work; in integrated neighborhoods, and in public spaces. At the same time, middle-class blacks must also think about managing their interactions with blacks from the lower classes. Like those of Barth's European ethnics, these interactions with other racial and class groupings shape middle-class blacks' conceptions of who they are.

But Barth's key insight was that members of the same ethnic group may think differently about how to nurture and sustain their ethnic identity. These differences stem from members' regional locations, he argued. Studying the Pathan ethnic group, some of whom live in Afghanistan and others farther south in West Pakistan, Barth discovered that the Pathans draw boundaries between themselves and others on the basis of *virtue* as manifested in three institutions: hospitality, the council, and seclusion. Hospitality involves entertaining guests lavishly, regardless of the guests' social stature; in doing so, the Pathan demonstrate their moral rectitude.

The council is charged with negotiating disputes in a way that reflects core Pathan values of egalitarianism and unanimity. Seclusion refers to the practice of celebrating sexuality, dominance, and patriarchy in the shadows of the public sphere before an all-male audience, rather than valorizing masculinity in the public sphere. These virtues constitute the basis for boundary drawing among the Pathan, a way for them to distinguish their ethnic group from others; however, this set of virtues is more useful in some regions of the country than in others. As a result, the salience of Pathan identity waxes and wanes with the location and organizational structure of the group's villages. Barth demonstrated convincingly that regional location affects how the Pathan think of themselves in ethnic terms, but he was not concerned with documenting the considerable effort that individual Pathans put forth on a daily basis to manage their ethnic identity or what it meant to them to have to do it in the first place.

To date, only a handful of studies have explored within-group variation in identity. An early work by the sociologist Michele Lamont, *Money, Morals, and Manners,* explores these boundary-drawing processes among upper-middle-class white men in the United States and France. What she finds is that both American and French men want to distinguish their group from the lower classes but engage in different types of boundary-work to do so. Americans define themselves in contradistinction to the lower classes based on moral boundaries (assessments as to who is honest, hardworking, and ethical) and socioeconomic boundaries (indicators of social position, including wealth, occupational authority, and occupational status). American upper-middle-class men are less likely than the French, she argues, to exclude others based on cultural boundaries (as measured by educational attainment, tastes, and mastery of high culture).[10] Digging deeper into the sources of internal variation, Lamont compares all of the men according to occupational type (cultural specialist or social specialist) and industry (for-profit or nonprofit sector). The original pattern holds. American men rely more on socioeconomic boundaries to distinguish their group from the lower classes, whether they are cultural or social specialists and whether they work in the private or public sector. Similarly, French men employ cultural boundaries to do this work, regardless of their occupational type or industry type.

Do upper-middle-class black American men use socioeconomic boundaries to distinguish their group from others as their white counterparts do? A key weakness of Lamont's work is her failure to study upper-middle-class black men, especially since she draws direct comparisons between upper-middle-class and lower-middle-class men in a second pivotal study, *The Dignity of Working Men*. Drawing on interviews with both black and white working-class men, Lamont shows that in contrast to upper-middle-class men, both groups reject traditional economic indicators, relying instead on moral boundaries to raise their status relative to the upper classes. This finding raises questions as to whether the boundary-work of upper-middle-class American blacks would more closely resemble that of upper-middle-class American white men (who are motivated to draw both socioeconomic and moral boundaries) or lower-middle-class black men (who draw moral boundaries exclusively).

Blue-Chip Black also answers the call put forth by Lamont for empirical studies that explore the boundary-work carried out by upper-middle-class blacks.[11] Operating from the premise that the boundaries drawn by members of the upper-middle class "are likely to be more permanent, less crossable, and less resisted than the boundaries that exist between ethnic groups," Lamont implies, though she does not state directly, that upper-middle-class blacks and whites may be more similar than are upper-middle-class and lower-class blacks.[12] If this were true, it would mean that upper-middle-class blacks would, like their white upper-middle-class counterparts, use moral boundaries to buttress their already confident hold on a higher social standing. In American society, where pulling yourself up by your own bootstraps is valorized and freeloaders are looked down upon, the white men in Lamont's study use moral criteria to underscore the idea that their success is the result of their hard work and that they have played the American game and come out ahead. The perception that successful people are those who clawed their way to the front of the pack is critical, especially since parents' status position has implications for their children's well-being, as Lamont points out:

> Competition permeates everything in the American upper-middle class world. It even permeates the world of children; parents often make considerable financial sacrifices and efforts to have their children admitted to the "best schools," not only at the college level but at the elementary and high school levels as well. . . . [One informant said of the upper-middle class,] "They are all successful people. If the kids don't do well somehow, that's a reflection on them and somewhat detracts from themselves. So therefore their kids must be good, and they see to it."[13]

If it were true that upper-middle-class blacks and whites are more similar than upper-middle- and lower-class blacks, it would also mean that socioeconomic criteria shape the boundary-work of upper-middle-class black men just as they do that of upper-middle-class white men. Take money, for example. Money matters to upper-middle-class white men not merely for its accumulated value, but also for its symbolic value, because "money means above all freedom, control, and security, these being clearly circumscribed by level of personal income." Demonstrating one's success through visible measures of comfort and upper-middle-class living is a defining feature in the lives of upper-middle-class white men. This measure includes the usual suspects—material items such as an imposing home, luxury cars, and exotic vacations. But it also includes "the kids' ballet classes and piano lessons, and their tennis and computer camps, as well as the time spent at work vs. the time the adults spend golfing or enjoying other leisure-time activities." Membership in exclusive clubs is another way that the upper-middle-class white men in Lamont's study communicate their status position. Such membership "provides information on socioeconomic status to the extent that it signals the fact that one has achieved a certain income level, that one is committed to its accompanying lifestyle, and that one has been accepted by the 'right kinds of people.' "[14]

The idea that some class boundaries within the black community may be more impermeable than those between blacks and whites is not a new one. In *Unequal Childhoods*, sociologist Annette Lareau writes of the patterns of class transmission she found among her middle-class informants: "Middle class black and white children in my study did exhibit some key differences, yet the biggest gaps were not within social classes but . . . across them."[15] And long before Lamont and Lareau, William J. Wilson launched the race-class debate when he posited that the widening gulf between the black lower class, a group with little opportunity for upward mobility, and the black middle class, a group that has expanded enormously due largely to civil rights legislation, means that the lives of middle-class blacks are more similar to the white middle class than to those of the black lower classes.[16] So the idea is not new, but this is the first book to explore how different groups of middle-class blacks conceive of their status position and define themselves relative to whites and lower-class blacks across a number of distinct settings. I show that to fully understand this process, we need to examine the boundary-work of the black upper-middle class apart from that of the black middle class. In doing so, we begin to develop a new language to talk about class, one that speaks to differentiation within the black middle class.

To my knowledge, only one previous study investigates variations in how different groups of middle-class blacks conceive of their identity. Studying black executives in a large Philadelphia corporation, sociologist Elijah Anderson showed that the black workers can be classified according to two distinct identity formations: "the own" and "the wise." The "own" occupy positions low on the corporate hierarchy, are less integrated into the corporate culture, and are defined by their skin color and belief in racial unity. The "wise" hold "positions of authority and influence" in the company, have internalized the corporate culture, and function as supportive mentors to the "own."[17] Anderson's study is instructive because he shows that not all middle-class blacks conceive of their identity in the same way. However, because his study is limited to the workplace, we don't know whether the differentiation he found is transferable to other public settings frequented by middle-class blacks.

THE BLACK MIDDLE-CLASS TOOL KIT

The tool kit model draws attention to the material and nonmaterial forms of culture that help people to negotiate everyday life and to make sense of the actions of others. Material culture refers to the physical objects that people create and assign meaning to. A college diploma, for example, signifies an important credential to employers and helps them to sort out applicants by their level of training. Nonmaterial culture consists of the more abstract cultural objects that people create, from ideas to rituals to ceremonies. A bar mitzvah ceremony, for example, represents a sacred rite of passage for a young Jewish boy. Sociologists refer to these cultural forms—including the college diploma and the bar mitzvah—as symbols because they have a meaning that is more complex than their original function suggests. They represent the ways in which cultural meaning is transmitted and stored. We draw on these meanings in our everyday lives as the need arises. Taken together, these various symbols constitute a cultural repertoire, a set of cultural materials standing at the ready whenever we want or need to make use of them.[18] According to Ann Swidler:

> [It is] best to think of culture as a repertoire, like that of an actor, a musician, or a dancer. This image suggests that culture cultivates skills and habits in its users, so that one can be more or less good at the cultural repertoire one performs, and that such cultured capacities may exist both as discrete skills, habits and orientations, and, in larger assemblages, like the pieces a musician has mastered or the plays an actor has performed. It is in this sense that people have an array of cultural resources upon which they can draw. We can ask not only what pieces are in the repertoire but why some are performed at one time, some at another.[19]

Evidence suggests that blacks and whites not only engage different elements of the cultural tool kit, they draw from different types of tool kits altogether. From Mary Pattillo's study of a black neighborhood on the south side of Chicago, we learn that black people access a distinctly black cultural tool kit, composed of church rituals such as prayer, call-and-response, and religious material objects, which are put to use in public community meetings as an effective way to mobilize the neighborhood's residents. These church rituals are so pervasive in the black community that they are understood even by blacks who are not regular churchgoers. Pattillo concludes that this specific strategy of employing religious tools in secular settings is a distinguishing feature of civic life in black Chicago. She argues that political meetings and events held in comparable white Chicago communities do not incorporate prayer, testimony, or other church rituals as black civic events do.[20] I build on Pattillo's finding by showing that the racially distinct black cultural tool kit is further distinguished by social class.

Just as blacks in Chicago engage a tool kit in which cultural content and meaning are not dispersed beyond the boundaries of the black world, the middle-class blacks in this study access a tool kit reflective of the black middle-class experience. My focus here is strictly on the social identities that make up the black middle-class tool kit, not the many other cultural symbols that may be relevant to the black middle-class experience. The black middle-class tool kit is composed of public identities, status-based identities, racial and class-based identities, and suburban identities. Middle-class blacks employ these identities instrumentally to establish their position in American society relative to white strangers, their white middle-class neighbors, lower-class blacks, and one another. In public settings, where they are likely to encounter white strangers who are not automatically aware of their class position, middle-class blacks assert public identities in order to manage these interactions effectively, to demonstrate their middle-class status, and to ensure a carefree outing. A key strategy involves differentiating their group from lower-class blacks and amplifying similarities with the white middle class. The groups of blacks in this study do not vary in their use of public identities. Public identities are necessary in a racialized society and will remain necessary so long as the public perception of who is middle-class in the United States does not include black people. Status-based identities are critical to the intergenerational reproduction of a middle-class status. Middle-class blacks differ by economic status in their perceptions of how to transmit or reproduce their social status. These status differences give rise to two different groups of middle-class blacks, the elite black middle class and the core black middle class. The last three identities housed in the black middle class tool kit emerge from middle-class blacks' interactions with others in their suburban settings. Racial identities reflect parents' perceptions about how best to prepare their children for the white world while maintaining connections to other blacks. Parents living in predominantly white suburbs think differently about this process than do parents living in majority-black suburban communities. Class-based identities reflect the tension between hip hop culture and the middle-class culture parents hope to socialize their children into. Suburban identities capture the community issues that facilitate alliances between middle-class blacks and their white neighbors. The set of identities housed in the black middle-class tool kit should be incorporated into our definition of what it means to be black and middle-class along with standard indicators such as income, occupation, education, and home ownership.

It is possible that the social identities I describe and connect to middle-class blacks may resonate with other groups as well. Latinos are slated to overtake blacks as the largest minority group in the United States by 2050. As reports of increasing discrimination directed toward Latinos come to light, researchers may find that the model that I've outlined also reflects the Latino experience in the United States. Similarly, I suspect lower-class blacks also possess a host of social identities reflective of their class position and lifestyle. But because my sample includes neither Latinos or lower-class blacks, I limit my discussion to the black middle class and leave it to other social scientists to test the model among other racial, ethnic, or class groupings.

CONSTRUCTION SITES AND BLACK IDENTITIES

Ascribed and achieved characteristics like race and class aren't the only factors that determine which identities middle-class blacks pluck from their tool kit. People tend to think of the construction of social identities primarily in terms of individual characteristics (e.g., class, gender, age, race), but in my view, this perspective is incomplete. There is compelling evidence that the neighborhood context can also have a profound influence on the formation of a sense of who one is as a middle-class black person. Context matters greatly because it affects the situations that middle-class blacks are likely to confront and the strategies they use to deal with such situations. In neighborhoods, the social organization of the community helps to determine what boundaries are drawn and under what circumstances. For example, in the lower-middle-class black neighborhood depicted in Mary Pattillo's Chicago study, black residents are ambivalent about drawing rigid boundaries against social deviants such as drug dealers because they, too, are well-known members of the general community.[21]

Neighborhoods and other arenas where identities are negotiated over and over again by individuals are what sociologists Stephen Cornell and Douglas Hartmann term "construction sites."[22] Within these settings, people establish criteria that serve as the basis for establishing boundaries. Among the same individuals, these criteria may vary from one setting to another.[23] This makes perfect sense given that the roles that individuals play change as they move from one setting to another. A surgeon is simply a mother or father on returning home to the family at the end of the workday. Other types of identities are also context-specific. Through her study of the play patterns of children attending an elementary school, Barrie Thorne determined that gender is an identity that waxes and wanes; it is salient in some situations but discounted in others.[24] She writes, "A 'boy' will always be a 'boy' and that fact will enter all his experiences. But in some interactions, he may be much more aware of that strand of his identity than in others, just as his ethnicity or age may be more relevant in some situations than others." We know this intuitively, but few studies have been attentive to variability in actions of the same individuals across a variety of different contexts or "construction sites." No ethnographic treatment of the black middle class has contrasted different types of middle-class black communities in the same study.

Sociologists Joe Feagin and Melvin Sikes conducted interviews with more than 200 middle-class blacks in their exhaustive investigation of how middle-class blacks manage their identities in a variety of contexts, from the workplace to colleges to neighborhoods to public recreational and social settings. But because the authors do not trace the experience of the same individuals across these different settings, the study cannot determine whether their informants' racial identities matter more in some contexts than in others.[25] We are left with the impression that the only reason middle-class blacks care so much about a racial identity is that they have to defend themselves against racism at every turn. Negotiating racism is important, but the middle-class blacks in this study are invested in their racial identities for another equally important reason: they enjoy interacting with other blacks.

Scholars have focused so much on the burden of blackness that they have devoted scant attention to the possibility that there is something enjoyable about being black and participating in a community of blacks.

To identify the conditions under which a black racial identity is an advantage or a liability, I draw a distinction between public and private construction sites. The public spaces presented here include shopping centers, the workplace, and the housing market in the greater Washington, D.C., metropolitan area—construction sites that figure most centrally in the everyday lives of the black middle class. Identity construction processes in public spaces differ according to blacks' familiarity with the whites they encounter in these settings. By contrast, in their suburban communities, middle-class blacks' white neighbors know a great deal about them—where they work, where they vacation, where they shop, and their general status in the community. Moreover, suburban blacks in Lakeview, Riverton, and Sherwood Park share a common class background with their white neighbors. But in public spaces, middle-class blacks meet up with unfamiliar whites who do not know them well, and they therefore must develop strategies to manage racial stigmatization in the public sphere, should they encounter it. By exploring the identity work of the same people across a variety of different settings, I demonstrate (just as Barrie Thorne did in her analysis of gender) that the salience of black racial identity varies from one context to another.

OVERVIEW OF THE BOOK

The first two chapters lay the foundation for a discussion of variation in the identity options of middle-class black suburbanites. Chapter 1 discusses the literature on black middle-class identity. I review how the group has been operationalized in previous studies and explain why this definition is inadequate.

Chapter 2 establishes the role that suburban developers play in orchestrating community life. Through the rules and regulations that they attached to homeowners' deeds, developers in Lakeview, Riverton, and Sherwood Park imposed a set of core values on suburban residents, a practice that distinguishes Washington's suburbs from the District, where, in the absence of developers, residents themselves assume responsibility for determining the community's personality. Differences in developers' visions of what constitutes an ideal middle-class suburban lifestyle resulted in diverse suburban communities that house different groups of middle-class blacks and structure their social identities in different ways.

The remaining chapters present each of the social identities stored in the black middle class tool kit and, with the exception of chapter 3, outline how different groups of middle-class blacks choose from these identities. Chapter 3 explores an under-studied component of racial stigma theory: the degree to which middle-class blacks resort to signaling their class position, the use of what I call *public identities*, as a legitimate strategy for negotiating racial discrimination in three sectors of the public sphere: the marketplace, the workplace, and while house-hunting. I challenge the prevailing view, in which middle-class blacks' tendency to successfully play up their middle-class status is discounted. Indeed, the middle-class blacks in this study believe that they get what they want—a trouble-free shopping experience, loyalty from white subordinates, and access to homes put up for sale—when they demonstrate to whites that they are truly members of the middle class. Scholars need to look more at the identity strategies of the same individuals across contexts that are shared by all members of the black middle classes.

Chapter 4 examines how perceptions of economic stability shape the status identities that middle-class blacks assert. Blacks in Lakeview, Riverton, and Sherwood Park are all concerned about actively maintaining their status position relative to other groups, but they go about this process differently. Sherwood Park blacks view their economic circumstances as stable and secure; therefore, they think about their status in the context of status reproduction, spending responsibly on themselves and lavishly on their children as a way of preparing them to replicate their parents' lifestyle for themselves as adults. Riverton and Lakeview blacks report feeling financially burdened; thus, they think about their status in terms of protecting what they have, leading them to spend responsibly on themselves and conservatively on their children. Based on these lifestyle differences, I characterize Sherwood Park blacks as members of the elite black middle class and Riverton and Lakeview blacks as members of the core black middle class. In summary, this chapter shows that the identities of middle-class blacks vary according to economic status.

In the next two chapters, I turn to the identity negotiation strategies employed by middle-class blacks within their suburban communities, contrasting the experience of living in a predominantly white suburb with that of living in a majority-black community. Chapter 5 establishes the missing link between an affinity for black spaces and the alternative assimilation trajectories of middle-class blacks. Although the middle-class blacks in this study routinely travel back and forth across black-white boundaries, they are nevertheless concerned with nurturing meaningful connections to the black world. Blacks in both majority-white Lakeview and predominantly black Riverton perceive the black world as an important site for the construction of black racial identities, but residential location leads them to privilege different segments of the black world. In Riverton, black families are not unusual; therefore, Riverton residents rely on their black subdivision—a geographical community—to suture a black racial identity. By contrast, in Lakeview, a black family is often the only black presence in the community; therefore, Lakeview residents report taking additional steps, relying on black social organizations—an ideological community—to accomplish the same goal. In short, middle-class blacks rely on the black world as an important site for socializing, even if they live in a white suburb, a selective pattern of assimilation which I term *strategic assimilation*. Identity studies should direct more attention to variation in how middle-class blacks sustain racial identities.

Chapter 6 reveals variation in the construction of suburban identities by outlining the conditions under which black and white suburbanites in Prince George's County and Fairfax County form alliances on the basis of shared interests. In majority-black Prince George's County, where Riverton and Sherwood Park residents grapple with an inadequate tax base, a troubled school system, and the imminent threat of a large-scale tourist development, suburban identities are constructed on the basis of residential location. Black and white residents in upscale Sherwood Park avoid the public schools (with the exception of special magnet programs) and generally support the controversial tourist development, National Harbor, since they live far enough away from the site to avoid being affected by the introduction of stadium lighting and the projected increase in traffic, noise, and pollution. By contrast, black and white Riverton residents desire to improve the public school system from within and vehemently object to National Harbor. Indeed, many Riverton residents will lose their homes if the county carries out its plan to improve access to National Harbor by expanding a residential street to four lanes from two. In predominantly white Lakeview, suburban identities are constructed on the basis of age cohorts. Older residents are resistant to development and neighborhood improvement projects, while younger residents tend to support these changes.

The conclusion revisits the black middle-class tool kit, explaining why it is a better theoretical framework for understanding the identity options of the black middle classes than other approaches. Analyzing middle-class blacks' reliance on the tool kit shows that while there are important differences between middle-class whites and blacks, there are also real and meaningful divisions within the black middle class itself between the elite black middle class and the core black middle class.

1

Defining the Post-Integration Black Middle Classes

In the United States it is common knowledge that there are stark, un-relenting divisions between the black underclass and the black mid-dle class.[1] Indeed, class polarization between the two groups is so per-vasive that we often assume the central fault line in the black world is that between the black poor and the black middle class. But the experi-ences of the people in this book suggest that this common marker may not constitute the primary fault line differentiating blacks from one an-other in years to come. Ever-deepening divisions exist within the black middle class itself; these fault lines are under-studied and therefore not well-known. In this chapter, I show that there are distinct groups of middle-class blacks in the United States: lower-middle-class blacks, the focus of most sociological studies; and middle-class blacks and upper-middle-class blacks, who, by comparison, have received far less atten-tion. Studies of the former group inform much of what we know about the black middle class. These studies imply an undifferentiated class; in-deed, a unifying thread throughout studies of the former group is that despite appreciable differences in their income, occupation, and educa-tional attainment, members of the black lower-middle class share a common daily experience that does not differ significantly from the ex-perience of being a member of the black working class or the black poor. At the same time, many existing studies report that the middle-class blacks and whites do not experience their middle-class status in the same way.[2]

This popular perception of the black middle-class experience as nearly indistinguishable from the everyday lives of lower-class blacks arises in part because scholars engaged in community-based studies have tended to study lower-middle-class blacks who are living in urban centers or in older suburbs contiguous with these urban centers, communities that are characterized by many of the same problems that immobilize the inner cities: high unemployment, drugs, teenage pregnancy, high rates of poverty, inferior shopping districts, low-performing school districts, poor municipal services, and white flight. It also arises due to a more general problem: the black middle-class has not been properly defined in the sociological literature. This misspecification not only conceals growing heterogeneity within the group, it leads researchers to draw erroneous conclusions about the group—findings that are derived from data on individuals who would be more accurately characterized as black working class. In practice, the black lower-middle class and the black middle class have been unevenly studied and, as a result, the two groups are often confounded in the sociological literature.

In order to properly understand what it means to be a middle-class black person in America, we need a new study—a detailed analysis of the under-studied groups: middle-class blacks who do *not* live in or near blighted urban neighborhoods. Admittedly, the suburban communities depicted in this book are exceptions to the rule in terms of where most blacks live, regardless of class. Because most neighborhoods in the United States are racially segregated, the vast majority of middle-class blacks live in communities alongside lower-class blacks, communities like those typically studied by sociologists. But recent studies suggest that the pattern of imposed racial residential segregation which dominated the twentieth century may be changing due to two new trends in the spatial patterns of Americans. First, the number of stable, integrated neighborhoods is slowly increasing in the United States.[3] Second, growing numbers of middle-class blacks are opting to settle in majority-black, distinctly middle-class suburban enclaves.[4] If these disparate trends continue unabated, the types of middle-class communities I portray here are likely to become less and less exceptional over time. As sociologist Robert Adelman explained with regard to the first trend, "A new residential dynamic for African Americans may be in the making."[5]

The variety of residential communities now available to middle-class blacks has important implications for how these individuals conceive of their identities. Looking at middle-class blacks who live in completely different settings than those typically studied by sociologists, areas where poor and working-class blacks are *not* present, I find strong evidence of variation *within* the black middle class in terms of how members of this diverse group perceive themselves and others. In short, I agree with established studies asserting that one's place of residence can have an important effect on identity; however, my comparative data allow me to show something even more theoretically compelling: that living in particular *kinds* of suburban communities results in *different* effects on identity.

In this chapter, I begin by outlining the indicators that have been used in previous studies to define the black middle class and identifying some of the problems that these standard measures pose. I then take up the topic of the misspecification of class—the tendency among scholars to blur lines between the black lower-middle class and the black working class, and, more central to my argument, the problem of failing to distinguish between the experiences and perceptions of lower-middle-class blacks and those of middle- and upper-class blacks. I use national data from the census to suggest a way to define the black middle class differently, so that hidden distinctions between different groups of middle-class blacks are accounted for. In the last section of the chapter, I compare and contrast the three suburban communities that make up this study as a way of foreshadowing the argument developed in the remainder of the book. I show that difference in residence has an important effect on how middle-class blacks think about their identity as well as implications for how social scientists should begin to think about operationalizing the black middle class. Blacks in Lakeview, Riverton, and Sherwood Park are engaged in different kinds of identity work, both across the three groups and vis-à-vis blacks who live in the kinds of residential areas more commonly available to blacks in the United States.

DEFINING THE BLACK MIDDLE CLASS PRIOR TO THE 1960s

After emancipation, the group that emerged as the elite among blacks was conspicuous in its departure from the standard markers of upward mobility—income, occupation, and educational attainment. Instead, boundaries drawn by members of the black elite class against other blacks stemmed from the class structure instituted under the system of slavery. Although slavery was undergirded by the one-drop rule (a cultural definition of blackness in which one drop of black blood makes an individual black), in practice, a pattern of stratification emerged in which slaves with white ancestry benefited from their lighter skin color and white features in at least three ways.[6] First, mulattoes were more likely to be put to work as house servants—cooks, butlers, and chauffeurs—while darker-skinned blacks were most often relegated to back-breaking physical labor in the fields. Second, in their household positions, mulattoes were exposed to the lifestyles and culture of upper-class whites, a lifestyle they would seek to imitate after emancipation. Third, in their capacity as personal servants to white slaveowners, mulattoes learned a trade or skill that they would eventually parlay into a stable career serving white clients once slavery was abolished.

It was clear to house servants and field hands alike that light skin and white features were valuable currency in the slavery era. Whites treated mulattoes as though they were superior to dark-skinned blacks with pronounced African features, and mulattoes internalized this image. According to Verna Keith and Cedric Herring, mulattoes' physical likeness to whites blurred the boundary between the two groups. Even so, the one-drop rule prevented mulattoes from evolving into a distinct buffer group here in the United States as they did in South Africa, Latin America, and the Caribbean, although mulattoes did form the foundation for the black middle class. All accounts indicate that mulattoes were overrepresented among free blacks during the era of slavery (since many were freed by their slavemaster fathers or allowed to earn money to purchase their freedom) as well as among the black upper crust after emancipation.[7]

The class differentiation produced under enslavement thrived for many years thereafter, assuming a new form after World War I, the period when the Great Migration brought southern blacks into the North in unprecedented numbers. The 1924 National Origins Quota Act reduced from a torrent to a trickle the number of white immigrants lured from their European homelands by the promise of untold economic opportunities in the United States, and black migrants from the South began to move into low-skilled occupations up north that had long been dominated by immigrants from southern and eastern Europe.[8] As a result of these marked demographic changes, the proportion of the black population concentrated in the agricultural industry declined precipitously, and a new group of middle-class blacks, those who earned their living providing essential services to a burgeoning, segregated black community, emerged. Their occupations ranged from doctors to ministers to teachers to insurance agents to funeral directors, services that northern whites refused to provide to a black clientele.[9] By the first quarter of the twentieth century, the definition of the black elite had changed from a group composed primarily of those with white ancestry to a far more heterogeneous class category.

We tend to think of the black class structure during this early period in terms of only two groups: the predominantly mulatto elite, and everyone else. But mulattoes sought more than mere social and physical distance from the black masses.[10] As a result of the social, economic, and ancestral privileges afforded their group during enslavement, mulattoes also drew sharp boundaries between their group and the nouveau-riche, monoracial blacks who had managed to gain entry into the black middle class. The former group was acknowledged as the spokespersons for the black community, wielding considerable power and influence until World War I. A very small percentage of the mulatto elite worked in professional occupations as doctors, lawyers, or civil servants. Most were employed in roles that did not require formal education, such as caterers, barbers, headwaiters, shoemakers, tailors, blacksmiths, and cooks; all of these roles catered to wealthy whites. While none of the mulatto elite could be considered upper-class in the sense that whites were, their coveted occupations carried a high degree of prestige among the black masses to whom these career options were closed.[11]

For these reasons, membership in the mulatto elite was based on neither demonstrable wealth nor occupational status. Instead, mulattoes were embraced or excluded on the basis of family name and ancestry, an extension of the very same criteria that had pitted house slaves against field slaves. As one member of the mulatto elite explained, "The aristocracy of which I write is based on birth. It is a club whose passwords are 'Who are your people?' "[12] It was not enough to be merely mulatto *or* from an accomplished family. One needed to fulfill both conditions in order to gain entry into the group. Ancestry was reflected in skin color, so much so that prominent dark-skinned blacks (along with the black masses) were often snubbed by the mulatto elite. A mulatto woman from an old elite family recalled how her family's aversion to dark skin precluded her from marrying the celebrated poet Paul Lawrence Dunbar, with whom she had begun a love affair. E. Franklin Frazier writes, "When her mother thought she was falling in love with the black poet Dunbar, her mother immediately told her that no matter how great a poet Dunbar was, a person as black as he could not become a member of their family."[13] The mulatto elite passed down light skin and white features from one generation to the next by selecting marriage partners from within their own small circle.[14]

Wealth was also not as important in determining membership in the mulatto elite as a lifestyle imitative of upper-class whites and elitist tastes and values. Just as their wealthy, white employers had, the mulatto elite stressed marriage, etiquette, and good taste. As a group, they disapproved of black English, which they labeled "dialect language," as well as "any vulgar display of wealth, overdressing, and mad rush for amusements."[15] Instead, they sought to align themselves as closely as possible with whites and white culture. The mulatto elite lived in white neighborhoods or elite sections of black neighborhoods, worked for white clients, and privileged the lifestyle of the white upper class. These attempts to weaken the boundary between their group and whites meant that the group would reinforce boundaries against upwardly mobile dark-skinned blacks and lower-class blacks. "Having adopted the values of white society and culture as their own, the black elite not only strove to emulate the whites with whom they frequently came into contact but also felt the need to separate themselves from the black masses and even the new black elite that began to emerge at the turn of the century."[16]

The mulatto elite may have regretted this decision, as their standing in the black community diminished substantially after World War I. A new white upper class was evolving, composed of upwardly mobile individuals who had no historical connection to the planter class or allegiance to former mulatto servants and therefore shunned them. Seeking social and physical distance from mulattoes, this new white upper class preferred predominantly white neighborhoods and founded their own educational institutions and social clubs, from which mulattoes were excluded.[17] By 1915, as the black population in the North grew exponentially and serving whites lost its cachet, the mulatto elite was replaced by black professionals and small business owners, the parvenu. With prescient resolve, the parvenu had already begun to cater to the swelling population of northern blacks. In this way, the nouveau riche differed from the mulatto elite; the basis for their class position was achievement rather than ancestry.

While the lives of the mulatto elite were defined by ongoing contact with whites through their employment as personal servants, the lives of the emergent black middle class were defined by the reinforcement and strengthening of black-white boundaries in the form of Jim Crow legislation, racial residential segregation, and social exclusion. Ironically, racial segregation presented upwardly mobile blacks—particularly those with an entrepreneurial vision—with a rare opportunity to ascend into the black middle class. Some scholars argue that certain members of the emergent black middle class were heavily invested in maintaining racially segregated neighborhoods. For one thing, an isolated black community allowed black professionals and small businessmen to monopolize the market for goods and services. If blacks could not depend on the services of white doctors, lawyers, real estate agents, or undertakers; buy life insurance from mainstream companies; or rely on white journalists to report on black communities, they would have to seek out blacks trained to perform these services. The emergent black middle class and their black clients were mutually dependent on one another.[18] Politicians also benefited from a concentration of blacks—and votes—in a segregated space. Others suggest the emergent black middle class worried that the black lower class was not equipped to interact with whites in the white world and were opposed to racial integration based on the supposed inferiority of the black lower classes. Implicit in this line of reasoning is the emergent black middle class's disappointment in whites' stubborn refusal to consider their group apart from the uncultured lower classes. As a black newspaper editor lamented, "The white people draw the line at the wrong point and put all of us in the same class."[19]

But the emergent black middle class experienced more distinctions than the one that separated it from the black lower class. Occupational differentiation led to deep-seated divisions between upper-middle-class and lower-middle-class blacks. While ancestry and light skin structured the lives of the mulatto elite, achievement and refinement structured the lives of the emergent black middle class. Specifically, educational attainment set the emergent black middle class apart from the mulatto elite, and focusing on educational attainment was one way that members of the emergent black middle class erected boundaries within their own group. Drake and Cayton observed, "Persons who wish to circulate near the 'top' [of the class structure], whatever they lack in money or job, must have enough education to avoid grammatical blunders, and to allow them to converse intelligently. Ignorant 'breaks' and inability to cite evidence of education—formal and informal—can bar a person permanently from the top."[20]

The occupational choices of upwardly mobile blacks began to expand slowly with the founding and growth of a key educational source for ambitious blacks: black colleges. During the Civil War, black and white northern missionaries traveled to the South to tutor slaves who had escaped into the protective custody of the Union Army. In 1865, the federal government, through the establishment of the Freedman's Bureau and under the leadership of its commissioner, General O. O. Howard, committed resources to building public schools for former slaves. At their founding, many of these schools were referred to as "colleges" or "universities," even though their curriculum at the time was the equivalent of a high school education. Howard University, the namesake of the commissioner, was the only Freedman's Bureau "college" to actually mature into university status shortly after its opening in 1867. Other colleges were founded by the American Missionary Association (Hampton University), by northern white philanthropists (Spelman College, the namesake of Laura Spelman Rockefeller), or by blacks (Tuskegee Institute).[21] By 1900, 99 of the country's current 117 historically black colleges had been established, including Morehouse University, the only four-year institution for black males, in 1867.[22]

Early on, very few blacks were matriculating at these institutions, a reality that severely limited the growth of the black middle class. Taken together, the ninety-nine black colleges had a combined enrollment of fewer than three thousand students at the turn of the century.[23] Some scholars conclude from these paltry enrollments that higher education was a low priority for blacks in the late nineteenth and early twentieth centuries. Others argue that the agricultural economy in the South, and economic hardship more generally, meant that black children rarely received a full year of primary schooling, as they were needed in the fields. However much they may have valued education, most southern blacks in the late nineteenth and early twentieth centuries were not in a position to take full advantage of the most rudimentary schooling, to say nothing of higher education.[24]

Student enrollment in black colleges began to rise in 1915 and increased dramatically in the 1940s, concomitant with unprecedented increases in the financial contributions earmarked for black colleges from both black and white institutions. Founded in 1944, the United Negro College Fund raised $750,000 for black colleges in its first year alone. Major contributions also poured in from an improbable source: southern states. After contributing only $422,356 in 1914, southern states allocated a whopping $10,881,932 to black colleges in 1947, a sum representing 30 percent of their total budget allocation for higher education. Their generosity has been attributed to the desire on the part of southern states to maintain segregated schools. After a 1938 Supreme Court ruling in which the state of Missouri was instructed to either admit blacks to the University of Missouri Law School or to provide them with their own institution, southern states elected to uphold racial segregation by investing in black colleges.[25]

From 1915 to 1940, black college enrollment rose from about 5,000 students to nearly 40,000, and by the 1960s, 105,000 students were enrolled in black colleges.[26] The effect of rising college attendance is evident in the shift in the black class structure. The percentage of blacks working as professionals increased from 1.4 percent in 1910 to 4.7 percent in 1960. The most dramatic shifts in the size of the black middle class are found in clerical occupations. Fewer than 1 percent of blacks held clerical positions in 1910; by 1960, 7.3 percent did.[27] At that same time, the implementation of New Deal policies opened up federal government jobs to blacks, generating occupational differentiation within the black middle class itself. College-educated blacks continued to enter the black middle class in small numbers in professional roles such as statisticians, economists, and librarians. Others occupied lower-middle-class positions, including office managers, secretaries, clerks, stenographers, and postal workers.[28] Here again, one's position within the black middle class was based not on income, since black professionals earned substantially less working in the racially segregated black community than their white counterparts did working in mainstream society, but on the status that education conferred. Within the black population, Drake and Cayton noted, "job status and earning power are often far out of line. . . . A stenographer earns much less than a foundry worker, but enjoys a higher social status. A prize-fighter makes considerably more than a doctor, but does not have so much prestige. Pullman porters and mail carriers receive a larger and steadier income than some dentists and physicians, but are not ranked so high socially."[29]

Education carried a good deal of weight in southern states too. Maynard Jackson Sr., the father of the first black Atlanta mayor, Maynard Jackson Jr., was held in high esteem by the Atlanta black community because he was well-educated and pastored a prominent Baptist church. However, Maynard Sr. had very little disposable income. At the time of death, his widow and children struggled to make ends meet.[30] As education grew in importance, it began to supplant ancestry as the central determination of membership in the black middle class. Moreover, monoracial black men who had earned college degrees and become successful black professionals began to marry women from the mulatto elite, thereby anchoring their membership in the emergent black middle class.[31]

THE POST-INTEGRATION BLACK MIDDLE CLASS

In the aftermath of the Civil Rights Act of 1964, federal policy that barred discrimination in employment or education on the basis of race or gender, a "real" black middle class began to evolve—meaning simply that with greater access to both education and white-collar jobs, more blacks gradually achieved a middle-class status closely aligned with conventional indicators of class position. The category "black middle class"—and the kinds of distinctions blacks made vis-à-vis one another—gradually became more rooted in education, occupation, and income and less tied with skin color and ancestry. Even so, today's black middle class is defined very differently in different community studies of the black middle class. Most of these studies rely on family income, some on occupational status, others on educational attainment, and still others on the class composition of the neighborhood or some combination of these indicators. Clearly, categorizing individuals in black communities by class position is more of an art than a science, since along with the objective markers of income, occupation, and educational attainment, the effects of historically determined indices of status and prestige (outlined above) continue to complicate class position. But confusion about who is middle-class and which neighborhoods clear the middle class hurdle has resulted in a skewed understanding of the ways in which middle-class blacks think about and experience their identities as black people in America.

As existing studies show, residents of lower-middle-class black communities experience the frustration of attaining a middle-class status as indicated by the standard social indicators (for example, income, occupation, and education) and then finding that the rewards that should accompany this achieved status—such as safe and desirable housing in a good neighborhood, good public schools, social distance from the poor and public housing, and respectful treatment from public officials—are not automatically granted to them.[32] Even though blacks in lower-middle-class neighborhoods attempt to distinguish themselves from black working-class and poor black residents, their class-based identity is often frustratingly invisible to others in their neighborhood settings. For these reasons, sociologists argue that middle-class blacks do not experience daily life in the same way that middle-class whites do.

Commonalities in the everyday experiences of blacks across class lines are of great interest because they do not conform to conventional understandings of the relationship between upward mobility and integration into mainstream society. Many middle-class blacks depicted in existing studies have done all the right things, following the rules, but have not met with widespread acceptance, leading Feagin to conclude, "No matter how affluent and influential, a black person cannot escape the stigma of being black."[33] The experiences of this group are also of interest because they highlight the degree to which ongoing discrimination and racial residential segregation trump class advantage in many communities across the United States, negatively affecting the quality of life of middle-class blacks. However, these reported commonalities among blacks, while useful in terms of drawing attention to persistent inequality, have incorrectly shaped our understanding of black middle-class identity by generalizing from the black lower-middle class to draw conclusions about the black middle class as a whole.

One way in which existing studies of the black middle class are misleading is that they center around the close (sometimes involuntary) ties between lower-middle-class blacks and lower-class blacks. In urban areas, residential segregation causes middle-class blacks to have to share their neighborhood with working-class and poor blacks, or to live in communities contiguous with these neighborhoods. Within these communities, residents face challenges that suburban residents of homogeneous middle-class communities, black or white, do not confront. Like most members of the middle class, urban black middle-class residents would like to think only about middle-class concerns, such as maintaining quality schools, property values, and the overall well-being of the community. But in urban centers and near-urban suburbs, residents must think about problems that middle-class blacks in different types of settings do not. Existing studies show that urban lower-middle-class blacks battle gangs, drug dealers, escalating drug use, the threat of Section 8 renters, violence, and the city government's attempts to plop public housing within their community's borders.[34]

In urban areas, black middle-class life is defined by the group's close proximity to the lower classes, and these shared associations limit the social usefulness of their middle-class status. Social scientists describe the life chances of the black middle class as inextricably bound up with that of the black lower classes.[35] Because middle-class blacks are forced to live in predominantly black communities along with working-class and poor blacks, scholars argue, different classes of blacks are dependent on the same (often poor) municipal services. As Pattillo observes in a study of a community on the South Side of Chicago:

even the predominantly middle-class areas remain tied to the core ghetto. Administrative boundaries have no regard for the neighborhoods established by the black middle class. High schools service neighborhoods with a diversity of residents. Police districts are responsible for the residents of housing projects as well as those who live in owner-occupied single-family homes. Supermarkets, parks, nightclubs, scout troops, churches, and beaches all serve a heterogeneous black population. . . . The middle-class way of life is in constant jeopardy in black middle-class neighborhoods because of the unique nature of their composition and location.[36]

Sociologist Bruce Haynes observes a similar phenomenon among the black middle-class residents of suburban Runyon Heights. He describes them as "locked into a common fate with the working-class" with respect to political tensions between public officials and the community regarding the distribution of resources. He notes that Runyon Heights residents organized first against the segregation and isolation of a largely black elementary school due to redistricting, and subsequently against the school board's decision to shut down the neighborhood school entirely. And sociologist Monique Taylor observed after a water main break in Harlem that residents from various classes worked together, helping their neighbors to collect water from the fire hydrant and tote it into their homes. Taylor concluded, "Sharing the block with a suspected crackhouse means that apartment dwellers and home owners together experience temporary disaster as a shared crisis."[37]

By defining the black middle class as inclusive of those residents employed in working-class occupations, social scientists lend support to the notion that the black middle class and the black lower classes are inextricably bound to one another by commonly held perceptions of *linked fate*, a term coined by the political scientist Michael Dawson. He argues that in response to persistent racial inequality, middle-class blacks condition their fate on the perceived life chances of the average black. The status of blacks as a group then becomes the standard by which individual middle-class blacks evaluate their own opportunities for upward mobility and economic success. However, as political scientist Cathy Cohen makes clear, the linked fate model is sustained only to the extent that blacks amplify out-group differences between themselves and whites while discounting within-group differences among blacks.[38] Thus, the linked fate approach adopted in community-based studies of the black lower-middle class does help us to understand how this group differs substantially from their white counterparts, but it also conceals many important differences and distinctions among members of the black population, specifically variation within the black middle class.

In the next section, I explain how middle-class status is defined in this study. The definition that I outline is the one that is of most interest to my respondents, highlighting gradations within the black middle class.

DEFINING THE BLACK MIDDLE CLASSES TODAY

Income is the most straightforward and frequently employed definition of middle-class position, but social scientists vary widely in their use of this social indicator. As a result, their measures often mask huge disparities within the black middle class. For example, in *The Hidden Cost of Being African American,* sociologist Thomas Shapiro's middle-class sample is composed of families whose income ranges from a mere $17,000 annually all the way up to $79,000. In his study of the Runyon Heights community, Bruce Haynes establishes a middle-class status based on a median family income of $43,500, which is not only well above the 1990 national median family income ($35,353) but also significantly higher than the national *black* median family income ($21,423). Similarly, Pattillo reports that the median income in Groveland, an urban community in Chicago, is $39,500, a figure twice the city's poverty level—a standard baseline for establishing a middle-class position.[39]

Yet a median *family* income of right around $40,000, while consistent with the national median family income in 1990, is a very low barometer of middle-class status.[40] It could mean, for instance, that each parent earns barely $20,000 annually. Without question, Pattillo's trenchant analysis of the Groveland community and its residents provides insight into the ways in which the fate of lower-middle-class blacks is inextricably bound with that of the black poor, but because the median income in Groveland community is more representative of the lower-middle class, the study cannot fully address the concerns and experiences of a black middle-class population.

By contrast, the middle-class blacks in the current study consider an *individual* income of $50,000 the baseline standard for entry into the black middle class. When asked, "Would you describe yourself as middle-class, upper-middle-class, or upper-class?" nearly everyone reported in the end that they considered themselves middle-class. However, their responses reflected the kind of worrisome imprecision about who is middle-class that we see in the existing literature. For example,

Michelle, a research analyst and Sherwood Park resident, looked unsure for a moment and then responded, "If you define it by dollars, my husband and I both make over $50,000, so, I don't know, what is that?" Similarly, Audrey, who lives in Lakeview, believes that she and her family "should fall in the middle," but she's uncertain about how her perception accords with other middle-class people. "I don't know how people classify themselves," she begins hesitantly. "What are they basing it on? Are they basing it on location, income? I'm not totally sure." Like Michelle, Audrey, who is recently retired from a long career as a real estate agent, turns first to income to try to justify her decision to locate her family "in the middle." "I know," she says with conviction, "that I'm not in the low-income bracket, okay, when you're basing it just on income." Then, shifting from income to spending, Audrey distinguishes herself from the *upper*-middle class: "I feel that we live *modest*, but not anything more than that." And Lydia, a Sherwood Park resident who earns well over the baseline income for this study working as an engineer, argues that one cannot establish a middle-class lifestyle in the Washington, D.C., area on less than $50,000 per year:

> I would probably describe myself as middle-class, but the IRS has a different idea. [She laughs openly.] See, I don't go with what the IRS says. I would say, if you ask me, I would say I live in a middle-class community. But the IRS has different ideas about what is considered middle, upper, based on what your tax should be. So somebody needs to straighten them out! [She laughs.] The IRS considers, they make their [determination] base[d] on somewhere like Tougaloo, Mississippi, where $50,000 will buy you a really nice home and a really nice life. Whereas here, you're like on poverty row. You can't survive on that kind of money. They don't consider the fact that you live in a major metropolitan area where things cost three and four times what they do in like, Kansas. . . . So we get to be poor, but the IRS thinks we're rich.

Lydia is not really poor, and neither are the other middle-class blacks in this study, though they joke about it. Sherwood Park residents Nathaniel and Lisa, married computer scientists, laughed as they claimed, "We describe ourselves as *working*-class! Yeah, *working*-class. If you gotta get up and go to work every day, you're working-class!" Describing her family facetiously as "one paycheck away from poverty," Charlotte, like Nathaniel and Lisa, connects her class position to the fact that she has to work to help support her family. "I don't care what you are, if you have to work every day, you are po' [poor]! I don't care how much money you make!"

To be sure, only a small segment of the U.S. population earns over $50,000 annually—18 percent of white workers and 9 percent of black workers in 2000 (see figure 1). Apart from the classification preferences expressed by the people in this study, there are analytical benefits to separating middle-class blacks who earn more than $50,000 from those who earn less. For one thing, high earners, particularly those who hold college degrees, have seen their incomes rise steadily from one decade to the next since the 1970s, while lower-wage earners have seen their incomes decline.[41] Income disparities between those at the bottom of the income distribution and those at the top were most stark in states with exceedingly high wage earners, such as New York. There the median income increased by 54.1 percent, rising from $56,812 in the late 1970s to an astonishing $161,858 in the late 1990s.[42] Put simply, people at and near the bottom have had to figure out how to make it on much less since the 1970s, while people closer to the top have been able to maintain the standard of living they've enjoyed for the last three decades. This disparity in the growth of income over time helps to explain why lower-middle-class blacks experience their class position differently than middle- and upper-middle-class blacks do.

Distinguishing blacks who earn more than $50,000 annually from those who earn less is useful for a second reason, namely, that this type of analysis provides insight into the relative composition of the middle classes by race. Table 1 contrasts the earnings of whites and blacks broken down into three categories of middle-class position. The majority of middle-class people fall into the lower-middle-class category, whether they are white (53 percent) or black (65 percent). The gap between whites and blacks narrows when we consider the upper income categories, which are the focus of this study. Whites earning between $50,000 and $99,999 constitute 37 percent of the white middle class, while blacks in this income group make up 31 percent of the black middle class. 10 percent of whites are upper-middle-class and upper-class, compared with 4 percent of blacks. These comparisons show that the incomes of white and black middle-class individuals converge more at the top of the middle class structure than at the bottom. In terms of the composition of middle class categories, lower-middle-class blacks differ more from lower-middle-class whites than middle-class blacks differ from middle-class whites.

Blacks who earn more than $50,000 are set apart from lower-middle-class blacks on yet another indicator of middle-class status: wealth. National studies show that the black-white income gap has narrowed over time, but the wealth gap has not. In the United States, income is tied to achievement. Most Americans believe that people with more training,

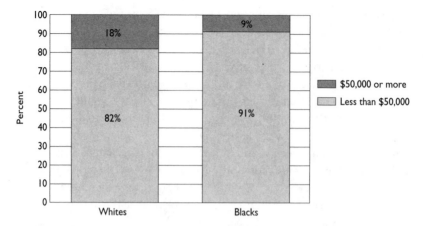

Figure 1. Percentage of white and black U.S. population eighteen years and older with income above and below $50,000, 2000. Source: U.S. Census Bureau, 2000 Survey (PINC-02, Part 25 and Part 49).

skills, and education deserve to earn more than those who are less accomplished. Consequently, the narrowing of the black-white wage gap lends credence to the idea that our society is meritocractic.[43] But wealth is different. It is not earned, but passed down from one generation to the next. Inherited wealth is what allows many families to afford a middle-class lifestyle, one that would be well out of reach if they were forced to rely only on what their achievements could provide.[44] More often than not, the families who stand to inherit wealth are white, which means that whites are more likely than blacks to be cushioned by the safety net of wealth should their income be wiped out by a layoff, poor business decisions, or simply bad luck. Because this safety net is not visible in the analysis of income differentials, scholars concerned with racial inequality now suggest that we should consider wealth alongside income in our determinations of who is or is not middle-class.

Families who have accumulated wealth do not use it "to purchase milk and shoes and other life necessities. More often it is used to create opportunities, secure a desired stature and standard of living, or pass that class status along to one's children."[45] In this way, wealth "can serve to create or reinforce class identity."[46] We can learn even more than we already know from national studies of wealth about the relationship between wealth and class position by examining how different groups of middle-class blacks use assets to transmit and reproduce their class position. Most middle-class families identify their home as their most valuable asset. In existing community-based studies of the black middle class, some authors highlight home ownership. Bruce Haynes notes that in Runyon Heights, 56 percent of residents are homeowners; in Pattillo's Groveland, 75 percent of residents are. In this regard, both black communities are atypical. Nationally, 52 percent of blacks earning between $30,000 and $49,999 own their own homes, compared with 70 percent of their white counterparts in the same income category. Indeed, as figure 2 shows, not only do whites and blacks differ in their patterns of home ownership, but different groups of the black middle class do as well. Consistent with existing studies, in every income category, more whites than blacks are homeowners; however, this differential is smallest among high earners (income over $100,000 annually). Moreover, whereas only 52 percent of blacks in the $30,000–49,999 income category own their own homes, 66 percent of blacks earning more than $50,000 do, as do 80 percent of those earning more than $100,000. We need to consider these intraclass distinctions along with racial disparities in our assessments of the wealth gap.

Sociological studies also include occupation as an indicator of who is middle-class. They tend to collapse white-collar occupations—professionals, managers, and supervisors—into the same broad middle-class category as clerical and sales workers. In most ethnographic studies, clerical and sales workers constitute the majority of the sample, with black professionals making up a negligible portion. I don't dispute the fact that, historically, many occupations that are actually working-class positions were considered middle-class by the black community. Porters and postal clerks, for example, were widely perceived as veritable middle-class occupations. But now that the black class structure has expanded enormously, there is good reason to rethink the tendency to characterize many working-class occupations as middle-class. In contemporary studies of black middle-class communities, sociologists tend to appropriate the occupational categories that signaled a middle-class status years ago and apply them to today's society. These blacks are actually what LeMasters terms "blue-collar aristocrats" rather than members of the middle class.[47]

For instance, in his historical account of the first blacks to move into Runyon Heights, a predominantly black community in Yonkers, a suburb of New York, Bruce Haynes notes that early on, the suburb was composed of working-class blacks whose positions carried an elevated status in the black community. "Due to the skewed occupational structure," he writes, "blue-collar occupations like carpenter, coachman, and railroad porter could carry middle-class status, particularly if the individual was a homeowner in a respectable community." And this schema

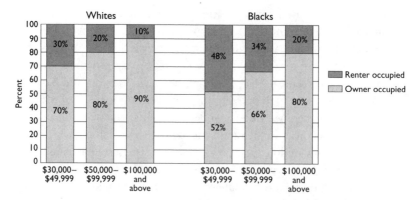

Figure 2. Percentage of U.S. households occupied by owners and renters, by race and income, 2000. Source: U.S. Census Bureau, Current Population Survey (HINC-01, Part 2 and Part 3).

informs Haynes's current understanding of who should be categorized as a member of the black middle class. After World War II, incoming Runyon Heights residents were better educated than their predecessors, working, as a result, in lower-middle-class occupations as teachers, nurses, clerical workers, and salesmen, rather than working-class occupations. In practice, these lower-middle-class workers were virtually indistinguishable from the black lower classes as they fought along with the black working class to compel white employers to hire blacks. In this way, "the divide between the working-class and the middle class was blurred. . . . Nondiscriminatory hiring practices would benefit all occupational classes, so the black classes organized during the 1940s, taking their message directly to employers." Today, Runyon Heights is composed largely of lower-middle-class residents—social workers, teachers, and government workers—with only a tiny proportion of residents holding middle-class managerial or professional occupations as lawyers, computer consultants, and small business owners.[48]

Another popular indicator of middle-class status is educational attainment. Generally, social scientists equate a college degree with being middle-class, but nearly all the existing studies of the black middle class have fudged a bit on this measure, leading to imprecise definitions of who falls where within the middle class. Only 20 percent of residents in Pattillo's Groveland are college graduates. Given the correlation between education and occupation, the 80 percent who are not college graduates are likely concentrated in low-level sales and clerical positions rather than the more exclusive managerial and executive positions sociologists

Sharon Collins and Elijah Anderson adopt as indicators of a middle-class status. According to anthropologist Stephen Gregory, residents of working- and middle-class Corona are "well-educated," although he doesn't state that they are college graduates. Other scholars either do not include educational attainment in their determination of middle-class status, acknowledge "some college" as a sufficient measure, or accept one member's college degree as a measure of the family's middle-class position.[49]

A college degree is associated with higher and more stable earnings, good indications that an individual is actually middle-class. Table 2 shows educational attainment by race and income. Attaining a college degree is positively correlated with income: 13 percent of the black lower-middle class hold college degrees, 18 percent of the black core middle class are college graduates, and 28 percent of the black elite middle class earned college degrees. Among whites, 16 percent of the lower-middle class hold college degrees, 22 percent of the core middle class are college graduates, and 34 percent of high earners earned college degrees. Note that the differences between the black middle classes are greater than the differences between blacks and whites for each of the income categories.

In addition to these standard measures, most studies establish a neighborhood as middle-class based on its resemblance to the neighborhood of the average middle-class black. Pattillo describes Groveland as a middle-class neighborhood based in part on its location "as a kind of buffer between core black poverty areas and whites." But the typical neighborhood of the average middle-class black is changing. In suburbia, the neighborhood of a middle-class black looks different. It may be heavily black, Haynes observes, but, like Runyon Heights, it may be "surrounded by many virtually all-white working and middle-class residential areas," not predominantly black and poor communities, a phenomenon that has important implications for how black residents conceive of their identity.[50]

The social identities employed by different groups of blacks constitute another variable that should become a standard component of our definition of the black middle class. I view these identities as housed in a black middle-class tool kit and argue that residential location helps to determine how and under what circumstances groups of middle-class blacks construct and assert these identities. Like income, occupation, and education, an individual's ability to convincingly portray distinct identities as a way of signaling social position is an important element of social class.

In the introduction to this book, I noted that some middle-class black

TABLE 2. EDUCATIONAL ATTAINMENT, BY RACE AND INCOME, 2000

In percentages

WHITES			
	$30,000–$49,999	*$50,000–$99,999*	*$100,000 or above*
Less than BA/BS			
<9th grade	5	2	1
9th–12th grade	8	4	2
High school graduate	36	30	15
Some college	20	20	14
Two-year degree	9	10	8
BA/BS or higher			
Bachelor's degree	16	22	34
Master's degree	4	8	16
Professional degree	1	2	6
Doctorate	1	2	5
N	17,712	25,961	12,359

BLACKS			
	$30,000–$49,999	*$50,000–$99,999*	*$100,000 or above*
Less than BA/BS			
<9th grade	3	2	1
9th–12th grade	9	7	3
High school graduate	38	30	17
Some college	22	24	20
Two-year degree	10	10	10
BA/BS or higher			
Bachelor's degree	13	18	28
Master's degree	4	7	14
Professional degree	0.6	1	5
Doctorate	0.3	1	1
N	2,854	27,457	803

SOURCE: U.S. Census Bureau, Current Population Survey (HINC-01, Part 2 and Part 3).

families live lifestyles that mirror in many ways the lifestyles of middle-class whites. These shared lifestyle characteristics—the aesthetic quality of middle-class neighborhoods, the spacious homes, the attention to leisure and recreation—all factor into what I mean by a revised definition of the black middle class. Overlap between black and white middle-class people on these measures is a key distinction between the middle-class blacks in my sample and the blacks portrayed in previous studies of the black middle class. Because income is the source of this enviable black middle-class lifestyle, and because income is determined by one's education and occupational status, I employ these measures as well. In doing so, I demonstrate that while generally, as Pattillo notes, "a more appropriate socioeconomic label for members of the black middle class is 'lower middle class,'"[51] a growing proportion of blacks exist for whom this label is an inadequate fit. Inconsistent measures of which neighborhoods and black residents are middle-class has led to confusion about how to establish the boundaries of the black middle-class and a failure to identify gradations within it. I am suggesting that we think about defining the black middle-class differently than scholars have in previous studies, focusing more keenly on the criteria that help to distinguish the black lower-middle class from the black middle class.

The comparisons that I've drawn here using census data show that it is possible to speak of distinct groups of middle-class blacks. Socioeconomic indicators, lifestyle decisions, and the varied spatial patterns of middle-class blacks suggest that there are good reasons to divide the black middle class into distinct groups—those individuals earning less than $50,000, whom I deem lower-middle-class; those individuals earning more than $50,000 but less than $100,000, who I argue constitute the core black middle class; and those individuals earning more than $100,000, whom I characterize as the elite black middle class. Black high-wage earners merit greater attention from social scientists interested in identity precisely because they are less likely to endure the chronic economic and social challenges of everyday life that many lower-middle-class blacks experience in their neighborhood settings. In other words, these high-wage-earning blacks are engaged in a different type of identity project than those who earn significantly less.

We tend to think of suburbs as havens for the white middle and upper-middle classes, and census data support this general perception. However, just as other indicators of middle-class position vary among the black middle classes, so too does suburbanization. Only 35 percent of

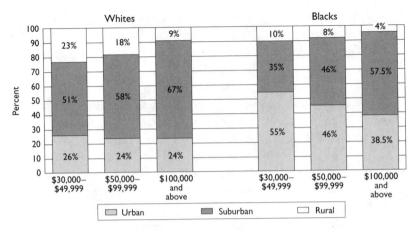

Figure 3. Percentage of U.S. households located in central cities, in suburbs, and in rural areas, by race and income, 2000. Source: U.S. Census Bureau, Current Population Survey (HINC-01, Part 2 and Part 3).

lower-middle-class blacks lived in suburbs in 2000, compared to 51 percent of whites in their income category (see figure 3). The place-of-residence gap also narrows as income rises: 46 percent of the core black middle class live in suburbs, compared to 58 percent of whites. And in the highest income category, 58 percent of blacks are suburbanites, compared with 67 percent of whites. In the next section, I explain how the suburbs in this study differ from those studied most often by sociologists.

MIDDLE-CLASS-BLACK OUT-MIGRATION

Opportunities for sociologists to explore the experiences of the core and elite black middle classes are linked to debates over where middle-class blacks live. These debates have been framed within the context of black out-migration theory. The theory suggests there is a positive correlation between racial progress, rising socioeconomic status, and geographic mobility. As conceived by sociologist William J. Wilson, the theory posits that new opportunities generated by civil rights legislation created a "class-selective" migration, allowing middle-class blacks (followed by working-class blacks) to flee heavily black, predominantly poor neighborhoods, presumably settling into the majority-white suburbs of the nation's largest cities. Importantly, Wilson did not track the migration patterns of middle-class blacks directly and makes no concrete claims about the specific location or characteristics of their new neighborhoods. Instead, he showed that in cities with the largest concentrations of poor people (for example, New York, Chicago, Philadelphia, Detroit, and Los Angeles), the total population declined by 9 percent during the 1970s, while the poor population increased by 22 percent.[52]

Where did middle-class blacks go? Critics of the black out-migration theory agree that middle-class blacks left the mostly black, overwhelmingly poor neighborhoods lodged in the central city but disagree that they ended up in the white, middle-class suburbs in the large numbers alluded to by Wilson. Political economist Paul Jargowsky argues that members of the black middle class settled in middle-class *black* neighborhoods, apart from the black poor. Pattillo contends that black middle-class neighborhoods are contiguous with poor black neighborhoods. Thus, middle-class blacks who manage to escape the geographical " 'hood" don't get very far away from its social and economic threats.[53] Douglas Massey and Nancy Denton present compelling evidence that persistent racial residential segregation severely limits the residential options of blacks, even when they are middle-class. A middle-class status doesn't automatically translate into better housing. Indeed, they show that in most U.S. cities, middle-class blacks are as segregated from middle-class whites as poor blacks are from poor whites.[54] They argue further that most middle-class blacks continue to live in neighborhoods that do not reflect their status position—predominantly black communities in close proximity to the black poor. These distressed black neighborhoods are the research focus of most existing community-based studies of the black middle class.

Other scholars show that middle-class blacks have managed to escape the ghetto and move into white neighborhoods, but whites' unwillingness to remain in communities with a visible black presence has tipped the racial composition of these communities toward majority black. According to sociologist Lincoln Quillian, "Middle-class blacks have been moving into white neighborhoods at rates high enough to increase their numbers there, but declining white populations in neighborhoods with substantial black populations have prevented a large increase in the share of blacks in white nonpoor neighborhoods."[55]

To be sure, the vast majority of middle-class blacks do live in residential communities that are less desirable than those of their middle-class white counterparts, and where they live has real and identifiable costs for their everyday lives. Most often, these communities are heavily black. Generally, houses appreciate more slowly in black middle-class neighborhoods than they do in white communities, public transportation is less efficient, quality food and clothing stores are often absent, and home and car insurance rates are higher. Even in suburbia, where Alba, Logan, and Schults report middle-class black suburbanites do receive a payoff for being middle-class, because they live in suburbs with a larger percentage of white neighbors than lower-class blacks, the authors still identify a drawback: their white neighbors earn significantly less than the middle-class black residents, and thus, middle-class blacks still do not live in communities with whites who share their class position.[56]

But in the years since the out-migration thesis was proposed, three important changes in the spatial patterns of middle-class blacks have occurred, changes that point to a need for social scientists to devote more attention to variation in the experiences of a different group of middle-class blacks, namely, those whose residential location constitutes an exception to the general rule. First, the percentage of blacks living in the suburbs of the country's largest cities has increased from a small minority of the suburban population in the 1970s to a sizable mass, particularly in metropolitan areas with large concentrations of middle-class blacks (see table 3). Social and political pressure from the civil rights movement and fair housing organizations coupled with an explosion of new housing construction have contributed to notable increases in the percentage of blacks living in suburbia. Secondly, middle-class, *distinctly black* suburban enclaves are growing in popularity. These exclusive communities are most likely to crop up in metropolitan areas where middle-class blacks are concentrated, such as Atlanta; Washington, D.C.; Houston; and St. Louis. Within these suburban enclaves, middle-class blacks isolate themselves from the black poor and buffer themselves from racial slights that might arise in comparable white, middle-class suburban communities.[57] Third, the kinds of suburban communities where middle-class blacks now settle vary in terms of the quality of their housing stock, racial composition, appreciation values, proximity to the poor, availability of municipal services, and general aesthetic appeal. The assumption that majority-white, middle-class neighborhoods are the most appealing places for middle-class blacks to live is misguided in the current period, just as the stereotype that predominantly black neighborhoods are inherently dangerous places for middle-class blacks to live is also not invariantly true.[58]

The kinds of suburban communities now available to middle-class blacks in the Washington, D.C., metropolitan area are as diverse as the black middle class itself. Lakeview and Riverton are both middle-class suburbs, but living in predominantly white Lakeview presents a different set of opportunities and challenges to middle-class blacks as they

TABLE 3. PERCENTAGE OF BLACK POPULATION
RESIDING IN SUBURBS, SELECT METROPOLITAN
AREAS, 1970–2000

Metropolitan Area	1970	1980	1990	2000
Chicago	10.39	16.16	18.36	32.42
Cleveland	13.41	27.36	33.83	50.57
Detroit	13.23	14.83	17.40	32.50
New York	6.89	8.10	6.54	17.48
Philadelphia	22.54	27.78	32.00	21.77
Atlanta	26.64	43.24	64.08	78.51
Baltimore	14.29	22.62	29.19	70.05
Washington, D.C.	24.97	47.48	61.64	82.71
Dallas	36.41	36.76	27.64	57.24
Houston	18.69	16.82	25.03	37.37
Phoenix	14.82	22.01	31.04	43.59

SOURCE: U.S. Census and the American Housing Survey.

manage their social identities than does living in majority-black River-ton. Upper-middle-class, heavily black Sherwood Park presents an altogether different set of challenges. Sherwood Park residents recognize that they are geographically located in the larger Riverton community, but see their subdivision as set apart from the other, less exclusive (though still middle-class) Riverton subdivisions. In the remainder of this chapter, I highlight important differences in blacks' migration to Prince George's County, Maryland, and Fairfax County, Virginia, and explain how their place of residence bears on the identity options of middle-class black suburbanites. I begin with a brief description of suburbanization processes in the two counties, and then move on to a detailed description of the three sites that make up this study. While Lakeview, Riverton, and Sherwood Park are rare residential locations for middle-class blacks today, as more blacks attain middle- and upper-middle-class status, there are good reasons to believe that these upwardly mobile blacks will select suburban communities like the ones I describe in this book.

FAIRFAX COUNTY, VIRGINIA

Lakeview, located in majority-white Fairfax County, is one suburban community where middle-class blacks have managed to settle, albeit in small numbers.[59] The bulk of Fairfax County's middle-class black population are transplants—newcomers to the Washington, D.C., area, not local blacks spilling over from the central city.[60] Most of this group re-located due to a promotion or entirely new job assignment. Unlike many northern and midwestern cities—Boston, Chicago, Philadelphia, and New York—Washington's economy is grounded in government jobs and personal service occupations, not manufacturing. Because of its close proximity (less than ten miles) to the central city, Fairfax County appeals to black federal employees seeking to minimize their daily commute. From 1970 to 1980, the black population in Fairfax rose from 16,381 to 35,802, an increase of 118 percent, reflecting the expansion of the federal government coupled with transplants hired to fill new positions.[61]

Prior to the 1960s, the tremendous growth in Fairfax County's population was fueled in part by white flight from D.C. in response to the Supreme Court's 1954 *Brown v. the Board of Education of Topeka* decision declaring racially segregated public schools unconstitutional. Virginia's governor, Thomas B. Stanley, directed blacks emboldened by the *Brown* decision to disregard the ruling. "I shall use every legal means at my command," he declared, "to continue segregated schools in Virginia." Governor Stanley appointed a state commission to consider the dilemma. The commission proposed that local leaders, not the federal government, should dictate a plan for integration and that the state should offer tuition grants to whites so that their children might attend private schools or public schools in jurisdictions committed to preserving segregation. Whites voted in favor of this resolution; blacks rejected it. Having passed, the resolution empowered Governor Stanley to deny state funds to schools that sought to comply with the *Brown* decision. Despite the Supreme Court's ruling that public schools desegregate, not a single black student in Virginia attended a white public school during the 1956–1957 school year. The resolution was revoked by the Virginia Supreme Court in 1959. Public schools that had been shut down in protest were ordered to reopen, and the state was forced to fund all public schools, including those prone to integrating.[62]

Today, Fairfax County public schools enjoy a national reputation for excellence that middle-class blacks appear to value highly. In recent years, the number of black students in Fairfax County public schools has increased substantially, from 4,214 blacks in 1970 to 8,530 blacks in 1980.[63] But because black students are more likely to be suspended and less likely to be placed in honors or Advanced Placement courses, black parents have lodged complaints that the school system is, if not inherently racist, insensitive to blacks.

In addition to the potential for racial tension in the schools, black home-seekers interested in Fairfax County have met with opposition in the form of restrictive zoning laws designed to limit construction of apartment buildings and other multifamily housing units that would appeal to lower-income families. On the one hand, these laws have helped to maintain a middle-class presence in Fairfax. At the same time, they discourage lower-class blacks who cannot afford single-family housing. These factors—job growth, quality schools, and a commitment to single-family housing—help to explain black suburbanization in Fairfax County and also address the low proportion of blacks in the county overall.

PRINCE GEORGE'S COUNTY, MARYLAND

Prince George's County is the only county in the country in which the median income of residents continued to rise as the suburb transitioned from majority white to majority black. This statistic alone distinguishes Prince George's County from the typical black suburban county. Suburbs in predominantly black counties are often older communities, contiguous with the central city and characterized by a high percentage of poor residents, a weak tax base, poor municipal services, exceptionally high density, and deteriorating housing stock.[64] As Logan and Schneider argue, because it is unlikely that many blacks would prefer these unfavorable conditions, the neighborhood characteristics in most of the nation's black suburbs reflect ongoing racial discrimination in the housing market.[65] Thus, the average black suburbanite lacks reasonable housing alternatives to their current suburb.

Although most suburban blacks live in suburbs that are virtually indistinguishable from the central city in terms of deleterious neighborhood characteristics, some middle-class blacks live in suburbs that more closely resemble white middle-class communities.[66] It is from studying majority-white and predominantly black suburban middle-class communities such as those found in Fairfax County and Prince George's County, rather than poorer black neighborhoods, that we will draw the most fruitful data on the black middle class. In Prince George's County, predominantly black, solidly middle-class suburbs are increasing in popularity, prestige, and influence, and therefore merit the attention of social scientists.[67] Within these suburban enclaves, one finds a dizzying array of subdivisions ranging from middle-middle class to upper-middle class. While none of the Prince George's County residents in this study are forced to grapple with drug dealers, gang members, or the encroachment of public housing in their subdivisions, as residents in Pattillo's Chicago community or Haynes's Yonkers suburb do, residents in the Riverton subdivisions are affected differently by the problems that do plague the county—an inferior public school system and relentless strip malls, among other structural maladies. I examine differences in Prince George's County residents' perceptions of their community's most salient problems in chapter 6.

Today, scholars and journalists alike think of Prince George's County as the quintessential black middle-class suburb, but it didn't start out that way. From its founding in the seventeenth century until the 1960s, Prince George's County was an overwhelmingly white, working-class community, with the exception of the slave population. Blacks began trickling into the county in the 1960s, spilling over into contiguous suburbs located just inside the beltway from predominantly black sections of southeast D.C. "As black families moved in, whites moved out," historian Andrew Wiese writes. "The result was a swift process of racial turnover much like the one that had transformed northeast Washington in the 1940s and 1950s. By the early seventies, African Americans were on their way to a majority in neat residential suburbs all along the city line."[68] This classic pattern of neighborhood succession—upwardly mobile blacks taking over the abandoned suburban neighborhoods of working-class whites—surged on, showing no signs of abating in the 1970s, as distraught white residents fled deeper into the bowels of the county with a parade of black home-seekers trailing closely behind. In 1970, white residents made up 85 percent of the population of Prince George's County and blacks a mere 14 percent. By 1990, the white population had dwindled to 43 percent and the black population had risen to 52 percent.[69]

Three factors quickened the pace of black suburbanization in Prince George's County. First, in 1972, Sylvester Vaughns, along with seven other black parents, sued the county, charging that a segregated school system was unconscionable. Twenty-two years prior, the National Association for the Advancement of Colored People (NAACP) won their legal battle against segregated schools in the 1954 *Brown v. the Board of Education* decision. However, like many southern communities, the Prince George's County school administration ignored the court's ruling to desegregate "with all deliberate speed." Instead, Prince George's County deliberately encouraged segregation, constructing brand-new schools for whites and for blacks well after the *Brown* ruling, despite a chorus of criticism from black residents. Given the county's failure to enforce *Brown,* the NAACP joined the 1972 suit brought forth by the eight black parents. The NAACP/parents coalition prevailed, and court-ordered busing was instituted in Prince George's County in December 1972.[70] By the 1980s, when the county had a majority-black presence, it no longer made sense to enforce court-ordered busing, and the ruling was overturned at the urging of blacks. Today, the Prince George's County school system is heavily black, although, as I discuss in chapter 6, high-income black parents avoid traditional classrooms in favor of magnet schools or elite private schools.

Second, beginning in the 1970s, the Prince George's County police department finally agreed to hire black officers. Other American cities with large black populations had hired black police officers decades before. For example, eight black men were hired by Atlanta's police force back in 1947. Atlanta's black policemen were restricted to patrolling black neighborhoods and were not authorized to arrest whites, but their presence did have symbolic meaning for black residents.[71] Known for its brutality against black residents, Prince George's County's police department was hit with a suit alleging discrimination in hiring as well. In response, the department reluctantly recruited blacks, and by the 1980s, 12 percent of the police department was black.[72]

Third, Prince George's County provided generous incentives, in the form of tax breaks, to encourage developers to construct affordable new housing developments within the county's borders. Blacks seeking reasonably priced homes in the Washington, D.C., area can find them in Prince George's County, where new housing construction has outpaced neighborhood succession as the primary form of suburbanization. Rather than taking over communities once dominated by working-class whites, middle-class blacks are now moving into developments constructed specifically for them.[73]

Developers make no attempt to hide the fact that a home of the same model is priced significantly lower in Prince George's County than in surrounding counties.[74] Michael, a Prince George's County resident, remembers that he "saw the same house [as the one he eventually bought in Prince George's County] in Montgomery County. Our house is on like an acre and a third . . . something like that. We saw the *exact* model . . . up in Montgomery County on . . . [a] lot which is a quarter-acre. . . . It was like forty thousand dollars more—the difference between Montgomery County and Fairfax County. Same house, same model, forty thousand dollars more. You can do the economics."

These differences in black suburbanization trends serve as an excellent example of the kind of diversity stemming from residential location that we find within the black middle class. By studying more than one residential community, it is possible to compare and contrast the experiences of the two groups of blacks that make up America's black middle class. In doing so, we will uncover what has been right before our eyes all along: the numerous boundaries that elite and core middle-class blacks maintain to distinguish themselves from one another.

CONCLUSION

Why is a new study on the black middle class needed? We have learned a great deal about the dynamics between members of various classes within the urban communities depicted in existing community-based studies of the black middle class, and we know a fair amount about identity-related issues among members of a single specific class within these communities, whether that single class is the black poor, black working-class, or black lower-middle class. This is valuable information, but it has skewed our understanding of what it means to be a middle-class black in the contemporary United States.

By first stipulating what I mean by middle class (baseline criteria including income, education, occupation, wealth, and use of the black middle-class tool kit), and then looking at middle-class blacks who live in completely different settings than those studied most often by sociologists, I discover something new. Unlike urban settings, suburbia has no "third places" such as coffee shops, bookstores, or cafes where residents gather informally to mingle with their neighbors.[75] Different kinds of suburbs make up for the lack of public spaces and public interaction in different ways. Difference in residence, it turns out, is very important because it has a significant effect on how the blacks in this study perceive themselves and others. Indeed, groups of middle-class blacks who live in different types of suburban communities engage in different kinds of identity work. In this book, place of residence has a consciously shaped meaning, defined by housing developers and their sales staff as well as by the kind of identity work individuals do and don't need to perform in their specific suburban communities. I turn to these constructed meanings in the next chapter.

2

Social Organization in Washington's Suburbia

The middle-class blacks in this study live in placid suburban subdivisions. They don't open their front doors to find people of dubious character congregating on their stoops; they don't worry about how to negotiate sidewalks blocked by clumps of suspicious-looking strangers; and they aren't concerned that when night falls their cars will be broken into or vandalized.[1] There are no strangers wandering aimlessly through Lakeview, Riverton, or Sherwood Park. Indeed, any kind of street activity is rare here: much of the social activity in middle-class suburbia happens behind closed doors, not on street corners.[2] Why this is so may be traced, in part, to the role of suburban developers.

A distinguishing characteristic of suburbia is that the developer's original vision plays a significant role in shaping community life long after the homes have been constructed and the work crews and sales staff have moved on to new sites. It is the suburban developer who initially establishes the personality and character of the community, stipulating the house sizes and styles, the selling prices, the spacing between homes, the layout of the streets, and the placement of common areas. These structural features determine not only what kind of people will move into the subdivision but also the conditions under which they will interact with one another. For instance, large homes with spacious yards appeal to wealthier home-seekers. At the same time, the vast distance between such homes means that residents are not likely to run into one another unless they make a deliberate effort to do so. Similarly, developer-specified regulations affect community members' social interactions and behaviors. In some subdivisions, rules are explicitly encoded in covenants and rigorously enforced; in others, they are merely verbally acknowledged by residents and loosely upheld through tradition and peer pressure. Thus, in order to understand variation in the social identities of middle-class black suburbanites in Lakeview, Riverton, and Sherwood Park, we need to know more about the communities themselves.

Middle-class blacks in the Washington, D.C., area inhabit a variety of desirable suburban spaces, communities that vary in terms of their racial composition, class composition, proximity to the poor, and internal governing systems. Many of these current subdivisions bear little resemblance to the declining suburbs middle-class blacks were confined to in the early years of racial integration in the housing market.[3] To varying degrees, the communities of Lakeview, Riverton, and Sherwood Park each bear the imprint of Levittown, New York, the first large-scale suburban subdivision built in the United States. For that reason, this chapter begins by tracing the ways in which specific innovations in suburban development pioneered by the Levitt brothers in postwar America continue to shape builders' visions and practices today. The discussion then moves to each of the three subdivisions in turn to assess the impact of their respective builders' visions of middle-class values and standards on present-day community life. Key similarities and differences in the structural characteristics of the three developments are identified, factors that influence how each community's middle-class black residents conceive of their racial and class-based identities.

LEVITTOWN: A MODEL FOR SUBURBAN DEVELOPERS

The sociologist Herbert Gans did not exaggerate when he declared that the famed Levittown subdivisions were "undoubtedly the prototype" for subsequent suburban developments constructed in the post–World War II era.[4] The construction industry had stagnated during the war years, and builders were unable to respond quickly enough to meet the tremendous demand for houses created by the exceedingly high marriage and birth rates that followed the end of the war. The Levitt brothers' solution was inventive. Utilizing principals of "scientific management," they routinized home construction, an approach that made it possible to build more than thirty houses per day. Prefabricated walls, flooring, and roofs were shipped to the subdivision site, where trained workers quickly snapped the homes together.[5] Dubbed "the Henry Ford of housing," William Levitt supervised the construction and opening of the first Levittown on Long Island, New York, in 1947. With 17,400 homes, it was the nation's largest suburban subdivision constructed by a single builder. Still basking in their initial success, the Levitts went on to build a second Levittown near Philadelphia in the early 1950s that comprised 16,000 homes, and a third in New Jersey in 1958.[6]

Levittown's massive scale and innovative building principles provided a template for the modern American suburban subdivision. Nearly every study of post–World War II suburban life credits the Levitts with establishing construction procedures that made suburban home ownership profitable for builders and possible for young, moderate-income families. When whites abandoned central cities in droves beginning in the 1950s, they were moving into suburban subdivisions patterned after the Levitts' enormously successful model. But the Levitts' influence on the modern subdivision extends well beyond guidelines dictating the optimal physical environment to which builders should aspire. The Levitts sought to institute and sustain a particular lifestyle in their subdivisions, one that reflected "the ways of middle-class civility and manners."[7] To ensure that their vision of middle-class life was realized and sustained, they introduced a series of innovations, all of which remain among suburban builders' standard practices today.

One strategy the Levitts used to mold middle-class desire was to expose potential buyers to an array of appealing design features and rooms full of gleaming new furniture that the buyers may not have needed, but that they would immediately recognize that they *wanted*. Unlike the vast majority of builders, the Levitts erected full-size model homes, stocked with modern appliances and furniture (all donated by Macy's, General Electric, and Bendix in return for the right to use the Levitt name to market their products), as a way to persuade buyers that Levittown was the right place for them. The Levitt brothers gambled that as home-seekers walked through the models, touching coveted appliances and absorbing the tasteful decorating style, they would conclude that their own cramped apartments were hopelessly inadequate and antiquated. Even if the home-seekers didn't purchase a home that day, the brothers believed "the model would linger in their minds and soften them up for future homeownership."[8] Following the Levitts' hugely successful example, contemporary suburban developers furnish model homes lavishly, suggesting to potential home-seekers that they belong in the subdivision and deserve the opulent lifestyle laid out before them.

Generating the hefty down payment and collateral necessary to qualify for a mortgage was a formidable barrier to home ownership for many aspiring middle-class families in the early postwar years. A second important innovation of the Levitts was to install their own sales staff onsite to market the homes, thus rendering real estate agents unnecessary; they also helped buyers with financing by accepting very small down payments, thus bypassing the loan bottlenecks characteristic of commercial banking arrangements. Few home-seekers could resist the combined effects of the glib sales staff and the beckoning opportunity to assume the luxurious life offered by the model homes. With a down payment of only a hundred dollars on a house that could be obtained for a mere seven thousand dollars (the equivalent of $63,282 today), young families persuaded themselves that it was more economical to buy a Levitt home than to continue renting.[9] Today's suburban builders also employ their own sales staff, who help arrange financing for potential buyers who find the subdivision desirable but unaffordable at first glance.

A third strategy the Levitts used was to gloss over potentially troublesome distinctions stemming from occupational status by selling everyone the same style house. "In a place like Levittown, whether a household's breadwinner was a mechanic, factory worker, low-level engineer, white-collar employee, salesman, or small businessman scarcely mattered. . . . What mattered was that his home bore the trappings of a middle-class life."[10] Both the Long Island and Philadelphia subdivisions contained a single model: the four-room, Cape Cod–style home that was the Levitts' signature structure. These 750-square-foot homes, tiny by today's standards, contained a living room, a kitchen, a bath, two bedrooms, and an attic. They were enormously popular. According to historian Kenneth Jackson, "This early Levitt house was as basic to post–World War II suburban development as the Model T had been to the automobile."[11]

Over time, the Levitts did vary the style of their homes slightly, in one subdivision. The Cape Cod–style homes in the first two subdivisions had appealed primarily to working-class and lower-middle-class homeseekers. The Levitts and their staff designated this group "marginal buyers," that is, people who, in the absence of government assistance, wouldn't be able to afford a Levitt home. The Levitts hoped to reduce the number of marginal buyers in their New Jersey Levittown by offering three different models, rather than just one. In addition to the Cape

Cod home, they built a more expensive ranch style and a still more expensive two-story, colonial-style house.[12] With this "mixed housing," the Levitts became the first developers to successfully introduce a variety of housing styles in a single subdivision, a move that highlighted the presence of middle-class and lower-middle-class families within the same community. This innovation marked the emergence of a class structure in the New Jersey Levittown. In the Washington, D.C., area today, suburban developers also tend to offer a limited variety of models within the same subdivision, though they do so primarily to break up the monotony that offering only a single model would confer.

The final Levitt innovation, and perhaps the most significant one for this study, was the brothers' imposition of neighborhood covenants designed to regulate the lifestyles of Levittown residents and sustain a middle-class standard. For example, residents who wished to hang clothing outside to dry could do so only under the condition that they used the collapsible clothes racks provided by the Levitts. Traditional clotheslines were forbidden. Fences were prohibited as well. Families who failed to maintain their lawns as the subdivision covenants required learned that the Levitts would have the grass cut, and would then forward the bill to the recalcitrant homeowners.[13] Contemporary suburban developers use similar kinds of neighborhood covenants as a convenient way to preserve their preferred vision of suburban community life.

Along with these four enduring innovations, the Levitts also maintained a steadfast commitment to a racially inequitable aspect of community life long after it was ruled unconstitutional by the Supreme Court. The restrictive covenants written into the deeds of Levittown homes constituted racial residential segregation sanctioned by the federal government. Following prescriptions published under the banner of the Federal Housing Administration (FHA), in which neighborhoods segregated by race and class were openly encouraged, the Levitts adopted a "whites only" policy, requiring potential homeowners to agree "not to permit the premises to be used or occupied by any person other than members of the Caucasian race."[14] Ten years after restrictive covenants had been outlawed by the 1948 Supreme Court ruling in *Shelley v. Kramer,* the Levitts insisted on trying to maintain racial segregation in their subdivisions. A company representative pointed to the state's complicity as a partial explanation for the ongoing racial exclusion: "Our firm is liberal and progressive, but we don't want to be singled out or used as the firm which should start the other builders off. If there is no other builder who can keep Negroes out, we will not do so either; we will go with the group if the state makes us, but we don't want to lose millions by being the first. . . . We could not afford to take such losses."[15]

Of course, the Levitts previously had shown themselves to be more than willing to "start the builders off" in other respects, and eager to undertake the appreciable financial risks that accompanied their debut as builders of the first large-scale suburban subdivision in the nation. Their business practices strongly influenced smaller, lesser-known builders, and the Levitts' innovations—in the construction industry, in home marketing and sales, and in the establishment of neighborhood covenants—have all been adopted by builders today. The threat of federal sanctions finally moved the Levitts to agree to integrate their communities, beginning with the New Jersey Levittown. But the damage had already been done. Feeling unwelcome, black families did not flock to Levittown in large numbers, and these subdivisions remain predominantly white today. Had the Levitts been as determined to lead the industry in rejecting racial exclusion as they were in developing technological advances, middle-class blacks may have enjoyed suburban communities commensurate with their status position long before the 1970s.

FAIRFAX COUNTY

LAKEVIEW

Lakeview, a middle-class, predominantly white community composed of a historically rich conglomerate of subdivisions, is located in predominantly white Fairfax County, Virginia. Among Washingtonians, it is widely considered one of the most desirable suburban communities for professional families. Constructed beginning in the late 1950s and 1960s, Lakeview is dominated by modest ranch- and Cape Cod–style homes, with a small sprinkling of newer, two-story homes, all positioned on quarter-acre lots. Sidewalks and small, manicured front lawns buffer the houses from the street. There is very little space between homes. Narrow driveways delineate one lot from another, but a good number of the older homes do not have garages. Many of the homeowners have lined their driveways with shrubbery or have planted colorful flowers along the borders of their lawns. Shutters and front doors painted a variety of bright, inviting colors personalize the houses. These cosmetic home improvements help distinguish Lakeview from the typical cookie-cutter suburb.

The streets of the Lakeview subdivisions flank a single main roadway

Figure 4. Lakeview home distinguished by flower border, potted plants, and the American flag. Photo by Eric Shoaf.

in a modified grid pattern. Residents, who range from retirees to couples with young families, live in close proximity to a well-stocked, professionally staffed local library, two elementary schools, a middle school, a public park with a small playground, a slew of restaurants and discount stores (including Wal-Mart), and a large soccer field where local intramural teams compete. Property values in Lakeview are high and continue to escalate.

Longtime Lakeview residents Matt and Elizabeth, now in their seventies, are representative of the original Lakeview homeowners—white, professional men married to stay-at-home moms. Matt, whose thin build, gray hair, and glasses give him a bookish appearance, recently retired from a successful career as a structural engineer. Elizabeth, who has been married to Matt for fifty years, is slim and fit-looking. Her salt-and-pepper hair is stylishly cut, flattering her thin face. The couple raised their four children—two boys and two girls—in Lakeview. Photos depicting the children as youngsters decorate the small tables that stand at each end of a light blue, oversized sofa. Matt seems to relish opportunities to talk about the history and growth of the neighborhood; Elizabeth is generally quiet, but her shy manner gives way periodically when she energetically interjects information to clarify or extend a point Matt has made.

Only five homes in the Lakeview community were finished and ready for occupancy when Matt and Elizabeth moved into their cozy, three-bedroom bungalow in 1960. There were equally few restaurants and shopping malls in the early years. "There was one McDonald's," Elizabeth recalls, ". . . and one other restaurant that I can think of, and then there was a Dixie Pig, a little barbecue place. . . . There were none of these big malls. No Landmark. No Tysons [Corner]." Matt credits former president Dwight D. Eisenhower with spurring both the explosive growth and what has proven to be the enduring popularity of the Lakeview subdivisions. Soon after they moved into their new home, Matt explains, the Capital Beltway, one link in Eisenhower's intricate plan for an interstate highway, was completed: "Thank God for good ol' Dwight Eisenhower. If not for him, this national highway system wouldn't exist, 'cause Congress was against it, and he overrode it and signed it into law. . . . And that had a dramatic effect, because from the time that beltway was opened, this whole area started to grow and it hasn't stopped yet."[16]

The beltway encircles the Washington, D.C., metropolitan area and thus allows Lakeview residents to travel efficiently from the southern tip of the greater metro area northeast toward Maryland, or northwest to places like Tysons Corner Center, an enormous upscale shopping mall. Of course, the new highway also acted as a pipeline, funneling prospective home buyers from distant neighborhoods toward Lakeview. What the beltway did not bring was racial diversity. Though there was no overt, organized objection to black residents (i.e., no racial covenants or other written prohibitions), no blacks lived in Lakeview until the early 1970s, a few years after the 1968 Fair Housing Act had made its way through Congress.[17] "I've never known any restrictions for anybody living in here," Matt tells me, reflecting thoughtfully. He remembers two "mixed families" and one black family from his early years in the subdivision, but none of these families had moved in before 1969. Some older black couples I spoke with pointed out that the suburbs didn't open up to middle-class blacks until long after the Fair Housing Act had become law. For example, June and Randall, now in their late sixties, relocated to the Washington, D.C., area in 1961 to accept new jobs as high school teachers. June is petite and speaks in a soft, melodic voice; Randall is very tall, about 6' 4", and speaks in a booming voice. They have two adult children, a son and a daughter. Although, like Matt and Elizabeth, they had wanted a home in Lakeview, June recalls with disappointment, "There wasn't a section that we could buy in" because "this was before integration."[18] Another black Lakeview resident, fifty-two-year-old Charlotte, and her husband purchased their four-bedroom Lakeview home in 1976 and raised five children there. Charlotte recalls that ten years earlier, in 1966, Lakeview had been off-limits to blacks: "A lot of it has to do with your racial—with how integration was passed. Because when we first got married [in 1966] . . . D.C. was where most African Americans lived, because that was the area which was open. You didn't have these other areas. . . . Integration hadn't reached that point. So most people lived in the D.C. area. Then, about 1970, things started to open up [to blacks]."

Today, blacks continue to live in Lakeview subdivisions, but still in very small numbers. When Audrey, now a sixty-two-year-old retired real estate agent, and her husband purchased their bright yellow, two-story colonial in the early 1970s, they were the first black family to move into this newer Lakeview subdivision. Audrey is short and stout; her hair is a mass of tiny curls. As we sit in her immaculate, monochromatic living room (a range of yellows defines the space—from pale yellow carpet to gold, floor-length draperies), she describes those first years. "There were very few blacks, none in this general area. We kind of broke the barrier," she says, with a slight chuckle. Eventually, another black family bought in their subdivision, but when the adults in that family retired and moved farther south, Audrey's family again became the only black residents. Her son and daughter did not have black playmates in their subdivision. Despite this racial isolation, Audrey has never felt uncomfortable in Lakeview: "We were very well accepted when we moved here. We've always been accepted and included." Describing a social pattern familiar to suburbanites across the United States, she asserts of her neighbors:

> We know that they're there if we need them. If anything ever happened, if there's an illness or anything like that, they look out for you. . . . If I need something, then they'll come over. Like if I've run out of flour, you don't feel that you can't go next door to get it, that kind of thing. I never will forget, I never had a hand can opener. And all of a sudden the [electric] can opener broke. We didn't have a [hand] can opener in the house! [She laughs.] I've never had one before. I had an electric one. I was just dumbfounded! We didn't have a [hand] can opener! So then my neighbor was saying that she's never had anything but that kind! So she showed us the kind we needed to get.

Today, blacks and whites in Lakeview share a characteristic that sociologists argue is essential to sustaining an integrated neighborhood— a similar standard of living.[19] The newer residents "are mostly mid-level civil servants," according to Steve, a white fifty-two-year-old resident.

Trained as a political scientist, Steve detoured from the academic track and now works as a researcher for the federal government. He has lived in Lakeview with his wife and two daughters for fourteen years. Small acts of kindness, such as the can opener incident recounted by Audrey, help unite Lakeview residents and reinforce an awareness of their shared class position.

Social organization in Lakeview is structured through a neighborhood association that reflects the practical aspects of a mainstream, middle-class lifestyle. The association has an interesting history. Lakeview's original developer had been committed to constructing homes that exceeded code specifications, but the homes were so well-built and used such high-quality materials that he couldn't recover the money he'd put into them. He went bankrupt before all the sections of the development had been completed. Out of concern for the community's future value, the developer worked with residents to start the neighborhood association. For their part, residents hoped the organization would represent the community's interests to the next developer. Both aims are encapsulated in the neighborhood association's concern for property values, a key element of a mainstream, middle-class lifestyle. The association sponsors an annual contest to select the most attractive yard, which is administered by the community's garden club. Although most members of the club are elderly, they gamely continue to judge the best front yard and the best holiday decorations each year. Cheery signs mounted on wooden sticks mark the winning yards. According to Blanche, an older white resident who has served as garden club president, the yard-judging contest "encourages everyone to take really, really good care of his property . . . to say, 'I take pride in my home.'"

The neighborhood association's efforts to reinforce Lakeview's version of a middle-class lifestyle focus on promoting social activities rather than on enforcing rules. There are no covenants in Lakeview—residents may paint their homes whatever color they like, landscape as they choose, and structurally alter their homes, provided such changes do not violate Fairfax County building codes. Despite the neighborhood association's lack of enforcement authority, disputes among residents have been few. Steve, who is a past president of the association, remembers an incident involving a resident who parked a large boat in his driveway. Neighbors complained. Eventually, he moved out (for reasons unrelated to the boat squabble). It was an ideal solution since, as Steve admits, if the man had not moved, "I don't think there would have been anything to do" about the boat.

The fact that all residents are automatically members of the neighborhood association is another way in which Lakeview preserves its middle-class lifestyle. Everyone is "requested to pay" the nominal annual dues (eight dollars per family in 1997), but the few families who do not pay are not excluded from membership. Lakeview's low annual dues result in social activities that are modest compared to activities held in more upscale subdivisions like Sherwood Park. Events sponsored by the neighborhood association often draw on individual residents' resources. An older resident, for example, thinks back fondly on previous neighbors who were members of the military. Whenever Lakeview held a big event, they would supply whatever was needed for the party from the military's ample stash. The neighborhood association also relies on residents' talents rather than calling in professional entertainers. For years, Matt donned a Santa Claus costume at Christmastime and entered each house in the community, bringing treats for the children. Other popular neighborhood events, such as the semiannual cleanup drive and the annual yard sale, require only a minimal investment of association funds (e.g., the price of the newspaper ad announcing the date and time of the sale).

A small portion of the neighborhood association's accumulated funds is used to cater the annual dinner. At one time, this event more closely resembled a barbecue or a block party. It was held outside in June in one of the subdivision's cul-de-sacs. Some of the older residents complained that the weather was too hot for this kind of outdoor get-together. Now the dinner is held on a Sunday evening at the end of June inside a church about a mile from the subdivision. The party I attended began at 5:30 P.M., and most of the attendees were elderly and white, with a few exceptions. Two younger interracial couples and their children attended, but no black couples were present. The catered dinner targeted adult tastes and preferences and included exceptionally thick hamburgers, potato salad, corn on the cob, chunky cookies, and a variety of canned soft drinks. There were no special foods for children. Some of the parents came prepared: they brought along snack-size baggies of goldfish crackers and bite-size carrots for their children. A small playground beyond the recreation room's French doors provided the only source of entertainment. From the neighborhood association's perspective, the pleasure derived from sitting at circular tables and chatting with neighbors over dinner required no further enhancement.

Most of the other social events sponsored by the association, including a Halloween party, Christmas caroling, an Easter parade, and an Easter egg hunt, underscore a specifically white, middle-class, Christian lifestyle. The racial and religious diversity represented by Lakeview's few black, interracial, and Jewish families is downplayed in community life. Steve, who is Unitarian, muses over the seemingly absentminded nature of the community's failure to acknowledge its own diversity: "This is a somewhat diverse community, but not really. So when people have, like, Christmas caroling, they don't think about Jews—or [when there is the] Easter egg hunt, anything like that. It just doesn't click. . . . It's funny, . . . I wouldn't say this is a really diverse neighborhood, both culturally and racially." In its "diverse, but not really" approach to social organization, the Lakeview community is much like the average, middle-class suburban community in America. It is a modern-day Levittown. The developer's decision to emphasize uniformity by building homes nearly identical in their structural likeness attracted large numbers of residents who tend to focus on the community's economic homogeneity as the basis for the its mainstream, middle-class framework. Lakeview's racial and religious diversity are not incorporated into the community's character. In this way, living in Lakeview differs dramatically from living in Riverton.

PRINCE GEORGE'S COUNTY
RIVERTON

Riverton is a middle-class, predominantly black collection of subdivisions located in Prince George's County, Maryland, across the Potomac River from Fairfax County. Many whites in the greater Washington, D.C., area view Riverton as an undesirable place to live. A wooded central roadway cuts through the Riverton community for about two miles, providing access to the various subdivisions. Shopping centers stand at both ends of this roadway. The one at the east end contains a Food Lion grocery store, a Subway sandwich shop, a Kentucky Fried Chicken, and a gas station. At the other end, where the homeowners are of lower income, there is a Safeway grocery store, a McDonald's, a Dollar Store, several generic stores, and another gas station. Between the two endpoints, there is a 7-Eleven convenience store and the local elementary school. Public transportation to and from Riverton is limited to a single city bus route, with buses that run on weekdays during morning and afternoon rush hour only. Residents tend to drive wherever they are going; it is rare to see someone walking along Riverton's streets. In late fall, residents drive carefully to avoid colliding with deer that dart out suddenly onto the main roadway. The class composition of Riverton varies—ranging from lower-middle class to upper-middle class—and so too do the cost and quality of the housing stock. There are Georgian colonial, Cape Cod, split-foyer, and ranch-style homes. Riverton bears little resemblance to the typical pre-1970s black suburban community, which tends to be contiguous with the central city and where residents live in undesirable housing and endure inferior municipal services.

In the 1970s, only a few years after Prince George's County opened up to black home-seekers, Riverton acquired a reputation as the most desirable suburb for successful blacks. Forty-five-year-old Lydia, who lives with her husband and three children in the Sherwood Park section of Riverton, is a rich source of information about the area's history. She was raised in a working-class neighborhood in Washington, D.C., and remembers that, "growing up, you knew about [Riverton] because that was where the black elite lived." What began as a small, exclusive community expanded over time into the current loose assortment of subdivisions, spilling well beyond its original boundaries. Riverton residents continue to distinguish the elite portions of the development—including Sherwood Park—from other parts of the expanded section elsewhere along the main roadway. "This is what I was told," Lydia explains: "If you live to the left [of the main road], that's not considered an exclusive neighborhood. Whereas if you live to the right [Sherwood Park is one of the newer subdivisions located on the right], they think that you have money, because you live—the more expensive homes are to the right. So the street becomes like a boundary."

The symbolic significance of this physical boundary is respected by residents on both sides of the street. The prevailing view is that most middle-class blacks can afford to live somewhere in Riverton, but only black white-collar *professionals* reside in Sherwood Park. Terry, a thirty-two-year-old hospital administrator who, with her husband and two young daughters, lives about a half-mile from Sherwood Park, insists anyone can live in her subdivision: "A bus driver lives across the street, a firefighter. Nobody says you have to have that college degree. . . . That's why I'm saying you can be proud to be a janitor. Janitors can live out here." Janitors may live in the subdivisions that extend beyond Sherwood Park, but there are no janitors living in Sherwood Park. Kevin, a high school football coach, who, like Terry, lives in Riverton but not in Sherwood Park, warned me that "bougie [bourgeois] people live out there." For their part, some Sherwood Park residents jokingly refer to the other Riverton subdivisions as "the black middle-class ghetto."

Figure 5. Riverton home. Photo by Eric Shoaf.

Community life on the left side of the main Riverton roadway is characterized by a desire to uphold middle-class standards, but the levels of success in this regard vary across the individual subdivisions. Each subdivision has its own neighborhood (as opposed to homeowner) association. Jared, a systems administrator for the federal government, notes that the neighborhood association in his subdivision seems especially concerned with "one-on-one stuff. For instance, 'Address XYZ is keeping a filthy lawn'—they'll single out individuals who are not meeting the standards." Like the organization in Lakeview, everyone who lives in Jared's subdivision is automatically an association member, and again, as in Lakeview, the annual dues, at twenty dollars per family, are low. Most important, there are no covenants. This lack of legal authority makes the neighborhood association leery of entering into battles with residents. "The standards are unspoken, really," Jared explains, adding that this "is why they have issues. People fight back by, 'Okay, you want to fuss with me about my unmanicured lawn, then I'll just let it grow.' They had a couple of those incidents, where people chose to let their properties go down." The consequences were limited to "just peer pressure."

Things are different in Terry's subdivision. There are potential consequences for violating rules: "We have a little man in a little white car, and he drives around and he gives you a little warning. He's a part of the neighborhood committee." Terry's mixed feelings about the "little man" are clear as she recounts her own run-in with him:

> We used to have a waterbed. My husband was gonna move it, but it stayed [outside] two days. Well, he rang the doorbell [and said], "Do you know you have that, that garbage out there?" Like we didn't know that. [He said,] "Are you planning on moving it? If you don't have anybody to move it, we have a list of names of people who come and haul stuff away." They don't like that, that sort of stuff—trash, bulk trash I should say—sitting out. Cars, abandoned cars, [are] quickly towed. Quickly. They'll have a tow truck come in and tow the car away.

Terry also reports that residents have received tickets for parking boats on the street. But, she says, her area is less restrictive than some of the newer neighborhoods: "From what I understand, when the new developments go up, you can't have a fence. Things like that have passed." There are no written covenants in Terry's subdivision. Verbal warnings from the "little man" are common, but tickets typically are a last resort.

Martin, a city administrator, lives with his wife and two children in a house less than a mile from Terry's, but on the right side of the main roadway. He joined forces with his neighbors and the developer to organize a neighborhood association that operates much like a homeowners' association. There are bylaws and standing committees (e.g., a welcoming committee, a beautification committee, etc.). Martin feels that the rules imposed by the association are not excessive. From his perspective, they simply protect the community from the untoward consequences of any given individual's poor taste:

> Oh, it's not a whole bunch [of rules]. It's like if you want to build a structure, like a fence or things of that nature, the beautification committee—the plans had to be submitted to the neighborhood association, because they want to make sure, you know. . . . We have sprawling lawns and stuff like that, and if someone builds an ugly fence right in the middle of one of the yards . . . [the rules are] just to be able to have a say, just in case somebody has no taste at all. It's not really to try to keep people from doing what they want to do.

Overall, social organization in Riverton's subdivisions is centered around an adherence to "standards" that establish the community as middle-class. These standards, conceived by the developers and enforced (albeit weakly in some instances) by the neighborhood associations, aim to align the behavior of a diverse group of middle-class blacks to a baseline essential for a peaceful community life. In the absence of strict neighborhood covenants, neighborhood associations struggle to do this work.

By contrast, Sherwood Park is governed by a homeowners' association, an organization with substantially more authority and one that is more reflective of the developer's influence than the associations found in either Lakeview or Riverton.

SHERWOOD PARK

Sherwood Park is an upper-middle-class suburban community tucked away behind an expanse of trees off Riverton's main roadway. It is the kind of secluded community that strangers are likely to overlook as they speed past, despite the presence of a large, slightly faded sign proudly proclaiming the name of the subdivision and marking its main entry. A two-lane drive punctuated by an expansive rectangular island filled with fragrant, professionally maintained flowers leads into Sherwood Park. Aside from this landscaped island, there is no common space within the community. Just beyond the entryway, the subdivision's five spacious cul-de-sacs extend like elegant spokes from a gargantuan circular node on which additional homes are built. Prince George's County regulates the number and types of trees developers may remove (there are no restrictions on leveling pine trees, whereas hardwoods must be left standing). As a result, mature, shade-producing trees line Sherwood Park's streets and frame its homes. Two of the subdivision's cul-de-sacs back onto a creek, providing homeowners in these sections with waterfront property. Nearly every house in the subdivision has a brick facade (a few custom homes are exceptions) and is situated on at least one acre. Portable basketball hoops stand at the end of many of the homes' long, broad driveways. In total, seventy-eight imposing homes, seven occupied by white families, sit amid the deliberately picturesque landscape.

Outsiders often are surprised to learn that Sherwood Park is predominantly black. In 1987, when developers began constructing the subdivision, they intended to market the homes to upper-middle-class white home buyers. The first four couples to purchase homes, all from this targeted group, were certain, because the new development's sales manager and sales staff were white, that the community would be predominantly white, even though it was ensconced in a majority-black county.[20] But soon after white residents settled into the two completed cul-de-sacs, upper-middle-class blacks discovered Sherwood Park. They streamed in, inquiring about the availability of homes scheduled to be built in the remaining cul-de-sacs.

The influx of black homeowners in Sherwood Park led to significant

Figure 6. Sherwood Park home. A number of portable basketball hoops are scattered throughout the community. Photo by Eric Shoaf.

changes in the developers' marketing strategy. Once blacks began to acquire homes in the subdivision, the developers "decided that they had missed their market, and that their *real* market was the middle-class black who was looking for someplace [to] live with their own ethnic background friends," theorizes Andrew, a white, sixty-year-old public policy analyst and one of the first white residents. When he moved into the subdivision in 1989, Sherwood Park was about 24 percent black. In response to the spate of inquiries from blacks, the developers replaced the white sales group with a black staff, a move both black and white residents interpret as a deliberate effort to encourage black home-seekers and discourage white ones. Although it has been many years since Andrew bought his home in Sherwood Park, he remains angry that the developers failed to actively seek more whites. He alternates between pounding his fist on the breakfast table for emphasis and stabbing the air with his finger as he recalls how the subdivision's racial composition took shape. According to Andrew, "The entire sales staff in the subdivision . . . became black. *Everyone.* I saw it time after time. Whites would come up, and it was just an unwritten signal. They would walk in [to the model home] and look, and there wasn't a white face in sight. They would get back into the car, and sayonara." As Andrew anticipated, the racial composition of the Sherwood Park development changed "dramatically" following the staff switch, and it is now a predominantly black subdivision. Visibly upset, Andrew explains why he does not discuss his concerns about the subdivision's racial composition with his neighbors, punctuating his words for emphasis: "[The developers] made a marketing decision. And, you know, you don't *dare* make any comments, lest you be viewed as the wearer of the *white sheet,* for God's sake, and be, you know, *excoriated* by all those around you, and excised as being a cancer in the community, despite the fact that it just changed *dramatically.* . . . It became a *black* development."

The racial complexion of Sherwood Park changed as blacks began to move into the remaining cul-de-sacs, but the class composition of the community did not. Like their white counterparts, nearly all of Sherwood Park's black residents are college graduates working in professional occupations, typically as doctors, lawyers, executives, managers, or corporate partners. That life in Sherwood Park is defined by economic privilege and not hardship is reflected in the community's physical grandeur and in the residents' social activities.

In Sherwood Park, the distance between the homes is not merely ample; it is vast. Neighbors can't see into one another's windows, nor can they chat across front lawns or from porch to porch. As Lydia explains, contentedly, the homes afford a great deal of privacy: "I can go outside and sit on my deck, and nobody can see [me]. If I don't feel like talking to my neighbors, I don't have to talk to my neighbors, you know? That's what I like." Warren, a childless black resident and member of the homeowner association's board, agrees. "You don't wanna be too close to people," he cautions, pushing his glasses back up on his nose. "You want to have a certain amount of space." Ironically, the distance between homes in Sherwood Park appears to *facilitate* rather than hinder some emerging friendships. For instance, Michael really likes the neighbors immediately across the street from him. They are good friends, he reports,

> but, if they're sitting on their front porch, and I'm sitting on my front porch, and I want to talk to them, I'd actually have to go over there, because it's too far to yell. I mean it's *too* far to yell. I'm talking about a *good* distance. Not conducive for yelling. I mean, you might say, "Hey! Hey!" [He shouts this while throwing up his hand, pantomiming a greeting], you know, you just wave and say [to yourself], "I don't know what the hell he's sayin'!" [He laughs.] . . . And distance makes great friends.

The considerable distance between the homes means that Sherwood Park residents are spared the daily interactions with their neighbors so characteristic of concentrated urban areas. As John puts it, "It's not a community in the sense that we would all like for it to be—where you knew everybody else's business and you looked after everybody's kids, and you had a key to somebody's house, and you could go and turn off their television if they weren't home. We don't live like that." Moreover, residents don't tend to borrow a cup of sugar from their neighbors, nor are they likely to show up on one another's doorsteps unannounced. However, they do interact during neighborhood events.

Like the residents of Lakeview and Riverton, homeowners in Sherwood Park gather for an annual summer block party. The Sherwood Park version of this event, in keeping with the subdivision's posh profile, is more spectacular than the parties held in the other two communities. Traditionally, Sherwood Park's block party is well-attended by both black and white residents. The party I observed was held outside in late summer in the cul-de-sac of the homeowners' association president. The location of the party rotates annually from one cul-de-sac to another. It began in late afternoon, around four o'clock, and ended well after nine o'clock. In terms of both food and entertainment, the party aimed to please all comers. For the adults, there were pieces of crisply fried fish (cooked in a humongous deep fryer), a seemingly endless supply of sliced white bread, and assorted pastas and salads. A live rhythm and blues band played, enticing some residents into a spontaneous rendition of the electric slide, and there were door prizes, such as gift certificates for a dinner for two and movie tickets.

Most of the party's activities, however, catered to the subdivision's children. In addition to providing them with standard barbecue fare— hamburgers, hot dogs, and chips—the homeowners' association board also had arranged for a very special dessert. A Good Humor ice cream truck, complete with a uniformed Good Humor man and jingly sound track, made an appearance at the party. The children were very excited that they could "order" whatever they wanted from the truck's takeout window—and that they could go back to place another order as often as they wished. Younger children tended to select the Spider-Man popsicles; older children preferred the treats favored by adults, such as ice cream sandwiches or chocolate éclair bars. The children also enjoyed a performance by a professional magician and door prizes for Happy Meals at McDonald's. Without a doubt, though, for the younger children, the biggest draw was the moon bounce. A large, inflatable structure designed to resemble an oversized, tan-colored dog with an enormous belly, this party rental accommodated eight to ten bouncing children at a time.

Not surprisingly, a block party of this magnitude requires ample funding; the event I observed cost residents well over two thousand dollars. Sherwood Park's community activities—which, in addition to the block party, include a Fourth of July party, Yard of the Month awards, dumpster rentals (for spring and fall cleanups), and a Sunshine Fund (monies to defray the cost of purchasing flowers for sick and shut-in residents)—are all funded by its homeowners' association, the Neighborhood Review Board (NRB). Homeowners' associations are growing in popularity among builders of planned communities. They differ from neighborhood associations in important ways. Homeowners' associations are created by developers, not community members, and their primary purpose is to preserve property values by ensuring that the development is well-maintained. Once the development is fully occupied, developers typically cede power to an elected board of the community's homeowners. All individuals who purchase homes in these planned communities automatically become members of the homeowners' association.

Like homeowners' associations elsewhere, the NRB is governed by a set of covenants, legally enforceable rules and regulations drafted by the developers. Sherwood Park residents must pay a hundred dollars annually in homeowners' association dues, they must maintain their homes and yards, and they must not make any physical alterations to their homes without first securing approval from the NRB. At minimum, violators are subject to fines. At most, the NRB is authorized to initiate liens against violators' homes. To the extent that it effectively enforces these covenants, the NRB helps to preserve Sherwood Park's character and personality—big selling points, according to political scientist Evan McKenzie. Well-conceived covenants, he notes, "give the developer the power to create a distinct lifestyle in a development, which the developer can use as a powerful marketing tool."[21]

CONCLUSION

When the Levitts constructed first one Levittown, then another, then another, they couldn't have imagined that their model of suburban life would have such an enduring impact on suburban developers. This chapter has shown that a key organizing principle in suburbia is the imposition of the developer's vision of community life on home-seekers through the physical aspects of the community and through covenants incorporated into the homeowners' deeds, just as the Levitts did many decades earlier. These covenants set the standards for middle-class civility in a community. In Lakeview, the conventional model of suburban life, a sense of community is achieved by downplaying racial and religious distinctions in favor of mainstream norms. In Riverton, a sense of community results from everyone in the suburb doing their part to uphold middle-class standards. And in Sherwood Park, community life is sustained through an elegant setting and elite neighborhood activities. Subsequent chapters explore some of the ways in which the distinctive personalities of each of these suburban communities help shape the diversity found among their black middle-class residents. But before turning to the differences found within suburban residences, I examine how the blacks in this study think about their identities as they move about in public spaces.

3

Public Identities
Managing Race in Public Spaces

Instances of discrimination against blacks in stores, in the workplace, and in other public spaces occur every day, unobserved by potential sympathizers and unreported by black victims. As sociologist Joe Feagin's gripping study of the black middle-class experience shows, middle-class status does not automatically shield blacks from discrimination by whites in public spaces.[1] His interviewees' reports of being denied seating in restaurants, accosted while shopping, and harassed by police officers lead Feagin to conclude that a middle-class status does not protect blacks from the threat of racial discrimination.[2] Feagin's study documents the formal and informal mechanisms that contribute to persistent discrimination toward blacks in the public sphere. His perspective, which has been invaluable in shedding light on the dynamics of racial stratification in the United States, suggests that contemporary patterns of discrimination often prevent accomplished blacks from enjoying the taken-for-granted privileges associated with a middle-class status, such as a leisurely dinner out or a carefree shopping experience.

One problem with racial stigma theory, however, is that it downplays the arsenal of resources middle-class blacks have at their disposal to counter discriminatory treatment.[3] That such resources exist—and that blacks are willing and able to use them strategically in the workplace—

is demonstrated by Elijah Anderson in his recent study of corporate culture. Anderson identifies specific cultural resources black professionals employ to advance within the organization and to manage their interactions with co-workers.[4] The experiences of participants in my study suggest that the actions and strategies Anderson observed are not limited to the workplace. Middle-class blacks can use similar cultural resources to successfully signal their class position to whites in other public settings. This chapter demonstrates that despite the ever-present possibility of stigmatization, not all middle-class blacks feel as overwhelmed by and as ill-equipped to grapple with perceived discrimination as racial stigma theory implies. Some perceive themselves as active agents capable of orchestrating public interactions with whites to their advantage in a variety of public settings. Study participants from Lakeview, Riverton, and Sherwood Park describe how the strategic deployment of cultural capital, including language, mannerisms, clothing, and credentials, allows them to create what I call *public identities* that effectively lessen or short-circuit potential discriminatory treatment.

Unlike the *status-based identities* introduced in the previous chapter, in which middle-class blacks rely on wealth expressed through lifestyle distinctions to underscore symbolic differences between their social group and others, public identities are more purposeful, instrumental strategies that either reduce the probability of discrimination or curtail the extent of discrimination middle-class blacks face in their public interactions with white strangers. While middle-class blacks assert status-based identities primarily as a means of justifying their own attitudes toward other groups (the black poor, the white middle class, and the white upper class), they assert public identities in order to convince others— social strangers such as store clerks, workplace subordinates, and real estate agents—that they are legitimate members of the middle class. White Americans typically equate race with class and then reflexively consign all blacks to the lowest class levels. The experiences of middle-class blacks in my study suggest that those who actively correct the misapprehensions of white strangers reduce the likelihood of discriminatory treatment. This invocation of a public identity is a deliberate, conscious act—one that entails psychological costs as well as rewards. As Charlotte, an elementary school teacher and Lakeview resident, explains, black people "have two faces," and learn to distinguish self-presentation strategies suitable in the white world from self-presentation strategies useful in the black world. The continual enactment of a public self can be exhausting, and the perceived need to don a public identity that accurately telegraphs class status in order to secure smooth transactions in the white world can be infuriating. Jared, a Riverton resident, observes with a mixture of resignation and disgust, "If you're white and you're raggedy, don't matter. . . . But if I come out [to shop] in jeans, it's 'Oh, Southeast!' immediately. And you'll be treated differently." Forty-four-year-old Michelle, a program director at a research center, confesses that when she is engrossed in her work, she "slip[s] . . . every once and a while" and thinks of herself "just as a person with views and opinions," rather than as "the black girl." She berates herself for being a "jerk" whenever she momentarily forgets about her racial identity at her white-dominated workplace. Even in the post–civil rights era, "forgetting" one's racial identity is rarely an option for blacks. In predominantly white settings, "The world at large is a mirror for me every time I forget [that I am black and female]," Michelle states flatly.

Most middle-class whites, on the other hand, pay little overt attention to their own race or class. For them, most activities such as shopping, working as a manager, or buying a house are routinized, psychologically neutral, and relatively conflict free. Public challenges to their class status are rare. Middle-class blacks face a different reality. When they leave the familiarity of their upscale suburban communities, many of the accoutrements associated with their middle-class lifestyle fade from view.[5] Skin color persists. On occasions when race trumps class, blacks' everyday interactions with white store clerks, real estate agents, and office subordinates can become exercises in frustration or humiliation or both. Asserting public identities makes it possible for blacks to tip the balance of a public interaction so that class trumps race. Blacks who successfully bring their middle-class status firmly into focus pressure white strangers and workplace subordinates to adjust their own behaviors in light of this information. Public identities, then, are not so much prepared responses that permit individuals to skillfully avoid or ignore strangers or social deviants when in public as they are strategies for sustaining problem-free interactions involving strangers.[6] The use of public identities allows some middle-class blacks to complete their shopping without being accosted by store clerks or security guards, to supervise workplace subordinates effectively, and to disarm hostile real estate agents.

The first half of this chapter explores the construction of public identities and traces their origin. It explains how study participants representing all three research sites, most of whom grew up in working-class families, acquired the cultural capital necessary to assert public identities. The second half of the chapter outlines how middle-class blacks put public identities to work in three types of public interactions conducted in the Washington, D.C., area: shopping, managing work subordinates, and house-hunting. With respect to all three settings, the discussion draws on experiences reported by study participants; however, analysis of the third setting is supplemented by findings from my own undercover interactions with real estate agents when I posed as a home buyer. To date, no study has employed this methodology—combining participant observation with interview data—to understand how real estate agents relate to black home-seekers.

CONSTRUCTING PUBLIC IDENTITIES: BOUNDARY-WORK IN THE PUBLIC SPHERE

A key component of the public identities asserted by middle-class blacks is based on class and involves differentiating themselves from lower-class blacks through what I call *exclusionary* boundary-work. Washington-area middle-class blacks are firm in their belief that it is possible to minimize the probability of encountering racial discrimination if they can successfully convey their middle-class status to white strangers. To accomplish this feat, interviewees attempt to erect exclusionary boundaries against a bundle of stereotypes commonly associated with lower-class blacks. Exclusionary boundary-work is most readily apparent when middle-class blacks are shopping or managing employees in the workplace. Middle-class blacks also engage in *inclusionary* boundary-work in order to blur distinctions between themselves and white members of the middle class by emphasizing areas of consensus and shared experience. Efforts to highlight overlaps with the white middle class are common when middle-class blacks engage in house-hunting activities.

The construction and assertion of public identities varies according to social context and the basis of perceived discrimination. In the context of shopping, the middle-class blacks in this study perceive that race bias is operational, that is, that there is a failure by others to distinguish them from the black poor. Specifically, they know that whites wrongly assume that blacks are poor and that the poor are likely to be shoplifters. Consequently, when shopping, these middle-class blacks confront the stereotype of the street-savvy black shoplifter, which white store clerks often apply to blacks as a group.[7] To disassociate themselves from this negative image and signal that they "belong" in the store (i.e., that they have money, can afford the merchandise, and have no need to steal), study participants report that they dress with care. "People make decisions about you based on how you're dressed and what you look like,"

Michelle says. "Because I know that," she elaborates, "I choose my dress depending on what the environment is." Interviewees contend that their decisions to eschew clothing associated with urban popular culture—for example, oversized gold earrings, baggy jeans, and designer tennis shoes—maximize their chances of enjoying a trouble-free shopping experience and signal their respectability to white strangers. This kind of exclusionary boundary-work helps middle-class blacks establish *social differentiation*—they make clear to store personnel that they are *not* like the poor.

Evidence of social differentiation emerges in the workplace as well. Just as the professions have used educational credentials to limit membership and to bring legitimacy to their discipline, professional blacks underscore their authority as managers by highlighting credentials such as job title and professional status.[8] Holding positions of power, interviewees believe, makes them impervious to workplace discrimination.

In the context of house-hunting, middle-class blacks perceive that class, rather than race bias, operates. In order to maximize their range of residential options, public identities are constructed to be linked in an inclusionary manner with their white counterparts. With the dominant cultural code in mind, middle-class blacks rely on mainstream language and mannerisms to carry out interactions with real estate agents. In cases in which these interactions break down, respondents use their own resources and social networks to find an acceptable home on their own. Put simply, middle-class blacks engage in inclusionary boundary-work to establish *social unity*—to show that middle-class blacks are much like the white middle-class. These identity construction processes are mutually reinforcing in that they each help to affirm respondents' position as legitimate members of the American middle class.

As a result of their employment of public identities, the middle-class blacks in this study are pleased with their ability to successfully manage racial stigmatization in their interactions with white strangers in the public sphere, avoiding the kind of humiliation and frustration that Feagin's interviewees report experiencing routinely. Still, asserting public identities can be emotionally taxing at the personal level. Even when such strategies pay off, they can be tiring and irritating, exerting a potential psychological toll that informants either are unaware of or tend not to express. In this way, the middle-class blacks in this study differ from those interviewed by Feagin, who saw themselves as victims and didn't feel as confident that they could always do something to counter stigmatization. Feagin's respondents were overtly angry, and it is possible that the blacks in my study are more angry than they realize.

CULTURAL CAPITAL AND CULTURAL LITERACY

Cultural capital, a key signifier of middle-class status, constitutes the means by which public identities are staked out. Cultural capital theorists argue that an important mechanism in the reproduction of inequality is a lack of exposure to dominant cultural codes, behaviors, and practices.[9] Middle-class blacks have obviously secured a privileged position in the occupational structure. But cultural capital differs from such economic capital in that cultural capital indicates a "proficiency in and familiarity with dominant cultural codes and practices—for example, linguistic styles, aesthetic preferences, styles of interaction."[10] These signifiers of middle-class status are institutionalized and taken for granted as normative, hence the underlying assumption that groups that cannot activate cultural capital fall victim to systematic inequality. In previous studies, such marginalized groups have typically been poor and working-class.[11]

However, a recent study suggests that poor blacks and Latinos do rely on cultural resources to negotiate their social world. Through interviews with sixty-eight low-income high school youth and recent graduates, Prudence Carter shows that a nondominant form of cultural capital, which she calls *black cultural capital,* is of great importance to these young blacks because it allows them to signal their racial or ethnic authenticity to other black youth. The youth associated an appreciation for the newest rap artist and a command of black English with authentic blackness. Moreover, some of these students also deployed dominant cultural habits and signals, having been exposed to these cultural resources by dedicated teachers. Carter refers to this latter group of black youth as *cultural straddlers,* because they had learned how to move back and forth between minority and mainstream culture.[12]

Still, we know very little about the origins of the cultural capital middle-class blacks possess or about how they use it systematically to cope with discrimination.[13] Theorists typically investigate the impact of cultural capital in school settings, where they show that children from families whose lifestyles mirror the skills and preferences of the dominant culture are better prepared to negotiate the educational system (which is itself constitutive of the dominant culture) and ultimately achieve greater success in school.[14] In this chapter, I extend cultural capital's utility beyond the school setting to a variety of public settings frequented by middle-class blacks. The type of cultural literacy that is so critical to educational success may also be a crucial factor in middle-class blacks' ability to effectively negotiate interactions with whites in public settings.

How do middle-class blacks acquire the cultural capital necessary to activate public identities? According to Bourdieu, cultural capital is transmitted through one's family of origin. Children from high-status families are socialized into different dispositions (what Bourdieu calls "habitus") from children in low-status families. These dispositions reflect their distinct class position and ultimately dictate different tastes and preferences.[15] Growing up in a family with access to the cultural codes and resources of mainstream high culture produces children who are advantaged as adults, because possession of these cultural resources constitutes symbolic inclusion in the dominant culture and can be used to produce efficacious outcomes in interactions with other social groups.[16] From Bourdieu's perspective, people do not draw freely from an unrestricted set of cultural resources; their family's class position binds their cultural resources to those tastes, styles, and preferences consistent with their habitus. As a result, individuals who fail to acquire cultural capital early in life do not display the same natural feel for high culture as those who are born into it.[17]

Yet a growing number of studies question Bourdieu's claim that children learn early on from their parents whatever cultural capital they will have at their disposal later in life. Specifically, Paul DiMaggio asserts that high school students select from an expansive repertoire of cultural resources; John Mohr and DiMaggio demonstrate that girls acquire more cultural capital than boys in the same class position; and Bonnie Erickson argues that family of origin is only one factor—and not the most salient one—in the acquisition of cultural capital.[18] Each of these studies makes the same basic point, namely, that in his close attention to structural determinants, Bourdieu fails to explore how individuals play a role in shaping their own destinies. An alternative view is moving cultural analysis toward treatments that integrate structure and agency.[19] This alternative approach characterizes the process by which a group of middle-class blacks in the Washington, D.C., area acquires cultural capital.

FROM SOCIAL SURFERS TO SOCIAL CLIMBERS

The majority of the blacks in this study are first-generation middle-class or grew up in working-class families; therefore, they could not acquire cultural capital through the process outlined by Bourdieu. They were not in a position to inherit from their parents the ability to signal their class position to whites via mainstream cultural resources because their parents either did not have access to middle-class cultural resources or they had views about black-white interaction that were informed by Jim Crow laws and other pillars of racial segregation. The few interviewees who did grow up in the middle class question how much their parents, who went about their everyday lives almost exclusively in black communities, could have effectively prepared them to negotiate routine interactions with whites as equals.

For instance, John, now forty-six years old, grew up in "a little black Levittown."[20] Built in the South in the 1950s, all of the neat little bungalows in his suburban neighborhood were occupied by middle-class blacks. Perhaps reflecting his southern upbringing, John has an extraordinarily reserved personality. Occasionally, when he would tell a joke, it would take me by surprise. More often than not, he wears a pensive expression. In a southern accent punctuated by a cadence characteristic of an expert debater, John remembers that preachers, doctors, dentists, lawyers, and, overwhelmingly, teachers, lived together in this idyllic community, one that "was about as good as it got for black people" at the time. Living in relative isolation from white communities, John reports he and his black neighbors had little knowledge of what was happening in white neighborhoods or what whites were doing. Moreover, John feels his parents were not social climbers: "I describe my parents as 'social surfers.' We were on the low end of the economic curve of the neighborhood. They had no aspirations to move up. They just wanted to ride the wave." By John's recollection, his parents were complacent, completely unprepared for the kinds of fundamental changes in black-white interactions that the civil rights movement ushered in:

> My parents didn't have an appreciation for how much the world was changing. They thought that the world was going to be as it was in 1968 and get better, and that you didn't have to deal with those things. But on the other hand, they were very much trapped by thinking about the way the world was in 1948 and they never could embrace the change and take ad-

vantage of the changes that were taking place. My mom never felt comfortable going into a restaurant. . . . And it wasn't so much that the place was white. It just wasn't a part of her world.

Greg, now forty-nine years old, also found that his working-class parents were unprepared for an integrated world. A tall, extroverted man, Greg has a magnetic personality. He's the kind of fun guy that everyone in college would want to hang out with (in fact, he explains that he was very popular in college). Greg was raised in a small, predominantly white working-class town in the North. The blacks who lived there worked in racially segregated occupational niches: as domestics if they were women, and in the mills or as laborers if they were men. His own mother worked as a laundress at the local hospital, and Greg's dad was employed at the steel mill and moonlighted as a mason and painter. A by-product of living in such a small town is that "you knew everyone. The black folks that lived in [the town] were very, very close." But just as John's middle-class family had little interaction with white families, Greg's parents did not have egalitarian interactions with whites. Consequently, Greg reports that his parents' instruction that he be deferential did not serve him well in an integrated environment. His parents' "idea of getting along with whites was what folks would look upon today as subservient, I guess. Because, you know, they worked for white folks, and so they always used to say, 'You have to be respectful,' and da-da-da-da-da, and this kind of thing. So that's basically how they taught me to get along with whites. And then, through high school, when I went to college, I learned a different way of how to get along with whites."

As was the case with John's and Greg's parents, the attitudes of Charlotte's parents toward public interaction with whites were heavily influenced by the constraints of residential, occupational, and educational segregation. The small northern town where Charlotte spent most of her childhood had very few blacks. Her father, who is "very fair," was born there. To secure employment, many of his relatives, who were also "fair," would "pass for white." This practice "was very prevalent . . . because people couldn't get jobs" if they presented themselves as black. Chuckling, Charlotte recalls, "We would go down to Woolworth's, and we would see my aunt down there [working], and she would wink at us [she winks her own eye, imitating her aunt] because she was passing. And that was standard. They were family, but if you saw them out [on their job] it was kind of understood that, you know, [you] don't say, 'Hi, Aunt so-and-so,' because they would get fired. [She erupts in laughter.]

Oh yeah, there was passing! That's how it was. You'd see them and that was it."

The prejudice directed against black sales clerks was also evident in the school system and other social institutions. Charlotte is also very fair. At fifty-two years old, her bubbly, outgoing personality is balanced by her distressing account of her childhood experiences in the segregated North. Charlotte remembers that the "kids were so prejudiced. Games, they wouldn't take your hand. You wouldn't have anyone's house to go over to [to play]. When I was in junior high, we couldn't join any social clubs [except] band. . . . And when I was a little girl, we could only go to the movies on Wednesday, and [we had to] sit in the balcony." Eventually, Charlotte's parents moved the family to a larger city, one with more blacks. Despite her strained interactions with white classmates, Charlotte's parents did not discuss black-white interactions with her. Speculating, Charlotte determines they were exhausted from the considerable effort of maintaining themselves in a segregated society. As she explains, her parents were socialized into a different world than the one that her cohort experienced, and different still than the social world that her children are being socialized into:

> Back in those days, people talked to you differently. . . . When my parents and your mother's parents were coming up, they were just survivors. And they understood what was going on in terms of the racial issue—that they would have to work harder, to be more prepared, and do more to get the same job, or less than the same job, as their white counterparts. And I think that they were involved in that struggle so much that, when my generation was coming up, we were kind of also survivors in that, if you came home, and somebody beat you up—which happened—my mother, her answer to me going to an all-white school was to teach me how to fight. Yeah. Because you don't come home every day crying.

Today, Charlotte is an interventionist mother: "My generation, we were [saying to our kids], 'Now honey, these are the ramifications. If anything happens, Mother will [fix it].' " But as a child, it was different: "Mother was working. Daddy was working. They just didn't have *time* for that. Their life, in trying to survive and make it in a racial community, took *all* of their energy. And they taught their children . . . that we had to be strong, to stand out. And a lot of things were not verbalized. A lot was, again, 'I'll teach you to fight,' so when you get to school, 'you handle that.' "

John's parents avoided integrated institutions, Greg's parents advocated deference toward whites, and Charlotte's parents expected her to resolve racial conflict on her own, without their input. It is possible that Charlotte's parents were ill-prepared to confront her teachers. With the exception of Greg, none of the blacks interviewed for this study had parents who talked explicitly with them about how to get along with whites. And the advice dispensed by Greg's parents was so outdated that it was not useful in an integrated setting. Moreover, respondents' parents lacked early experience of integrated society, and, insofar as interviews reveal, they did not receive a lot of instruction in how to negotiate interracial relations by way of parental example.

While their parents' orientation centered around avoidance of whites and white settings, deference toward whites, and a general reluctance to confront authority figures, the blacks in this study were socialized into a different orientation through their interactions in predominantly white settings. This new orientation is characterized by the acknowledgment that you may be the only black in an integrated setting, a conscious decision to command respect from whites, and a willingness to confront authority figures, the gatekeepers of a middle-class lifestyle.

Many of the respondents in this study spoke of going to school in "*their* environment," meaning whites, or of being the only black in certain circumstances. In contrast to their parents, who tended to avoid white settings, these blacks fostered relationships with whites. Greg attended a predominantly white college, and at the time of his admission, he was the only black male there. He remembers getting to know some of the white males in his dorm:

> This was the '60s, so we'd talk about black-white relationships, those kinds of things. In those days what was big was encounter groups. They'd have these encounter groups and you'd sit there and they'd run you through things where you're supposed to get closeness. They'd ask you, "Do you really trust this person?" Then they'd ask you to do something where you'd have to put your total trust in the person. We used to just have sessions [where] we'd sit around and just talk. And one of the things that I found out, this one guy, Peter, who's a real good friend of mine—well, *became* a good friend of mine—just never had any exposure to black people. As he told me, there was only one black kid—he went to a school that had a graduating class of two thousand people; there was only one black kid. *One* black kid in his whole high school. I go, "You're kiddin' me?!" He says, "No." And so of course we lived in a dorm and we used to learn things. Like I'd always take a shower and put lotion on. Jergen's was big then. He says, "Greg, why do you always put Jergen's on?" I said, " 'Cause of ash!" [Peter says,] "What's ash?" Now I, like I said, I didn't grow up in the city.

I'm just a country black kid that just grew up in a small town. I said [he assumes an incredulous tone], "You don't know what ash is?!" So they tell me, "You mean dry skin?" Now I don't know nothin' about dry skin, but I knew what ash was! [I said,] "My momma always called it 'ash'!" [He laughs.] So, they sort of learned that. . . . [By the time] we graduated together, there was sort of a mutual exchange of ideas. They had learned a lot from me in the four years, and I had learned a lot from those guys.

The blacks in this study also differ from their parents in that they work in predominantly white settings where they have learned how to command respect from white coworkers. Dressed in a button-down shirt, slacks, and suspenders, Richard looks the part of the corporate vice president. He seems to be all about business as he joins me in the family's living room. This corporate demeanor spills over into our interview. With few exceptions, Richard provides only basic facts in response to my questions and checks his watch frequently. He perks up periodically, such as when he is talking to me about how to command respect:

> My boss's boss . . . one morning he called me and said, "Richard, this is a sales organization. I understand that your team carries over 50 percent of the revenue." And I said, "That's right." And he said, "I need you to come down and talk to me and explain that to me." This was about eight o'clock in the morning. And I said, "Well, I'll be glad to do that, but I need an hour." That's an old trick. Whenever your boss calls and tells you, "Oh, I need to see you right away," you never just stop what you're doing and go right in. 'Cause your time is important. It depends on what it is. But you should never get in the habit of just dropping your work. They've got to respect your time too. [Instead, say,] "Oh, I'll be happy to do that. But why don't we get together at such and such a time?" as opposed to stopping what you are doing. I'm used to working in that environment. I know what political moves to make, how to associate, it's just a part of me now. I've learned how to work the system.

The blacks in this study differ further from their parents in terms of their willingness to confront authority. This strategy proved especially useful in managing interactions with teachers. Parents sought again and again to negotiate on their child's behalf. Alana, tall and imposing, with her hair secured near the nape of her neck in a neat bun, learned how to successfully land her child in the classroom of the best teacher at the elementary school:

> Sometimes you have to use some strategies in terms of getting your kid out of the class[room of a bad teacher], not say, "Oh, the teacher can't teach."

You know, certain people's personalities don't click. And you can go up and describe certain personality characteristics of a teacher that you would like for your child. . . . I knew a couple who had said [referring to my daughter], "Oh, what grade is she going to be in? Well you want her to get so-and-so teacher." So I went up [to the school] and I was talking with the assistant principal, and . . . I think I might have asked, "Do you allow parents any say-so about what teacher they get?" And she said something about, "No, we try not to do that because that would complicate things. But we do allow parents to talk about characteristics that they would like in a teacher." So that's just indirect. I mean, if you know that [desirable] teacher's characteristics, you just describe them. I don't know, did I mention a couple [teachers] by name? [She pauses briefly to reflect.] Anyway, sure enough, my daughter got one of them when we got there.

These examples are evidence of clear generational differences between the blacks in my sample and their parents in terms of their access to the kind of cultural resources useful in managing interactions with whites.

John, Greg, Charlotte, and other blacks in my study were not endowed with the cultural capital useful in managing interactions with whites through their families of origin. As children, they were compelled to figure out these negotiations on their own through their immersion in white colleges, workplaces, and educational institutions, without involving their parents or other adults. They did so through two socialization processes that facilitate the construction of public identities: improvisation and script-switching.

IMPROVISATIONAL SOCIALIZATION

During childhood, the blacks in this study were socialized into a set of informal strategies that allowed them to negotiate on their own the racial discrimination they faced at that time. In contrast to their parents' strategies of avoidance, deference, and unwillingness to confront authority, interviewees were more likely to fight back surreptitiously. For example, they often challenged indirectly the authority of white teachers and authority figures. When these middle-class blacks employed improvisational strategies, they left the impression that they were obeying the rules when they were, in fact, circumventing rules and established practices. This phenomenon is typified by Brad, who told me how a white guidance counselor had discouraged his applying to college: "My high school counselor told me that I should not go to Michigan because I probably wouldn't make it, and I should go to a trade school. [That way] I would have a job, [and] I could support my family." He pauses, visibly upset. Then, with sarcasm, he adds, "She was great."

I asked him, "This was a black woman telling you this?" He answered, "Uh-uh, she was a white woman. Miss Blupper. I remember her name." Miss Blupper's lack of confidence in Brad's intellectual ability made him even more determined to go to college. Brad acquired on his own a knowledge of college rankings and the admissions process that his guidance counselor was unwilling to provide. He ended up graduating from high school early to attend the University of Michigan and went on to become a judge.

In addition to being discouraged from pursuing a college track by high school teachers, middle-class blacks frequently faced white teachers who were heavily invested in symbolically maintaining the racial boundaries that had been dismantled by desegregation policy. Looking back on his tenure as class president during his junior year at the predominantly white high school, Greg remembers that the tradition dictating who should escort the homecoming queen was abandoned by his white teacher when she realized that he was slotted to escort a white girl:

> My junior year in high school there was always the tradition that the juniors put on the prom for the seniors. . . . I was the class president, and I was 'spose to escort the queen. . . . Well, they made an exception that year. [He laughs.] Basically they said, well, they'd let me and my date lead the parade, and the queen and everybody else [were to] follow behind. Well, you know how I am, I'm saying, "What's up with this?" I'm 'spose to walk the queen, but the queen's white. They didn't want me walking a white queen. I guess they didn't want this black guy walking in with this white queen. So it's really funny that the girl that I happened to be dating at that time, she had naturally red hair, and [she was] just as white as almost snow. But she was black! Yeah, she was a black girl! [He laughs.] . . . So, anyway, I said, "I'll take her to the prom. I'll fake 'em all out." So I'm leading the prom, me [and the girl], we're going to the prom together. So nobody knew anything; so me and [the girl] showed up, and my, my, my, you talking about fine [attractive]!

Greg's ploy was effective, as the whites in attendance were, in fact, confused by his date's physical appearance. Greg recalls excitedly, "That [next] Monday, [I] come into school, [the kids are saying,] 'Greg, was she white? Greg, was she white?'" I asked Greg if his classmates didn't ask him that the night of the prom. He answered:

> No. In fact one of 'em—he's a good friend of mine now—he says, "Greg, I gotta ask you: that girl you brought to the prom, was she white?" I said, "Naw, man, she was black." [The friend replied,] "No she wasn't, man,

you kiddin' me!" I mean she had *real* red hair, you couldn't tell the difference, just could not tell the difference. But that was sort of my, not first exposure, but one that I really remember, and one that I said, "Well, I'm
gonna fight back." . . . Mrs. Colin was the teacher's name. I'll never forget
that little ol' mean lady. I said, "Well, I'll pay you back."

Greg decided to "pay back" the teacher not by using official channels
and reporting her to higher authorities or by insisting that in fact he
would escort the white queen as tradition dictated, but by devising a
scheme on his own that would both expose the absurdity of the black-
white boundary and preserve his dignity. Brad also circumvented official
channels in his quest for a college education.

By the time he entered high school, Greg possessed an insider's knowledge of mainstream culture; he knew whites would be baffled by the apparent racial identity of his fair-skinned date. He acquired this familiarity with dominant codes and practices through exposure to white
cultural norms in integrated settings, settings that required him to manage interactions with whites. Greg improvised strategies for managing
these interactions as the specific conflict arose, yet these incidents prepared him, as I will demonstrate, for later experiences with racial discrimination. Dealing with racial discrimination by using an improvisational approach is analogous to David Sudnow's description of learning
to become proficient on the piano: "You can't stop for long and think
through a next place to go. You have to keep on playing."[21] Similarly,
middle-class blacks seek to become proficient at wielding public identities. With each past experience of negotiating the color line seared in
their memories, this type of independence has its price. Charlotte expressed vivid childhood memories of the pain involved in resolving problems in a white high school on her own.

> I remember crying, and feeling like I wanted somebody to be there for me.
> But I also, at sixteen, was proud of myself, because I felt I could have gone
> anywhere and done anything. And I was the type of aggressive person who
> could stand up to people. And I always thought that that came directly
> from the fact that my mother and father *didn't* intervene, that I had to solve
> the problem myself. . . . [My sister] faced the same problems [at the white
> school]. It's surprising that we never would come home and talk about it.
> Because the problem was just understood. It wasn't so defined as [it is]
> now. It was just understood [back then] that you were black and this is
> what's gonna happen to you. You know, this is what you're gonna get.

Martin, now forty-nine, is tall and physically fit. He is the father of a
teenage boy and a seven-year old daughter and works as a city adminis-

trator. He grew up in the Washington, D.C., area, and he remembers how the lack of explicit direction from his parents about how to manage interactions with whites left him "ignorant" about the impact of racism. As a child, he unknowingly shopped in a segregated department store. "At that time you didn't shop in [stores] like Woody's; those were considered 'white' stores. They didn't tell you to get out [of the store] but it was just [understood] that black people didn't shop in it. . . . As a kid, I would go . . . buy my mom her Christmas gift. I would go to Woody's and buy her the perfumes and all. And I never felt anything [was wrong]. I guess I was ignorant." By the time Martin had gone away to college, his unawareness nearly resulted in violence, as he calmly explained:

> The first time that I felt any racism in my life that I can remember was when I went to [college], and we went out, a group of us, to eat. This was a place where they had a pool room in the back. And we sat there waiting to get waited on and people didn't wait on us. We kept calling the waitress, they didn't wait on us. Then maybe after about forty-five minutes, these [white] guys came out of the pool room. . . . They stood in the doorway just kind of looking at us. Then we kind of got it. We were the only black people there, and it was late at night, and we said, "Oh, *this* is what it is." We had ventured to another part of town. . . . I was mad at first, because it was the first time that I had ever been denied anything. I felt that we should demand service. Then I thought about it. We probably would have gotten into a fight. That's why the guys from the pool room stood there. That was the first time I'd ever experienced racism. I remember going home and I felt, I really felt sick going back to the dorm. We talked about what we should have done, that we probably would have gotten killed.

More recently, Martin found himself waiting in vain for service once again, this time on vacation with his family in California:

> The other time it happened was when we were in San Diego. I think it was a Denny's [restaurant]. This was five years ago. . . . Everybody left the place and we were still there [waiting]. I went to the manager. I was so hot, aw man, I was so-o-o hot I could have exploded. Finally, we got waited on.

This time Martin was older, no longer a college student. The threat of physical violence was not imminent, and Martin was well aware that he could signal his class position by using strong language to persuade the manager of a white establishment to serve his family. However, this assurance did not diminish his anger at not being served in a timely fashion in the first place.

Based on their childhood experiences with racial discrimination, the middle-class blacks in this study learned early on that it was indeed possible to confront such discrimination, most effectively by doing it indirectly. In this way, these middle-class blacks have been socialized to deal with racial discrimination in a strikingly different manner than their parents. Still, since the interviewees were raised by parents who lacked these confrontational skills, improvisational strategies were fabricated out of the cultural materials that respondents had on hand at the time. They were children, so they could not openly disrespect a teacher or challenge a group of white rednecks; this was the 1950s and early 1960s, so they could not depend on official channels or third parties to represent the interests of blacks. From early childhood victories involving the use of improvisational strategies, middle-class blacks determined that they do not have to take discrimination lying down, a practice that shapes their beliefs about how to respond to discriminatory encounters in the present.

SCRIPT-SWITCHING

Script-switching processes refer to the strategies middle-class blacks employ to demonstrate that they are knowledgeable about middle-class lifestyles and to communicate their social position to others. Scripts are sets of expectations that are unconsciously activated by individuals in their everyday lives as a way of arriving at an appropriate response to a situation. According to Abelson, in order to "behave a script," an individual satisfies three conditions. First, the person demonstrates cognitive awareness of the specific script. For example, a person who invokes the "dentist visit script" already has a prior understanding of what it means to be a dental patient. Second, the script is embedded in a context. For the dental patient, a cavity or some other dental problem makes the dental visit relevant. Third, the person must be willing to "enter the script," that is, the person must be willing, in this case, to actually visit the dentist instead of ignoring the problem or pretending that it does not exist. People make crucial decisions about whether to "enter the script" based on prior experience with such matters—for example, if a tooth aches for a long time, it is a good idea to see a dentist.[22]

Scholars now recognize that blacks and whites tend to "behave" different kinds of scripts. For example, Thomas Kochman observed that blacks tend to communicate in an "emotionally intense, dynamic, and demonstrative" style, whereas whites tend to communicate in a "more modest and emotionally constrained" style.[23] Of course, Kochman's schema is a generalization of these racial groups. There are whites and blacks who do not fit neatly into the categories he lays out. But these exceptions do not erase the powerful impact of these stereotypes on every-day interactions across the color line. Because public interactions are governed by mainstream scripts, middle-class blacks are compelled to switch from black scripts to white scripts in public spaces. Thus, public interactions require a different presentation of self than those asserted in majority-black spaces. In short, the middle-class blacks sometimes downplay their racial identities in public interactions with whites. Jasmine is short, with a bouncy haircut in the shape of a trendy bob. She seems taller than she actually is because she is extroverted and somewhat bossy, whereas her husband Richard is quiet and shy. Jasmine, now forty-five, describes how she felt compelled to script-switch as a teenager when her parents enrolled her in a predominantly white high school:

> I remember wanting to do "the white thing" when I was there. I had iodine and baby oil, trying to get a tan, and why wasn't [my] hair blowing in the wind? They [the white girls] would be shaving their legs and that type of thing, and most African American girls aren't that particular. I felt I needed to be a part of them, I needed to do their thing. . . . To this day, I think I made the blend [between two cultures] pretty decent because I have plenty of friends who just hate going back to our high school reunion. They just see no purpose [in going], but I enjoyed it because I participated in every-thing. . . . I was homecoming queen, I was in their beauty pageant when no other black person would dare to be in their pageant. I was like, "If you can do it, I can do it!"

One way to better understand how the phenomenon of script-switching works is to consider an example of a middle-class black who apparently refuses to satisfy the third condition necessary for enacting a script: agreeing to "enter the script." Charlotte, speaking with admiration of a worker in a predominantly white school system with very few other black teachers, outlined how a black male art teacher who declined to script-switch was harassed by the white principal. "[The] white principal can't *stand* him, and I think it's because he's this big, black guy, and he's loud. You know, 'Hey, how ya doing!' Kind of like that. He's real down to earth, and I think they're kind of envious of him, because he's been in books, he's been in the [*Washington*] *Post,* he's been on TV, and they're trying to get their little doctorates. And they're always demean-ing him. . . . They are just awful to him."

According to Charlotte, this teacher is subjected to a different set of evaluation criteria than the other teachers working at the school. But be-cause Charlotte and the few other black teachers have not been mis-treated in the ways that she observes the black male teacher has been,

Charlotte feels that the white principal is reacting not so much to the art teacher's race as to his refusal to display the appropriate command of cultural capital—in short, to switch scripts. By Charlotte's account, the white principal interprets the art teacher's behavior as gauche, even though there may be no basis for this conclusion aside from the teacher's refusal to engage a white script. "He kinda doesn't make the—he's an artist, and he's eccentric, and he's just *him,* and he doesn't do the bullshit." Charlotte added parenthetically, "And see . . . they want that, they want him to do that."

As Charlotte's narrative makes clear, some middle-class blacks believe that social acceptance in the public sphere is contingent upon their ability to script-switch. They believe that they are less likely to be hassled in white settings if they are willing to script-switch. Blacks who refuse to do so or are uncomfortable doing so may be penalized, just as the teacher at Charlotte's school was targeted. At the same time, blacks who refuse to script-switch may elicit a certain amount of respect and admiration from script-switchers, simply for *not* acting one way in the white world and then being their "true selves" in the black world. They have but one identity to put forth. This conclusion implies that blacks who *do* choose to use public identities pay an emotional price not paid either by whites or by middle-class blacks who are less savvy or who are unwilling to put out the effort required to successfully signal their class status according to mainstream norms.

The art teacher's experience of maintaining a black script stands in marked contrast to Michelle's. She engages in a white script in order to hire a black man to work at her predominantly white company where she is the only black employee. Her company's established hiring script takes little notice of affirmative action legislation. Michelle realized, "They don't feel like they are mandated to have affirmative action. In fact, they [argue that they just] hire the best person. My husband says that if you really wanted to do that, you'd get a headhunting firm to make sure that that happens. [But] they basically just hire people that they know. I've heard that a lot. Hire people that you *know,* that you feel comfortable with." Aware of the hiring script, Michelle enters it when she is charged with hiring a new manager. She seems smug at having played the game and emerged victorious as she explains:

> I just hired a black person two weeks ago, and I just looked at everybody like, "Anybody got anything to say?" Black man. But no one had anything to say, because his credentials were so impeccable. They looked and they

looked, but besides myself, we're the two most qualified people in the company. This man is top-notch. He's the first black man who ever worked in this company in a managerial position. Ever. So I made a conscious decision to find a good, qualified person. Be it black, white, or anything. This person outshined a lot of folks.

Michelle switched to the established hiring script to employ a person whom *she* would be comfortable with, just as her white co-workers had done when they were in a position to control the hiring decision. In previous studies, researchers used the term "code-switching" to refer to the temporary appropriation of mainstream language by members of minority groups.[24] I adopt the term "script-switching" instead to emphasize that middle-class blacks do not merely adopt substitute phrasings of an alternative language; they temporarily take on a whole new substitute set of social roles to perform.[25] As Charlotte put it, "We live in this world, and its kind of like being black, you know, you have two faces. So you know how to present yourself in the white world, and you present yourself in the black world as yourself."

The middle-class blacks in this study do not want to take their black identities to work with them. The problem is that because the workplace is governed by the same preoccupation with race that guides public interactions in general, middle-class blacks find that some whites insert race into social interactions where blacks believe it is not relevant. Michelle's frustration is visible as she remembers a racially charged interaction with a co-worker:

I was in Georgia a couple weeks ago, and one of those times I forgot that I was female and black. We were getting ready for this big event. And me and this guy that work together all the time—white guy, great guy, funny guy, good friend. We come out, it's raining. The rain was coming down. The hotel was two, three blocks away. So I said, "Let's go, we gotta get back in time to change before the cocktail party tonight. But I've got the umbrella, don't worry, let's go." So I'm going out the door. It was coming down like cats and dogs. I mean, our shoes and pants were soaked. So I grabbed his arm, we got under the umbrella, hunkered down, fought the wind, and we got to the hotel. Halfway to the hotel he said [she pauses] something about, "Are you concerned about what people will say?" I didn't get it. It went right over my head. I'm going, "What are you talking about?" He said, "Well, this white guy and this black girl, arm in arm, walking down the street under an umbrella going to a hotel." I was like, my God, where did you come up with that idea? We're just two people . . . walking in the rain! When did I become "the black girl"? When did that happen? When did that happen? It probably was going on all the time, sitting on the plane, laughing and joking. And I'm thinking to myself, "This jerk!" And then I say to myself, "No, *you're* the jerk. You forgot." They aren't going to let you forget that. I was just a person in my mind. We were teammates. Why did I have to become "the black girl"? Why am I not your partner? But that's naive on my part. . . . Every once in a while . . . those subtle moments when you're not thinking [about racism] catch you off guard every once in a while.[26]

The specific identity that these blacks elect to assert during interactions in the public sphere is of great importance, as strangers and white co-workers may "assume that the character projected before them is all that there is to the individual."[27] Since most public interactions are brief and nonrepetitive, public spaces require individuals to articulate an image that fills in profound gaps in a stranger's perception of them. Filling in these gaps is potentially problematic for blacks because in the public imagination, a black identity is bound up with poverty status. Complicating matters further, this phenomenon may work differently for one group of blacks than it does for another.[28] While all blacks must confront a racially charged environment, what being middle-class—or, more finely put, high status—buys some blacks is a broader set of strategies to negotiate this terrain. In the next section, I examine how public identities are asserted by middle-class blacks while shopping, in the workplace, and while house-hunting. In doing so, I will be demonstrating the tendency among middle-class blacks to rely on their command of cultural capital to script-switch from a black cultural style to a white cultural style. I begin with the exclusionary boundaries erected while shopping and in the workplace, then move on to the inclusionary boundaries erected while house-hunting.

ASSERTING PUBLIC IDENTITIES

Undoubtedly, all persons attempting to cross class boundaries have to spend time thinking about clothing, language, tastes, and mannerisms; they risk being identified as a member of a lower class if they make a mistake. Concerns among the socially mobile about needing to properly appropriate the general skills and cultural styles of the middle class in a convincing way are well-documented in the sociological literature and in fictional accounts. However, middle-class blacks' ambiguous position in the racial hierarchy means that they have to spend more time thinking about what they will wear in public, work harder at pulling off a middle-class presentation of self, and be more demonstrative at it than

white middle-class people who are also exhibiting their status and negotiating for deference. Moreover, while the fault line for upwardly mobile whites today is strictly class, middle-class blacks must negotiate class
boundaries as well as the stereotypes associated with their racial group.[29]
In this section, I demonstrate how public identities are put to work in
three public spaces, each with its own distinct pattern of black-white interaction. While shopping and in the workplace, these middle-class
blacks employ public identities to establish their distinctiveness from the
black poor and from subordinate workers. In the context of house-
hunting, middle-class blacks perceive that class bias operates; therefore,
public identities are constructed to establish their overlap with the white
middle class.

EXCLUSIONARY BOUNDARY-WORK

SHOPPING   An obvious way for middle-class blacks to signal their class position is through physical appearance. Barthel writes, "One of the most
easily read signs of status is our appearance: our posture, our clothing,
our overall presentation of self."[30] In public interactions, strangers respond to one another on the basis of this conspicuous signifier. Anderson speculates that a black middle-class resident of a gentrified community was commonly perceived as a member of the underclass because he
"sometimes wore dark jackets and sunglasses," clothing not associated
with the middle class.[31] Clothing "serve[s] as a kind of visual metaphor
for identity," and we tend to hold preconceived notions as to which fash-
ions are associated with wealth and which with poverty.[32] Here again,
middle-class blacks' ability to signify the correct command of cultural
capital—through their selection of clothing—factors into the conclusions
whites draw regarding their performance and competence. Michelle's description of a brief exchange with a new client whom she had not met
before is an apt segue into a discussion of the role that clothing plays in
first impressions, because it suggests that clothing may factor into whites'
stereotyping of blacks. Michelle angrily recalls how she saw a colleague's expression visibly shift in the course of a conversation:

> I was working on a project, and I dressed down, and one of the VPs wanted
> me to meet someone else. This person came, I was dressed down, and I had
> my VP using language, explaining that I look one way, but I'm really
> muckity-muck. . . . [The colleague's] statement was so pompous initially, he
> didn't expect me to understand what he was talking about. He threw a cou-
> ple things out—he said something that was controversial [not established as

fact], and you know how black folks have to do, you've gotta quote statistics, theorists, then you see their faces change, they adjust their seat, "Oh, well, tell me what you think about this and this." See, if it was just my imagination, you could say [to me], well you're just sensitive about what [white] people think, but at the end he said, "I really enjoyed talking to you, you really know a lot about [the topic]." And I'm thinking, "What makes you think that I didn't? Was it what I had on?"

Michelle insists the man was condescending to her at the outset "just because I am black. He thought that I wouldn't understand what he was talking about because I am black." Yet it is difficult to sort out whether the man assumes as a matter of course that blacks are incompetent until proven otherwise, or whether Michelle's casual clothing did factor into his impression of her. Some middle-class blacks hope to avoid this kind of confusion by creating a look that intimates affluence through the erection of exclusionary boundaries. In real terms, this would mean selecting clothing that contrasts sharply with the attire associated with black popular culture. Philip, who wears a suit to his job as a corporate executive, observed: "Being black is a negative, particularly if you're not lookin' a certain way. You . . . go in an elevator dressed in what I have on now [he is wearing a blue polo shirt and white shorts], white women start holding their pocketbooks. But if I'm dressed like I normally go to work, then it's fine."

Philip implies that he can control the extent to which he will be evaluated on the basis of whites' stereotypes about poor blacks by the type of clothing he decides to wear to the store. If Philip decides to assert his public identity, he will shop in his suit. Once he begins to make purchases, additional signifiers of his social status such as credit cards and zip code assure the store clerk that he is a legitimate member of the middle class. Through his performance, Philip believes that he annuls a stigmatized racial identity. He believes that when he is dressed as a professional, whites see his class status first and respond to him as a member of that social group.[33]

The assurance of these additional middle-class signifiers allows middle-class blacks to occasionally engage in subversive expressions of their class identity, much to their delight. Terry complained that store clerks react negatively to blacks who are "dressed down" under the assumption that they cannot afford to buy anything. "Going into a store, somebody follows you around the store. But [store clerks] don't help you [at all] if you go into a specialty store. They just refuse to walk up to you. Then you see a white person walk in and they immediately run to help them." However, as a member of the middle class, Terry is pleased that she has the leisure time and the requisite skills to voice a complaint:

> Now lately I will write a complaint. I will find out who owns the store and write a complaint. Before I used to just tell the [sales]person, "I guess you didn't know who walked into your store. It's a shame that you treat people like this because you don't know how much money I have." I love going to expensive stores in jeans and a T-shirt. Because they don't know how much money you have. And, you know, I may have a thousand dollars to give away that day. [She laughs.] They just don't know. And the way people treat you, I think it's a shame, based on your appearance.

Convinced that a store clerk ignored her because her clothing belied her actual class status, Terry went on to test her suspicion by varying the style of clothing that she sports while shopping. Terry enjoys "dressing down," but this subversive presentation of self appears to be enjoyable precisely because she can shed this role at a moment's notice, reassuming her actual middle-class identity. She then drew on her resources as a member of the middle class to file a formal complaint.

Because their performance as members of the middle class is perceived as legitimate when they are clothed in a way that signifies their social status, these blacks believe that using this strategy helps them to avoid the discrimination that blacks of a lower-class status experience. This perception is illustrated by Michael, a stylish corporate manager who suggested that his appearance, coupled with his Sherwood Park zip code and his assets, lead others to draw the conclusion that he is middle-class. He boasted, "When I apply for anything [that requires using] credit, I just give my name, address. . . . You have to fill out the credit application . . . you put your address down there, then you put down your collateral, IRA, all that stuff. So I don't know if I've been discriminated against that way. I mean, I can go to the store and buy what I want to buy."

In cases of racial discrimination, blacks are typically precluded from achieving a desired goal, such as obtaining a desired product or entering a particular establishment. Since middle-class blacks in this study enter stores and "buy what they want to buy," (when they are dressed in a manner that reflects their social status), they conclude that they have not experienced racial discrimination.

This suggests that when interviewees "buy what they want to buy" without interference from whites, they have successfully conveyed their class position to store clerks. Jared, neatly dressed in creased tan slacks and a burnt-orange pullover, argued that whites are not penalized for dressing down—their identity is not strictly tied to clothing—but that blacks do not have this luxury: "When you're out in the world, you can be wearing grubbies and you'll be perceived in a particular way if you're black." When asked if it works that way for white people, he responded, "No, 'cause there's a saying, 'If you have money, it's okay to wear rags,' or however it goes. So that's how they view it. . . . Probably there are some signs, like those are old shoes, but those [old shoes] are Oceans, or whatever, and [therefore] it's okay."

Shoes were a key signifier of class position among many of the blacks in this study. Jared later commented on my own shoes. I was wearing dark brown oxfords, not terribly expensive, but probably the type of shoe that people would associate with the middle class. He said to me, "You go to *Har-vard,* you got money!" I quickly denied it, but Jared said, "Yeah, you do. Look at your shoes."

Others also suggested that when middle-class blacks are dressed down, that is, not engaging public identities, their shopping experience is often extremely unpleasant. Michelle attempted to shop while dressed down, and was dismissed by the store clerk: "I went somewhere and they tried to tell me how I couldn't afford something . . . I was in the mood to buy. They were saying, "Well, it might cost this or that." I mean I went there seriously looking to shop. But I wasn't dressed that way." In response to my question, "Was it clothing or race?" Michelle looked slightly puzzled, as if she hadn't consider this possibility, then waffled as to the explanation for the store clerk's behavior.

> Probably a mixture of both, I don't know. See, I don't know what it's like to be white and dressed poorly and [to] try and buy something. I've always had in my mind where someone told me that you could wear holey jeans as long as you have on two-hundred-dollar shoes. People know that you got money. That's when you're worried about what people think about you. But, you know, on a relaxed day, I don't care what they [white people] think. You either have the money or you don't.

Sorting out the store clerk's motivation is difficult for Michelle in part because whites' stereotypes of the face of poverty are conflated with race. When most whites think abstractly about the middle class, they see a white family, not a black one. This same image leads whites to associate poverty with blacks. In order for whites to believe that the blacks appearing before them are middle-class, they would have to erase the indelible image linking the concept "middle class" exclusively to whites. Middle-class blacks in the Washington, D.C., area convey this status by engaging their public identity, expressed through clothing that signals their middle-class status to others. In the workplace, middle-class blacks focus on a different form of cultural capital—professional title and credentials—to minimize racial tension in the workplace and to underscore their position as managers or supervisors.

THE WORKPLACE   Perhaps no public setting better reflects the cultural styles and preferences of the American mainstream than the corporate world. As Feagin and Sikes observe in *Living with Racism,* blacks "in corporate America are under constant pressure to adapt . . . to the values and ways of the white world."[34] Studies focused on some of the first blacks to enter corporate America after the civil rights movement revealed forms of discrimination that, while not indicative of overt racial hostility, nevertheless slowed blacks' upward progress along the corporate ladder. Ambitious corporate blacks found that they were relegated to minority markets or human resources positions, that they were consistently passed over for promotions notwithstanding stellar sales and performance ratings, and that their qualifications were incessantly scrutinized and undervalued with little or no justification.[35] With so few blacks in positions of authority in corporate America in the 1970s and early 1980s, there was little that blacks could do to improve their circumstances.

How do black professionals fare today? Despite significant increases in the number of black corporate managers, beginning in the mid-1980s, black professionals still confront racial discrimination in their work settings. White colleagues and clients still register surprise when they encounter corporate blacks who speak intelligently about the topic at hand, black managers still confront "glass ceilings," and black managers still endure subjective critiques assessing their "fit" with the corporate culture. I focus here on two such problems faced by black managers today: managing white subordinates and negotiating racial disputes. Like shopping sites, workplace settings are characterized by a low regard for black cultural styles. According to Mary Jackman, many whites perceive black cultural styles as "inappropriate for occupational tasks involving responsibility or authority."[36] This means that black managers' credibility resides in their ability to switch to the script associated with white cultural styles. Therefore, in the workplace, black managers assert public identities by demonstrating their command of the cultural capital appropriate for their title or position. Indeed, they must, since the workplace experiences of middle-class blacks are characterized by frequent episodes of discriminatory treatment.[37]

Michael, a corporate manager, has a dry sense of humor and enjoys putting people in their place. He established his role as an authority figure at the outset by highlighting impermeable boundaries between himself and his receptionist. One such boundary is the telephone. Clearly annoyed, Michael explained, "The receptionist, always bitches about answering telephones, but that's her job. She's the receptionist. I ain't *never* gonna answer the telephone." Michael does not answer his own telephone because his conception of a manager means that subordinates handle mundane details such as phone messages. Answering the phone would reduce his social status to that of a subordinate.

In his position as corporate manager, Michael says he has never experienced any racial discrimination. He attributes this feat to the weight of his title and his ability to utilize it. "On *this* job . . . I always came in with some authority. Hey, you know, like, 'I'm corporate manager. You all can do whatever you want to do, but remember, I'm the one that signs [off]. I'm the one that signs.' And, when you're the one that signs, you got the power. So even if they don't like you, they got to smile, which is okay by me." Greg used a similar strategy with white employees who resented having to work under him after his company was awarded a lucrative contract. He begins to smile as he remembers how he handled the conflict:

> There are two folks that I know of that are stone redneck. I mean they're the biggest rednecks you ever did see. They now came over to work for me. They couldn't accept that. So we had several briefings and I said, "Okay, here's how we're gonna do this and here's how we're gonna work." Well, the people they work for . . . were also big rednecks, so they just sort of go along together. Well, they refused—not openly refused, but just subtly. They wouldn't come to meetings. . . . I ended up basically saying to them, "Look, y'all can do what you want to do. But when it comes time for bonuses, and it comes time for yearly wages and all that kind of stuff, now you can go to Jim [white supervisor who reports to Greg], and he can tell you what to do and y'all can go do it. But if he doesn't tell me that you did it, I won't know. So when it comes time for your annual evaluation, I'll just say, 'Didn't do nothing.' So, it's y'all's fault." Well, then they sort of opened up.

These middle-class blacks handle racial conflicts on their own because they are convinced that they have the ability to resolve them and because the Equal Employment Opportunity Commission (EEOC) has established such a poor record in resolving disputes. As a result, middle-class blacks with a legitimate dispute "don't pursue it as a racial issue," Jared noticed, "even though [they] may know it is. [They] pursue it as a person not doing what they're supposed to [do], or something of that nature." He added:

> The EEO[C], that's a paper dragon. It was one of the rewards that we gained from the civil rights movement that never really worked. . . . Number one, you file a complaint. By the time they get to you, it's three years later. You

know how much damage they can do to you in three years?! You'll be sick of working in the mailroom! [He laughs.] . . . It's well known in the government that if you go to EEO[C], they'll get even with you. You'll find yourself not getting awards. Getting the dirt assignments. Suddenly, your job was cut, you're now in charge of, uh, the *mail*room, or whatever.

Philip noted that the EEOC process is sometimes effective, but agreed with Jared's contention that the beneficiary's career is left in shambles. "Sometimes they do find cause, and there's back pay involved, or a payment is involved. . . . In most cases . . . even though retaliation is against the law, there is subtle retaliation, so people move on. . . . Particularly if there's been a settlement—a major settlement—they move on. They know that there's going to be some form of retaliation."

Involving the EEOC can be a traumatic experience; therefore, some middle-class blacks weigh the benefits of their job against ongoing workplace discrimination. For example, Alana, who is forty-seven and works as an attorney, conceded:

> I definitely am not naive enough to believe that everything that happens is always tied to race. Never. But yet, there are some things. Yes, it's better, but it's not the way it could or should be. I'm not gonna say, "That's a fact of life; you've gotta just accept it," but there are times when you need to make a stand, and other times when it's not worth it. Because this job allows me to live a pretty decent lifestyle. So I can complain, but I can't complain too much. . . . We have a lot of freedom. It's a decent office space. There's parking in the basement [that] I don't have to pay for. So there are a lot of perks. Like I said, I can't complain too much. Could I be doing better? Maybe. But as someone said, you control your destiny somewhat. If this place has really gotten to you to that point, you can try to move on. If I was gonna do that, I should have done it a while back. I'm not a spring chicken. Could I make a change in my occupation? Probably not, and not have to work umpteen more years. See, I would prefer to retire, and then if I wanted to do something else, go ahead. Or start to think about doing something else and do it on the side.

In contrast to previous studies of middle-class blacks in the workplace, those surveyed here feel empowered to negotiate workplace discrimination. Situated in positions of power, middle-class blacks rely on public identities—for example, their role as supervisor or manager—to solidify their identities as persons of considerable social status. Once their status is established, these middle-class blacks are in a position to extinguish racial conflicts in the workplace. In other instances, middle-class blacks decide that such effort is "not worth it," and juxtapose the pleasant aspects of their high-status occupations against such racial incidents as they arise. Though racial discrimination in the workplace has hardly disappeared, black professionals have become more adept at using class-based resources to resolve these kinds of conflicts.

INCLUSIONARY BOUNDARY-WORK

HOUSE-HUNTING   The housing market is another public space where differences in the valuation of black and white cultural styles may contribute to persistent inequality. Evidence substantiating this claim is found in a recent study of racial steering conducted by Doug Massey and Garvey Lundy. They found that landlords and rental agents have the ability to distinguish between a "black" voice and a "white" voice when communicating with a potential renter by phone.[38] Moreover, the racial discrimination perpetuated by rental agents is bound up with class discrimination such that blacks speaking in black English (whom rental agents assume to be lower-class) are less likely to obtain a rental than blacks speaking standard English (whom rental agents assume to be middle-class). This form of discrimination is known as linguistic profiling.

In *American Apartheid*, Douglas Massey and Nancy Denton argue that middle-class blacks have not had the opportunity to live wherever they want, to live "where people of their means and resources usually locate."[39] They conclude that a major factor in blacks' exclusion is racial discrimination by real estate agents, who serve as the "gatekeepers" of predominantly white neighborhoods to which blacks, even those with the requisite resources, seldom gain entry.[40]

Yet middle-class blacks interviewed for this study insist that one of the benefits of being middle-class is the option of living in any neighborhood one desires. Their housing decisions are no longer restricted by the behavior of real estate agents. John, who chose the majority-black but upper-middle-class Sherwood Park community, explained, "We could have lived anywhere we wanted to. We could have afforded to live a lot of different places, but we chose here." He and most of the middle-class blacks in this study minimize the likelihood that they have experienced racial discrimination while house-hunting because, in so many other aspects of their lives, they use class-based resources to secure a desired good. How do blacks use their public identity while house-hunting? To manage their interactions with white real estate agents, these middle-class blacks place a good deal of emphasis on displays of cultural capital—particularly appropriate clothing, apt language, and knowledge of the housing market. Yet house-hunting is a more complicated site for the construction and use of public identity because in house-hunting, unlike shopping and the workplace, respondents are unsure as to whether real estate agents are responding to their race or their class.

The preoccupation with presenting a middle-class appearance is evident in Lydia's description of her experience while viewing a model home in a predominantly white suburban subdivision located in the same greater metropolitan area where she and her husband eventually bought a home. We tend to think about the housing market in the context of a match between a home-seeker and a real estate agent in which the agent orchestrates the housing search by introducing clients to the homes he or she wants them to view. But this traditional path is only one of the possible ways to find a home in the suburbs of D.C. Equally popular are model homes. In newer subdivisions, developers open a "model" to potential home-seekers well before the development is completed. These models are staffed with the developer's representatives. During an "open house," they discuss the home's features with home-seekers in an attempt to convince them to buy. The key difference between these agents and the ones home-seekers acquire on their own through real estate agencies is that the developer's representatives have no interaction with home-seekers prior to the Open House and therefore no opportunity to "prequalify" clients before they show up at the property. This is the context Lydia entered when she attempted to view a model home. In response to the question "Have you ever experienced racial discrimination while house-hunting?" Lydia replied:

> I guess I never really thought about that in terms of racial, but economically, I think I have been. I tend not to be a person that dresses up. [She chuckles.] A couple times I've gone looking for houses and I'll just wear sweatpants. And you go out looking for a house that's in expensive neighborhoods, I don't know what they expect me to drive up in. That has nothing to do with how much money I have in the bank. And I've had that happen . . . a couple times. . . . I went to a house. . . . I don't know what we were driving, probably an old beat-up car. So I pull into the driveway, and I had on sweatpants, my [baseball] hat, I go in and see the house. I'd asked [the real estate agent] about the house, asked her for the information, and I said I wanted to take a tour. She immediately said to me, "Is this your price range?" [Dramatic pause.] I asked her how much was the house. She told me, and it was my price range, no big deal.

I asked, "Was this a black real estate agent?" Lydia answered, "White. She wanted to discuss my income before she would show me the house.

Basically, I told her I'll take a look at the house, and I'll let her know when I'm finished."

Lydia felt that the real estate agent was attempting to discourage her from viewing the house. However, she believed that her choice of clothing, her baseball hat, and her old car all signaled the wrong social class status to the agent—not that the agent objected to black home-seekers. I attempted to clarify the kind of discrimination Lydia felt she had experienced by posing a follow-up question: "Is that standard procedure? Do real estate agents normally ask you how much you make before they show you the house?" Lydia responded, shaking her head slightly from side to side, "No, no. I had been looking at lots and lots of houses. And I *knew* what she was doing. It was her way of saying, 'Oh, *God*, who is this person coming in here?' Because when I was there, a white couple came in, and I stopped to listen to what [the agent] would say to them. None of that, none of that."

I asked, "Did they have on sweatpants too?"

"No, they were dressed up," she laughed.

I persisted, "But you think it was because you had on sweatpants, not because you were a black person?"

"I think she probably, maybe looked at me and felt maybe I didn't make enough money to afford the house. That was part of it. I'm not sure, looking at houses, that we ever experienced any kind of *racial* discrimination. Because the real estate agents we had . . . they all took us to predominantly white neighborhoods. It wasn't that they were trying to steer us toward any type of neighborhood. They were willing to take our money anywhere." She burst into laughter.

I asked, "So do you think you could have actually bought one of those houses if you'd wanted to?"

"Oh yeah, oh yeah."

Lydia had an opportunity to test her suspicion that the real estate agent associated her with the poor when a white couple arrived to view the same home, even though the white couple had been well-dressed, not like her, and no comparison that controlled on clothing had been possible. Lydia concluded that the agent assessed the couple more favorably based on the quality of their clothing, and to support her position, Lydia identified occasions when white real estate agents had accepted her middle-class performance as a legitimate expression of who she is, showing her expensive homes in white neighborhoods.

Lydia's account illustrates the difficulty in pinpointing racial discrimination in the housing market. She did go on to view the model home.

Though she was dressed in an overly casual way, Lydia used strong language to inform the real estate agent that she intended to tour the home. And the agent did not move to prevent her from walking through the model home. Consequently, in Lydia's view, the encounter did not qualify as a "racial" one. So long as they are permitted to view the homes of their choice, the middle-class blacks in this study do not perceive racial discrimination in the housing market as affecting their own housing choices. As Jared indicates, if they have experienced racial discrimination, they don't know it: "The best *I know of*, I haven't been discriminated against in looking for a house in [this area]." These middle-class blacks do believe that housing discrimination exists; they just do not believe their current housing options are constrained by it. They consciously engage public identities to negotiate the pitfalls of the Washington, D.C., area housing market.

For instance, Audrey, now sixty-four, remembers her disheartening experience with a real estate agent over twenty years ago, when she and her husband moved into the area from another city:

> The agent took us down south [of the city] mostly, to . . . where more of the blacks lived . . . where they seemed to be feeding the black people that came into the area. . . . And when she started out showing us property [south of the city] . . . we told her we wanted to be closer. The things she showed us [that were closer] . . . it was gettin' worse. The properties . . . weren't as nice. So when she showed us the properties [in a black and Hispanic low-income section], we kind of like almost accepted the fact that this was what you're going to be getting.

Audrey and her family moved into the undesirable housing, but "from that day on," she said, "we never stopped looking at houses. We took it upon ourselves to continue just to look, to explore different areas." A year later, they moved to a more attractive neighborhood. Now distrustful of real estate agents, Audrey drew on cultural knowledge she'd acquired on her own—about desirable neighborhoods, schools, and the housing market in general—to locate a home in a neighborhood more suited to her family's tastes. Acquiring this kind of detailed information takes leisure time and research skills.

Greg and his wife found that their real estate agent also directed them to undesirable housing when they returned to the United States from a work assignment in Taiwan. Greg remembers:

> The agent kept showing us older homes. . . . They were ten-year-old homes, twelve-year old homes, and they just weren't our style. . . . Some of the homes, they had beautician shops in the basement, and she thought that

was a great deal, you know, you could wash, you could style your hair. And I'm thinking, "I don't need that." So Andrea [his wife] just said, "I'm not interested in those." So we came here [to Sherwood Park] just on a whim, I guess. And they had a girl [real estate agent] named [Liz], she said, "Let me show you these," and we looked at 'em. We went, "Oh," and, "Ah, yeah, okay." Then Andrea just said, "Hey, that's what I want."

In each of these examples, middle-class blacks confront discrimination from real estate agents. Audrey and her husband were steered to a section of the city where many blacks already lived. Greg and his wife were shown older, less attractive homes within their general area of choice. But the fact that these families were able to successfully find a home that did appeal to them leads them to the conclusion that widespread discrimination against blacks no longer effectively bars blacks of their social status from entering the neighborhood of their choice. Recall John's comment: "We could have lived anywhere we wanted to. . . . We chose here." When real estate agents fail them, middle-class blacks simply find an attractive home by driving around on their own. As Audrey made clear, they "never stop looking," or they happen to find a desirable home "on a whim," as Greg and his wife did.

William, like Audrey, also battled with a prejudicial real estate agent thirty years ago. He generalizes from his experience back in 1976 to speculate about what blacks likely encounter as they search for housing now:

When we went to buy our first single-family home, we had wanted to look in certain places, but the [real estate agent] who was taking us around would always take us to other places. Or we would mark out a certain area, [but] when we went to see a house out there, she had to go up first. Once she left us in the car, the guy was outside, and she went up to the guy, and I'm just assuming that it was said that he would say that he had a contract on the house, that it was under contract. He was white, and this was an all-white neighborhood. So that was smart. . . . I said, "You know, I really believe that we're getting discriminated against," because every place we said we wanted to go, there was always a reason why we couldn't see it.

Frustrated with their agent's slow progress, William and his wife took it upon themselves to locate homes that were available during their more recent housing search five years ago by reading through the real estate section of the paper.

You look in the paper and say, "Okay, here's a place." . . . Then [the real estate agent] would say, "Oh, it's already under contract," or "The open house is not until *next* week"—[anything] to put off from the time that we really was available [to see the home]. So we just went on and got rid of her, and just rode around until we found a place. We stopped and went in and looked at the house, and said, "I want to live there." The owner was there, and we talked to him. He gave us the name of his agent.

William went on to purchase the home that he and his wife discovered while driving around on their own. He was one of only a few respondents to report that housing discrimination still affects the lives of middle-class blacks. "You can easily get discriminated against. Discrimination run rampant in [this area]," he warned. "In a nice, low-tone sort of way, I caught the redlining. They have certain areas they're not gonna introduce to you if they can get around it. . . . [That's] still the case."

The U.S. Department of Housing and Urban Development (HUD), the federal agency charged with monitoring fair housing complaints, employed testers to pinpoint the frequency and severity of housing discrimination.[41] Their researchers determined that blacks are usually shown the homes that are *advertised*, "but agents often deny minority customers access to available units about which they have not explicitly inquired." Given that the "actual housing search typically involves the inspection of units introduced to the customer by the agent, this type of denial constitutes an important limitation on minority access to housing."[42] Because black home-seekers who dispense with their real estate agents end up touring desirable neighborhoods on their own looking for visible "For Sale" signs, they may never become aware of those homes that go unadvertised.

There is some evidence that HUD's policies have had an impact on how real estate agents relate to black clients in the Washington, D.C., metropolitan area. I went with John to view model homes in a newly constructed subdivision in Prince George's County. John said to the agent, "Let me ask you a question. What percentage of the people who have bought out here are black?" The agent, a black woman dressed in a conservative blue suit and pumps, smiled sheepishly and said, "That's something that I'm not allowed to say. HUD does not allow us to discuss the race of homeowners." But as we toured the model home, it became apparent to whom the subdivision was being marketed. In addition to the black real estate agent, the model home was decorated in a manner that suggested that a black family lived there. The curtains bore a kente cloth motif. A ceiling border with the names of Dizzy Gillespie, Ella Fitzgerald, and Louis Armstrong ran the length of the music room.

The children's bedrooms held signifiers of a black lifestyle, such as a director's chair labeled with the name Howard University and books authored by well-known blacks such as W. E. B. DuBois and Maya Angelou. According to John, the race of the agent showing a particular model home is automatically "a tip-off. You don't put a black real estate person in a neighborhood . . . that you're selling to white people."

Jasmine, who resides in Lakeview and also worked as a real estate agent at one point, reiterated the awareness among agents that discussing racial composition of a neighborhood with home-seekers is illegal:

> You know, that's not a point of conversation that I enter into. It may be subtle conversation, but it is against the law. What I do is I give people neighborhood tours. . . . We drive around to neighborhoods that they can afford. "You can afford this neighborhood and you need to examine it on a weekend or during the daytime to determine what you're comfortable with." But you can't steer people; that's against the law. Discussing race in the car when you're showing a house is against the law. Don't do it. . . . You have to be very careful about that, because—I just had a class, we have continuing education courses on equal opportunity . . . because real estate companies are really being sued, and the Department of Housing and Urban Development will come to your open house arbitrarily to see, do you say the same thing to white clients that you say to black clients? Do you steer clients to neighborhoods that are lower in cost even though they could afford other neighborhoods?

Audrey, a retired real estate agent and Lakeview resident, agreed, adding that often home-seekers "would ask you about the racial composition of neighborhoods. You're not supposed to tell them. That's discriminatory. Of course, they have to go out and find that on their own. You can't say, 'This neighborhood has more Hispanics,' or 'This neighborhood has more blacks.' You can't do that." She went on to describe her telephone encounter with a home-seeker whom she believed to be a HUD auditor:

> They have had a lot of—what do you call them? People that go out and pretend, people that do kind of undercover stuff, pretend that they are interested in a property. . . . I've had it happen when I was on floor duty. And you can almost tell when you have somebody on the phone like that. It's the way that they ask you the questions, and you start thinking about it. It's the questions, because somebody that's just interested in buying a house, they don't ask the questions quite the same way. They are so specific, and then if you don't answer it, if you give them a roundabout answer, they'll come right back to it . . . to see what I'm going to say. They had a lot of people that were planted to do that. And that's how real estate agents got in trouble.

Jasmine and Audrey, study participants who had also worked in real estate, suggest that real estate agents are now more cognizant of the kinds of sanctions facing them should they continue to discriminate against black home-seekers, and that they have adjusted their behavior accordingly. However, when I posed as a home-seeker, I found that white and black agents practiced watered-down versions of racial steering, just as William insisted they did. A common way to discriminate against black home-seekers in Lakeview is to try to steer blacks away from newly constructed subdivisions, which are rare in Lakeview and therefore command top dollar, and toward "established" neighborhoods, where the racial composition has already been decided. In the summer of 1998, I pretended to be searching for a home at the Long and Foster realty office in closest proximity to Lakeview. There, I was assigned to a middle-age white man after a brief wait in the lobby. I introduced myself as a Boston transplant, someone searching for a home for myself and my fiancé, who was busy completing his residency requirements and would be happy with whatever decision I made. When I informed this real estate agent that I was interested in purchasing a new home, his response was:

> Why do you want a new house? You would do better with an older home. [He turned to a large, colorful map of the area that is mounted on the wall, then plants his index finger on an older community.] This area here is *exclusive*. Now, what do I mean by *"exclusive"*? These homes run $225[,000] to $250[,000]. They are existing homes. They're a good deal because they have a new bathroom, a new kitchen, and you would have *neighbors*. With a new subdivision, all you have is the *newness*. You don't know who your neighbors are. Now, if you *want* a new home, there are new homes going up in [an area further north. He slides his finger up to pinpoint the area.] . . . in your price range. But don't overlook the older homes. If you do, you'd be shortchanging yourself.

I continued to insist that what we wanted to buy was a new home. Clearly frustrated, the agent pulled out a small book with colored photos and prices of the latest listings. He flipped to the listings for new subdivisions, arranged the book more centrally on the table so that it was positioned between us, then said, "See, these single-family homes start at five hundred [thousand dollars]. There aren't any new homes in this area in your price range." The problem was that I had not given the agent a price range. Like the real estate agent who queried Lydia, the Long and Foster representative *assumed* that I could not afford the five-hundred-thousand-dollar homes, even after I had announced that my fiancé would be working at the local hospital as a surgeon. One might argue, in the real estate agent's defense, that a young surgeon does not earn enough to afford a five-hundred-thousand-dollar home. In that case, this interaction could not be characterized as an instance of racial steering. However, the Long and Foster real estate agent did not inquire as to other sources of income, for example, whether we were independently wealthy, whether we had investments, or whether our parents would provide us with the down payment, and so on. Moreover, depending on his or her area of specialization, a young surgeon might well earn enough to purchase such a home.

Among some real estate agents in Lakeview, "price range" is a euphemism for racial homogeneity. The bulk of the land in Lakeview is already built up; consequently, the few newly constructed subdivisions are squeezed onto small plots of land between existing homes. Lakeview real estate agents appear heavily invested in keeping these new subdivisions white. The Lakeview Long and Foster agent appeared invested in steering me to established neighborhoods, where small signs of integration were already under way, under the pretense that there one would immediately know "who your neighbors are." But by denying blacks access to the newer subdivisions, realtors assure those white home buyers that they, too, will always know who their neighbors are: white families much like themselves.

My experience with the Long and Foster agent helps to explain why so many of the middle-class blacks in this study who have had interactions with real estate agents that a reasonable person might deem discriminatory don't see it that way. Even though the Long and Foster agent tried to steer me away from where I wanted to live, he was very nice about it. In fact, he packaged sound real estate advice up with his brand of racial steering. For example, he informed me that I should be on the lookout for couples who are breaking up or families who are relocating because "the best buys are divorce, foreclosure, and death," as these families are in a rush to sell. He also volunteered, "See, this won't be your final home. So you have to think about getting in, but also getting out. Will you be able to sell your home? You don't want to buy a dog."

Identifying housing discrimination is further complicated by the fact that black real estate agents are involved in their own version of steering, promoting predominantly black neighborhoods to black home-seekers. When Terry and her husband, Riverton residents, searched for their first home in Chicago, Terry remembers their black real estate agent singling out several white communities that they should avoid, admonishing, "Oh, you don't want to live there. Black people don't live there." Michelle, who viewed with her husband homes in both Lakeview and Riverton before deciding on Sherwood Park, the upper-middle-class suburb in Riverton, noticed that the Riverton real estate agent, who was black, "only showed us homes in black neighborhoods." And when I posed as a home-seeker in Riverton, a black agent did ask me first, "What areas are you interested in?" But once I tossed out Harbor Place, a majority-black middle-class community located in Prince George's County, as a possibility, he expressed considerable enthusiasm, volunteering that Harbor Place "is a community of black professionals. It's the hottest area right now. It used to be Riverton, but now it's Harbor Place." To a layperson, his comments may seem innocuous, but recall Audrey's warning: "You can't say, 'This neighborhood has more blacks.' You can't do that" because "that's discriminatory."

In the Washington, D.C., metropolitan area, there are both black and white real estate agents who direct black home-seekers away from white neighborhoods. My undercover observations suggest that white agents who engage in racial steering may do so to prevent black home-seekers from encroaching on stable, white communities, while black agents who steer may do so to protect their black clients from predominantly white communities where they could possibly encounter hostile white neighbors. Because the tactics real estate agents now use to promote racially homogeneous neighborhoods are so subtle, it is very difficult for blacks to pinpoint discrimination and to label it as such.

In cases where respondents do recognize discriminatory practices, they rely on two strategies to secure desirable housing, both of which require middle-class blacks to assert public identities. Some blacks confront real estate agents directly, the option Lydia chose when she advised the agent that she would "take a look at the house, and . . . let her know when [she had] finished." Though she was "dressed down," Lydia used unmistakable language to articulate her middle-class identity to the agent. In short, Lydia attempted to show that she belonged there, viewing the model home, just as much as the well-dressed white couple. In doing so, she relied on the class conviction that her access to cultural capital effectively challenged the real estate agent's potential roadblock.

Other middle-class blacks forgo the agent-client relationship completely, locating homes on their own as they drive through potential neighborhoods. Many already have friends living in the neighborhoods where they find their homes. Through these social networks, they are made aware of homes coming up for sale. This strategy can be likened to the self-reliant script that middle-class blacks make use of in the work-place. In the workplace, these middle-class blacks place little faith in the EEOC to resolve racial conflicts; instead, they resolve them on their own. While house-hunting, they dispense with real estate agents who are un-willing to help them find adequate housing. To locate a home on one's own requires skill and resources: a car, a working knowledge of the area's neighborhoods, leisure time to search, and so on. Thus, the middle-class blacks in this study realize that racial discrimination persists in the housing market, but they do not feel that their housing options are severely limited by it. After all, in the end, Lakeview and Riverton resi-dents do locate a home that pleases them, and because they have no way to systematically assess whether their housing search compares unfa-vorably to that of their white counterparts, they tend to wave off the practices of prejudicial real estate agents as inconsequential in their hous-ing decisions. Relying on middle-class resources and networks to nego-tiate these public interactions and to secure their dream home is a rea-sonably satisfying solution.

THE SOCIAL COST OF BEING BLACK AND MIDDLE-CLASS

Why aren't the middle-class blacks in this study angrier about having to do the work of engaging public identities in the first place? As they tell their stories, in some cases their eyes flash with anger as they remember the offense. But most informants tell their stories matter-of-factly, as if what they endured happens routinely to black people. Although these middle-class blacks dwell more on their successes than on what these feats cost them, some of their comments suggest there is in fact a psy-chological cost. Recall that both Brad and Greg remembered clearly the names of high school teachers who discriminated against them, with Greg declaring, "I'll never forget that mean ol' lady." And Michelle de-scribed a "relaxed day" as one in which she doesn't care about what whites think, a day when she would show up at a store wearing what-ever she feels, not the more mainstream clothing that would facilitate as-serting a public identity.

The blacks in this study are not the only blacks who do not overtly express sustained anger about their encounters with whites in public spaces. Annette Lareau describes how a black upper-middle-class woman in her study responded to an interaction that the fieldworker perceived as racist. The woman, Christina, was prepared to buy a sled from a mom-and-pop hardware store. Drawing on a fieldworker's notes, Lareau writes:

> Her checkbook was on the counter top and she had a pen in hand before the [older woman] stopped her. "We no longer accept checks. Do you have a credit card?" . . . (I thought Christina was going to "go off." I certainly would have.) Christina remained calm . . . she looked the woman in the eye and spoke in a casual voice, "Yes, I do, but the last time I was here, I paid with a check." The woman also spoke casually, "Well, since it is holiday season, we are trying to limit the number of checks that we accept." . . . Christina looked at [her son] then smiled. . . . Speaking to the salesperson, she said, "Can you hold the sled for me?"[43]

According to the fieldworker, as they exited the store, Christine denied that the encounter was a racist one, retrieved a credit card from her husband, then went back and purchased the sled. It is possible that Christina was unfazed by the salesclerk's behavior because she did have a credit card and was capable of purchasing the sled through an alternative means of payment. Similarly, the middle-class blacks also get what they want in the end—a home that they love, a subordinate worker's deference—so they may focus more on the outcome and less on the sometimes stinging process of achieving it. Alternatively, middle-class blacks may believe that racism is a permanent part of life. Audrey's comment that the homes shown to her by a real estate agent engaged in racial steering were simply "what you're going to be getting" and Charlotte's recollection that "this is what you're gonna get" signal this kind of resignation. It is possible that blacks who earn more than fifty thousand dollars annually process racial discrimination through a different lens than lower-middle-class blacks do. Feagin's insightful study collapsed different groups of middle-class blacks into one broad category. Future research will need to draw conclusions from a sample that contrasts the experiences of lower-middle-class blacks with those from the upper classes to assess these kinds of distinctions.

CONCLUSION

Although what makes the evening news is corporate discrimination scandals—multimillion-dollar lawsuits filed against companies accused of engaging in various forms of modern racism—the everyday instances of racial discrimination experienced by middle-class blacks warrant additional attention from scholars and the public. Feagin's racial stigma theory suggests that a middle-class standing does not protect blacks from racial discrimination. However, I have shown that this conclusion may not be invariantly true. Middle-class blacks in the Washington, D.C., area use public identities to reduce the probability that racial discrimination will determine important outcomes in their lives. By examining how public identities are employed in various public settings, we gain insight into the informal strategies blacks develop as a result of their experiences in a racialized society. These informal strategies are far more common than the occasional discrimination suits filed by blacks and profiled in the media.

Public identities constitute a form of cultural capital in which blacks with the knowledge and skills valorized by the American mainstream are in a position to manipulate public interactions to their advantage. Previous studies have not examined how high-status minority group members come to possess cultural capital. I introduced two conceptual devices to explain this process and to connect the acquisition of cultural capital to the construction and assertion of public identities in adulthood: improvisational processes and script-switching. To assert public identities, middle-class blacks first acquire cultural capital through their childhood introduction to integrated settings and through their ongoing interactions in the American mainstream, where white cultural styles rule the day. These improvisational and script-switching socialization processes allow middle-class blacks to demonstrate their familiarity with the cultural codes and practices associated with the white middle class. I also show that the cultural capital so critical to doing well in school is influential beyond the school setting as well: in shopping malls, the workplace, and to some extent, with real estate agents.

Among these middle-class blacks, projecting public identities is an opportunity to shore up their status as a group that is not merely black, but distinctly black *and middle-class*. Interviewees noted that "the world is not fair" and that "people will look at [them] in special ways because [they] are black." But these middle-class blacks also tend to associate persistent racial discrimination in public spaces with lower-class blacks, not their class grouping. As members of the middle class, they firmly believe in their ability to engage in strategies that minimize the amount and severity of discrimination directed toward their group. On the rare occasions when they believe that they do experience discrimination—from sales clerks, for example—middle-class blacks associate the incidents with an inability on their part to effectively signal their class position to store employees.

The findings presented in this chapter do not negate the racial stigma paradigm. Rather, these findings call attention to a neglected aspect of the model, namely, the mobilization of class-related strategies as a bulwark against racial discrimination. Indeed, the data suggest that social class may figure more centrally in middle-class blacks' subjective understanding of their public interactions than previous studies allow.

4

Status-Based Identities
Protecting and Reproducing
Middle-Class Status

Right now," declares Brad, a forty-six-year-old judge and Sherwood Park resident, "the top priority for me is getting both of my sons through their educations, as far as they need to go. . . . I will do everything that I can to help [them be successful] . . . whether that's through academics, setting up a business, or whatever." Concerns about status reproduction—that is, Brad's desire to ensure that when they are adults, his children will have at their disposal a clear roadmap for attaining a class position as comfortable as his—guide his financial decisions. "I don't take a lot of chances," he confides, adding, "I will probably kick myself for not having been involved in the stock market for the last four or five years. But for me, that's risky money." Other Sherwood Park blacks similarly direct their attention to status reproduction. They are willing to defer their own material desires, if necessary, in order to provide their children with sufficient financial and educational resources to attain a middle-class lifestyle. For Brad, and Sherwood Park blacks generally, spending responsibly on themselves but lavishly on their children is a central component of their conception of status.

Middle-class blacks in Riverton and Lakeview, on the other hand, take a different approach. Concerns about protecting their own status position lead parents in these communities to spend responsibly on themselves and *cautiously* on their children. Kevin, a large, gregarious, high school football coach who lives in Riverton, jokes about packing his four children off to Piney Woods, a private school in Mississippi known for its strict disciplinary tactics, but he would not seriously consider sending them to private schools in the local area. "I ain't paying no five thousand dollars [annually for tuition]—I ain't tryin' to do that much hustlin'! Five thousand and they still in high school and I'm struggling to eat and stuff? Shoot, they can go up to that school up there," he declares, pointing a chubby forefinger in the direction of the public elementary school. For Kevin, the staggering cost of private schooling for his children (in fact, his estimate is well shy of the actual annual tuition rates at elite private schools in the Washington, D.C., metropolitan area) would deplete resources he feels he and his wife need if they are to maintain their current standard of living. Lakeview residents Jasmine and her husband Richard, both in their mid-forties, are equally adamant about not jeopardizing their retirement plans by overspending on their children's education. Jasmine, who is self-employed, and Richard, who is a corporate manager, expect their two teenage sons to go to college. But unlike the black parents in Sherwood Park, this couple will require their children to help pay for their own education. "I want money in the bank," Jasmine stresses, as she comments on neighbors who in her opinion are whittling away at their savings paying tuition at their children's private schools. Richard is even more direct. Recalling a conversation with his oldest son about college scholarships, he begins laughing heartily at the memory. "I ain't goin' use my retirement money!" Richard reports having told his son. "So *you* make it happen."

As Brad's, Kevin's, and Jasmine and Richard's comments demonstrate, not all members of the black middle class employ the same strategies to facilitate the transmission or reproduction of status. Differences like the ones between blacks in Sherwood Park on the one hand and those in Riverton and Lakeview on the other are the focus of this chapter. These different strategies stem from differences in wealth, the kinds of assets middle-class blacks rely on to create opportunities for themselves and their children. Although interview respondents in all three communities uniformly describe themselves as members of the middle class, analyzing their evaluations of their own lifestyles and those of others reveals that a status hierarchy based on lifestyle distinctions exists within the black middle class.[1] Blacks who spend lavishly on their children, like Brad and his neighbors in Sherwood Park, conceive of their status principally in the context of status reproduction. They see their spending as an investment in this process. Blacks in Riverton and Lakeview, like Kevin, Jasmine, and Richard, who spend more conservatively on their children, think about their status in terms of protecting what they have. They see spending regularly on luxuries like private school tuition as threatening their status position.

These are meaningful differences that highlight important diversity within the black middle class. Sherwood Park blacks assert status identities that reflect an *elite* black middle-class status, while Lakeview and Riverton blacks assert status identities that reflect membership in the *core* black middle class.[2] Intraclass status distinctions among blacks are not new. In *Black Metropolis,* Drake and Cayton's investigation of life in Chicago's Bronzeville section (see chapter 1 for a discussion of this and other classic studies of black communities), the authors note that "the way in which people spend their money is the most important measuring rod in American life, particularly among people within the same general income range." They argue that among the residents of Bronzeville, "a man's style of living—what he does with his money—[is] a very important index to social status. It is through the expenditure of money that his educational level and ultimate aspirations for himself and his family find expression."[3] The varied lifestyles of the black middle class tend to go unnoted today because most studies focus on comparisons between the black poor and the black (lower) middle class.[4]

Exploring the processes by which blacks in Riverton, Lakeview, and Sherwood Park conceptualize, maintain, and protect their status identities as they define the boundaries between themselves and others shows that blacks not only negotiate for status *across* class lines, as existing studies demonstrate, they also make status claims *within* class categories. The drama professor Keith Johnstone argues in his book *Impro* that we tend to be oblivious to claims for status in the absence of conflict. "In the park we'll notice the ducks squabbling," he submits, "but not how carefully they keep their distances when they are not."[5] This chapter redirects attention to these carefully maintained status divisions within the black middle class by comparing and contrasting the beliefs and behaviors of core and elite middle-class blacks with respect to three dimensions of status: work ethic, spending responsibly, and sacrificing for their children.

NO "SILVER SPOONS": DIFFERENT PERCEPTIONS OF HOW WORK MATTERS

Despite their affluence, Sherwood Park blacks repeatedly refer to themselves as "middle-class," in part because they share with Riverton and

Lakeview blacks a general belief in the American ethos that hard work and playing by the rules are prerequisites to securing a middle-class lifestyle.[6] Within that overarching similarity of beliefs, however, lie important differences. Riverton and Lakeview blacks are disdainful of people who try to avoid work. Like the working poor, respondents from these communities see work as a *moral obligation*. For them, conceptions of status involve defining the black middle class in relation to those who shirk their work obligations, those who, thanks to "this welfare business," feel free to "just sit home and not do anything." By contrast, Sherwood Park blacks see work not as a moral directive but rather as a *pathway to economic independence*. Frequently reflecting on the effort it took to reach their current class position—"you work for it"; "we paid our dues"—these respondents express great admiration for the very wealthy, people who need not work to maintain their high standard of living. Sherwood Park blacks' conceptions of status thus involve defining the black middle class in relation to the upper classes.

RIVERTON AND LAKEVIEW: WORK AS A MORAL OBLIGATION

In *No Shame in My Game,* cultural anthropologist Katherine Newman finds that Harlem's black working poor, many of whom live in the same house or apartment with chronically unemployed individuals, draw rigid moral boundaries between themselves and those who elect not to seek employment. Their status claims hinge on their membership on the right side of that moral boundary; for them, the harsh reality that their jobs pay paltry salaries and require little skill is offset by the fact that they are productive citizens who support themselves just as white-collar workers do. As one worker explained to Newman, "I'm not knocking welfare, but I know people that are on it that can get up and work. There's nothing wrong with them. . . . I don't think it's right because that's my tax dollars going for somebody who is lazy and don't wanna get up."[7]

Riverton and Lakeview blacks, although they hold better jobs and live much more comfortably than Harlem's working poor, express a similar resentment toward able-bodied people who do not work. They target welfare recipients in particular—not because they are poor, but because they think this group lacks both a strong work ethic and personal initiative, and they believe that welfare recipients feel justified in accumulating more resources than they are rightfully entitled to. Lakeview resident Audrey, retired from her career as a real estate agent, is representative of this perspective. When she and her husband moved into their home in a new Lakeview subdivision in 1971, they were the first black family to inhabit the subdivision. Their house, purchased for $101,000, has appreciated to an astounding $375,000. Audrey stresses that "what we have, we have worked hard for." Although she welcomes the work requirement introduced in the 1996 federal Personal Responsibility and Work Reconciliation Act, she feels the policy doesn't go far enough: "This welfare business, and the programs that they have available now, is not helping these people [the poor]. They're *expecting* it; we're not helping them to be responsible. . . . Welfare reform, I'm glad of it, but I still say that the people who continue to get the benefits that are available, most of 'em are the ones that really should be out in the workplace."

Again, like Harlem's working poor, blacks in Riverton and Lakeview believe that the poor should be required to perform some sort of work or public service in exchange for their government-provided assistance. Alana, an attorney who lives with her husband and two teenage children in Lakeview, insists that welfare recipients shouldn't be allowed to "just sit home and collect a check." In a tone betraying her agitation, she cautions me, "Now, you don't even want to get me [started] on the welfare and all that now," before continuing:

> I believe everybody should work. . . . Those people's circumstances have put them in that situation. So you might can't do everything that you want to do, but you can do more than just sit home and collect a check. Now, that infuriates me to no end. I believe there should be a work component attached to it. I'm not saying cut people off, by no means. But if it's no more than requiring these people to go into the local library and volunteer to put up some books—everybody can do something. One of the things that you hear all the time is the government doesn't have the money to fully staff libraries. In order to pick up your check, you can do something. If it's no more than require them to go pick up trash in the neighborhood. That's not beneath anybody. Because, like I said, our community goes out and does it [Lakeview has an annual community-wide clean-up day]. I don't think they should get a free ride.

Riverton and Lakeview's middle-class blacks strongly believe that no one should live "the good life" without working hard to achieve it. Alana does not want the government to simply "cut people off," but at the same time, she is adamant that people on public assistance should not end up better off than those who are willing to work:

> I see people coming into the grocery store using food stamps, driving big cars, wearing better clothes . . . and I have a problem with a family who is

struggling but keeping their head above water who can't afford to buy their kids what they want, such as nice clothes, [while] somebody on welfare whose mother or father is not hittin' a lick come into school wit' designer this and that, they go get free lunch, or reduced lunch. Or at Christmastime . . . there are people who go to the Salvation Army, get Christmas [presents] for their kids, then turn around and they go over to Eastern Union Mission and get [more] toys. They [charitable organizations] are not tied in [to one another]. I know it happens. The problem I have is the parent who is out trying [to make ends meet] does not qualify to get anything. So here their child may get this one little doll. And a parent who hasn't worked a lick, got welfare check, food stamps, everything, he'll qualify to go to Salvation Army and pick up a bag of toys.

Audrey, too, resents people who don't feel obligated to work. She worries that, owing to prolonged "abuse" by nonworking individuals, the government's coffers soon will be drained. Her primary fear is that there will be nothing left for working people like her. Audrey's fears about Medicaid shortages are also connected to the general theme that people who haven't "put in" to the system shouldn't be able to benefit from federal programs and services. She focuses her anger on immigrants:

The people that come across the waters, they come here knowing how to use the system. They know how to use the system. They get things just because they come here. We have people whose parents has put things in the system, they can't get it. And I don't think that that's fair. That's why the dollars that should be used into things that can help people move to the levels that they should be, it's not being used. That's why when I get older, and if I need to have Medicaid or Medicare, I'm not going to be able to get it, because they have too many people that come here and they give them Medicaid with no questions asked. They come here pregnant, they drop babies year after year after year—they automatically get these things just because they are here. To me, that's not a citizen. Just because you're born here, you're not a citizen. I think that you have to do more than just being born here.

Clearly, a willingness to work is an important aspect of status identity for Riverton and Lakeview blacks. They share with the black working poor the belief that holding down a job is a way to earn respect as a productive citizen. However, unlike the working poor, who erect boundaries against the unemployed in order to feel better about being constrained to employment in low-status occupations, Riverton and Lakeview blacks draw distinctions based on the principle that working is the only legitimate way to achieve a comfortable standard of living in this country. Riverton resident Terry, who juggles her job as a hospital administrator with her responsibilities as the mother of two girls, seven and eight years old, emphasizes that maintaining a middle-class status and its accoutrements requires motivation, self-discipline, and hard work:

> It is a nice neighborhood, but everybody here works to stay here. And those who don't work are usually retired, or did something well for themselves while they were young and don't have to do it anymore, or earning income in different ways. But everybody goes to work—*this is your reward for going to work.* You can live in a nice neighborhood if you work every day. And . . . you don't have to be—a bus driver lives across the street, a fire-fighter. Nobody says you have to have that college degree, but you have to be willing to go to work. You go to work and do what's right, you can live out here. It's nothing saying you can't. You know how people say, "You've arrived"? You ain't got nowhere. I go to work. I don't believe in that philos-ophy [of "you've arrived"]. . . . I really don't understand when people from the inner city think that we have "arrived." Nope, we go to work every day. . . . If you do that, you can get here too. You just have to prioritize what to do with your money.

SHERWOOD PARK: WORK AS A PATHWAY TO INDEPENDENCE

"The very rich . . . are different from you and me," F. Scott Fitzgerald fa-mously observed in the short story "The Rich Boy."[8] Indeed they are, agrees John, who informs me over a midweek lunch at the California Pizza Kitchen in Old Town Alexandria, Virginia, that there is "no such thing as a black *upper* class." (We have driven about ten miles to north-ern Virginia from John's imposing home in Sherwood Park because there are no suitable eat-in restaurants in his upper-middle-class, mostly black neighborhood.) "You can't be serious," I counter. "What about Oprah, Bill Cosby, and the Beatrice guy?" But John is talking about more than deep pockets, for he knows there are very wealthy black people. What he has in mind is *old* money: "We don't have any Rockefellers or Kennedys. We don't."

Apart from wealth that stretches back seamlessly across genera-tions, the most important characteristic distinguishing the wealthy from everyone else is their orientation toward work. Rich people work because they *want* to; poor(er) people work because they *have* to. Many of the richest blacks in the United States, including Oprah Winfrey, Bill Cosby, and Reginald Lewis (the now-deceased past owner of food giant TLC Beatrice International), come from working-class origins. They didn't inherit wealth from their families. Instead, they all worked extraordinarily hard for their money and success. For Sherwood Park blacks, that distinction is crucial. One reason they describe themselves as "middle-class" despite their ample incomes, college degrees, and jobs as professionals is that each of these characteristics reflects their own sustained effort, not a birthright. Lydia, married to a corporate manager and the mother of three children—two boys and a girl—nevertheless continues to work as an engineer. She sees "work[ing] for it" as an essential characteristic of her lifestyle: "We are reasonably successful, but that has to do with the fact that we paid our dues, we went to school, we pulled the all-nighters like everybody else. Yeah, we got an education, and we're willing to work, to put the time in. And that's how it works in this country. Either you get born with a silver spoon in your mouth, win the lottery, which I'm not against either—"

I interjected, "Are you hoping for that—to win the lottery?"

"No." She giggled, suggesting that it would be silly to plan your life around something so remote. "Only if it's like, thirty million! So you work for it. I guess with black folks, the option is you either hit the lottery or you work for it. Very few of us—there are some— . . . come from families with a lot of money."

Unlike members of the upper class, who derive status from their *volunteer* work and charitable endeavors, Sherwood Park blacks must work to maintain their lifestyles.[9] In that limited sense, they might be considered "middle-class." Recall Sherwood Park residents Nathaniel and Lisa, parents of two young boys, who jokingly claimed that they were "working-class" before characterizing themselves as middle-class. Like their neighbors, both Nathaniel and Lisa work long hours. Lydia and Michael insist on a middle-class label, too, and point to the fact that they both work as proof of their middle-class status. Michael argues that their opulent lifestyle is possible only because they are a two-income household: "One of the neighbors is a doctor. His wife stays home. Okay, I would consider *that* upper-middle class, because . . . they have enough income coming in where she does not need to work. My wife *needs* to work. We both need to maintain." Lydia, also comparing herself to her neighbors, agrees. "We probably make a lot less money than most people that live around here," she tells me with a laugh big enough to make her eyes crinkle at the corners. "Why do you think that?" I ask, since together Lydia and Michael make about what everyone else in the community earns. She answers:

> Oh, I *know* we do. I know what a lot of people around here do for a living. We're probably at the low end of what most people make. . . . A lot of people [out here] have more money than we do. We'll be able to send our

kids to college. Hope they get a scholarship, but I know Princeton's not going to give me any money; they think we have money. I just think I'm middle-class because I have to work every day. If I didn't have to work, maybe I'd be upper-class. But I have to go to work. I really don't think I have a choice to live the way I want to live; I couldn't live here and not work. Not the way I *want* to live.

The sheer effort involved in achieving their current class position distinguishes Sherwood Park blacks from members of the upper classes. This may be a key reason these blacks so consistently describe themselves as middle-class. As Brad explains, he and his neighbors trace their roots to the working class and lower-middle class; these backgrounds lead them to believe that they have little in common with the upper class: "I think I may have more in common with those families who have had to come from a much lower economic point. Old money out here, like in most places, is very comfortable with old money. . . . People who have to work or who come from . . . below the poverty line . . . I think there are more commonalities between people who come from places like that, because they cherish what they have, and they are not gaudy with it, but very protective of it." However, like those in the upper class, Sherwood Park blacks do not believe that work done out of necessity is either necessarily rewarding or a sign of prestige. They work, as Lydia's husband Michael puts it, because "we got bills to pay. It costs to live out here. Everybody's probably paying fifteen [hundred dollars in mortgage bills]-plus a month . . . and none of the houses are falling down; people got to pay to maintain 'em. . . . If you move out here, you got to have some money coming in to pay the note. Everybody out here has got to pay the house note." John, echoing Michael, tells me, "I work now to pay for violin lessons for Danielle [his daughter], and for the house, and for my car. . . . Almost everybody in our neighborhood are two-income households, and they work to be able to pay that mortgage" in an upscale subdivision.

What Sherwood Park blacks value beyond the general utility of holding down a job is the independence that working in a high-status position bestows. This seems especially important to the men. John's casual proposal of a midday, mid-workweek time slot to talk over a leisurely lunch indirectly—but unmistakably—signals his autonomy. Michael is explicit about the ways in which his job, which affords him control over his own work schedule, brings him closer to the upper class:

We aren't rich, but you need to do something that gives you some sense of independence, some sense of the ability to do what you want to do when you want to do it. . . . I have that freedom. . . . If it's a nice day out and some friends want to go fishing, then I can say, "Well, let me check my schedule," and then we can go. As a matter of fact, tomorrow's supposed to be a nice day. Well, I already called my partnas; we pullin' out [from work] at 12, 12:10 tomorrow to play. . . . You're going to have to work, but it's *how* you work and *how* you make your money [that is important].

Michael's claim that it's "how you work" that matters underlies his own and his neighbors' general construction of work as less a moral obligation and more a tool for achieving independence. Married to a surgeon, thirty-nine-year-old Tammy recounts how when they first moved to the subdivision nine years ago, she noticed that her husband's flexible work schedule was perplexing to some of her white neighbors in Sherwood Park, who weren't quite sure how someone so young could have so much free time on his hands:

My husband is a surgeon. . . . They start at 7 A.M. and basically get off at 3 P.M. because surgery is done in the morning. . . . When we first moved in, we were thirty, thirty-two, very young, black. I'm a stay-at-home mom, have a little baby, and we had this huge lawn, and for physical activity my husband would mow the lawn. He had a little riding mower, and he'd trim the lawn. . . . He'd come home [from the hospital] and do the lawn. And I'll always remember this. [A] young, white couple in the development—we were real friendly, we talked to everybody. But the husband came by and he started a conversation. "What does your husband do?" And I said, "Well, he's a surgeon." And he's like, "Oh-h-h-h. I was trying to figure out; I always see him doing his lawn during the day." And I just laughed it off. But what this person was saying to me was, "I feel so much better because I couldn't figure out how, as young as you guys are, you're not working. What kind of job does he have that he's home during the day, but he can afford this kind of house and his wife doesn't have to work?" . . . It was truly perplexing to him. Are they pushing drugs, did they win the lottery? How does a young black man have that kind of money? It's very interesting. If we were a young white couple and I was a stay-at-home mom with a young baby, you would just think my husband had a good-paying job. Period.

That economic independence is inextricably bound with purposeful decisions about career choice is clear when Sherwood Park blacks outline their aspirations for their children. They convey to their children that at least two career paths are possible and that the children will need to decide what kind of lifestyle they'd prefer to have and plan accordingly. In these discussions, a job at McDonald's is invoked frequently as the kind of low-skilled, dead-end work that everyone *should* avoid, but which could be the fate of those who fail to plan their futures and refuse to be selective about career choice. Snuggled into an oversized chair in her husband Brad's home office, Crystal, a stay-at-home mom, recounts a conversation her husband had with their teenage sons:

> Brad had a talk with them one time, and he said—I'm trying to remember how he put it—he said, "Listen, you can go to college, do well, be successful, get a good job, make a nice living, be able to go out to dinner, buy nice clothes. Or you can not do that—you have a choice—and have a little teeny apartment somewhere, take a bus, work at McDonald's. That's up to you, what you do." We'll see. I think that—we talk to them about trying to maintain the lifestyle, and also for them to understand that it took a lot of work to get here.

Michael is even more direct with his children. To give them an idea of what it takes to maintain their lifestyle, he shows them the bills that he and his wife pay each month:

> I told my oldest son, I said, "You can look at those people right behind the counter at McDonald's. They working hard, you know. What's the minimum wage? Six dollars an hour? Let's say it's six dollars. At the end of the day, if they work eight hours, they made, what, forty-eight dollars? Times five, two hundred forty dollars for the whole week. In a month they made a thousand dollars. Okay . . . this how much our house note is, okay? So you ain't living here [on that kind of salary]. You can't live [someplace like] here."

Michael grins with amused satisfaction as he remembers this discussion. Gradually, the grin morphs into unrestrained laughter as he continues with the recollection: " 'And by the way, this how much the car note is. So you ain't goin' be driving this car.' . . . And so, I'm saying, you need to be able to make some cash. . . . What I show them is that it costs, it costs to be where you are [currently]."

Sherwood Park blacks take every opportunity to remind their children that they need to give serious thought to how they will reproduce the lifestyle that they've grown accustomed to living under their parents' roof. Early on, children are encouraged to pursue occupations that facilitate economic independence. Crystal, for example, steered her son toward *owning* a business when he mentioned matter-of-factly as a youngster that he hoped to become a laborer someday: "I remember when they were younger, one of the kids said to me, 'Mommy, you know what I want to do when I grow up? I want to wash cars!' I said, 'That's fine, but you want to *own* the car wash, and then you can wash cars any time you want to, and when you don't feel like it, you don't have to.' I've always tried to stress to them that you don't have to be a doctor or a lawyer. In fact, that's a whole lot of work."

None of the Sherwood Park parents insist that their children pursue a *specific* occupation; their hope is that their children will never "be dependent upon other people," as fifty-two-year-old Philip, a corporate executive, and father of two girls, put it. Brad's thinking is similar. He began his career as a lawyer. Today, at age forty-six, he is not only a judge who earns over $200,000 a year, but also a published author and a popular speaker at local schools; his résumé, he told me, covers thirty pages. He does not, however, demand that his sons follow in his footsteps, nor does he expect them to match or exceed his many accomplishments. He simply advocates becoming a boss over becoming a worker. When I asked if he wanted his sons to do something like what he was doing, Brad responded, "If they want to. I most want them to do something that makes them happy . . . something that makes them an income that they can be comfortable supporting a family. . . . Damien is a motor head; he loves cars. But I only want him to take it to a level that he can have his own business and not be dependent upon other people to make a living."

In sum, for Sherwood Park blacks, work is a *pathway to independence* rather than the moral obligation it is for Riverton and Lakeview blacks.

"MORE MONTH LEFT THAN MONEY": SPENDING RESPONSIBLY

The ability to prioritize purchases and spend responsibly is a second dimension of middle-class blacks' definition of their status. No single purchase is more important than buying a home. Blacks from all three suburban communities stipulate that home ownership is central, distinguishing responsible consumers from spendthrifts, the fiscally shrewd middle class from the lower classes. However, beyond this initial status marker, the spending patterns of blacks in Sherwood Park differ in concrete ways from those of blacks in Riverton or Lakeview. The latter groups feel hugely burdened financially; therefore, they define spending responsibly in the context of a budget that prioritizes basics deemed essential to sustaining a middle-class lifestyle over luxuries like expensive cars and high-end electronics (items allegedly irresistible to the working class) or lavish vacations and second homes (purchases seen as typical of the upper class). Sherwood Park blacks, free from financial constraints, spend more liberally, purchasing necessities along with expensive luxuries that serve to make a comfortable life all the more comfortable. Despite their avoidance of the label upper-middle class, these blacks' consumption patterns generally conform to that class level. They define responsible spending as consumption decisions that help to reproduce their status. This definition is not constrictive, as most of what Sherwood Park blacks desire is well within their reach.

RIVERTON AND LAKEVIEW: PRIORITIZING ESSENTIALS

Riverton and Lakeview blacks believe that purchasing a home should take precedence over every other kind of purchase, especially a luxury car. Terry, a hospital administrator, evokes a critique popular in many black communities, namely, that working-class black men buy luxury cars but they live in low-grade rental properties (often with their mamas):

> Don't complain that you live in the ghetto, even though you go to work, when you're driving around in a Lexus. And I'm not even talking about getting it by illegal means. But if you prioritize that way, then you will never live in a nice neighborhood. It's [about] where your priorities are. It's just where your priorities are. I'd love a BMW; it's my dream car. I'll get one eventually. I'm not goin' cry over it. And I'm not goin' go get a six-hundred-dollar [per month] car note either. [She laughs.] It's not on the schedule. . . . If it's meant for me to have it, I'm goin' have one. If it's not, I'm not goin' sweat it either.

Like Terry, Kevin draws a sharp boundary between his status group and working-class blacks, who are said to prefer conspicuous consumption to responsible spending:

> One of the reasons they [car]jack a lot of these cars, 'cause in the back of their mind, they really think it's no way in they life they can get a Lexus. "Ain't no way in the world I'm-a get a four by four." So when my son graduates [from college] and he gets hisself a Lexus, [it's,] "Oh, he think he all that." As Chris Rock say, "low expectation negroes." That's what they got—low expectations. These guys will get a loan for a car quicker than they get a loan for a house.

Generally, living in an apartment invites suspicion and boundary-drawing from Riverton and Lakeview blacks. Alana, though, questions relying too broadly on this established status marker: "I'm not saying that everybody who lives in an apartment is not middle-class, but you don't have—and I guess, well, this is another generalization I'm making. If you don't own a home, [that] does not mean that you're not middle-class, but I think some of your middle-class values—you tend to find most people [long pause] owning something. [Long pause.] And that's not even true, now that I think about it."

In seeing themselves as different from the black working class, a group that reputedly engages in frivolous spending, thus thwarting their efforts to save up for a home, Riverton and Lakeview blacks are both similar to and different from the white middle class. They are similar because they spend responsibly, prioritizing owning a home over other major purchases. They are different because they perceive themselves as far less frugal than the white middle class. Terry brings this analysis to bear when describing one of her white co-workers: "This guy is a physician, making $198,000 a year. He got a car stolen from him. It was a '78 Oldsmobile!"

In order to determine the age of the car at the time of the theft, I asked, "Was this recently?"

Terry responded, "Recently. You would think this man had his Mercedes stolen, the way he was ranting and raving. 'I paid seven hundred fifty dollars for that car, and I can't believe somebody stole my car.' You would think [by] the way he was responding that this was a million-dollar car, the way he was responding. [He was saying,] 'But you don't understand! How can I replace that car?' He said, 'It only cost me seven hundred fifty dollars. I pay [virtually] no insurance on it. How can I replace that car?' Gorgeous home—you wouldn't know [going by the car]." Terry laughed. "[White people] prioritize things. They don't go buy the Mercedes first. They go buy their house."

In short, the lifestyle of Riverton and Lakeview middle-class blacks differs significantly from that of working-class blacks, overlaps partially with that of middle-class whites, and has virtually nothing in common with that of upper-class whites.

Often, outsiders' perceptions of the upper class are shaped through indirect access to this privileged group. But Charlotte, a gregarious fifty-two-year-old high school teacher, mother of five children, and Lakeview resident, gained an insider's perspective. She befriended an affable white woman from work, Sarah, whom Charlotte describes as " 'old money' [because] her mother's mother was a millionaire." Sarah, whose family is still living off the grandmother's money, is committed to educating youth and works "for chump change," according to Charlotte. Sarah married an IBM salesman in the early 1970s, and at that time her husband earned about $70,000 annually, while Sarah earned about $25,000. For Sarah, that household income constituted living "in poverty." She confessed to Charlotte back then, "I *cannot* live in poverty." Sarah *felt* poor until her father, who wanted her "to live in a certain manner," intervened, providing the couple with financial help.

It was from Sarah that Charlotte learned "how to really shop." The first time the two women went to the mall together, they were on a lunch break. Charlotte still recalls that excursion. In animated detail, she recounts how the trip transformed her perception of shopping:

> She said, "Let's go get some yogurt." I said, "Okay." She said, "But I have to go shopping." I said, "I don't think we have time." Her little girl at that time was about three or four. She said, "We'll have time." [Charlotte says this in an assured tone designed to convey Sarah's certainty.] So we go to Lord & Taylor and she walks up to the saleslady and says, "I'd like some things for my daughter. I'd like a coat and something for play, something for dress," and blah-blah-blah. The lady said, "No problem." [Then] she [Sarah] said [to me], "Let's go," and we went upstairs and had our yogurt. Then I said, "Do you have time to look for things [for your daughter]?" She said, "Yeah!" She came down, [looked at the things the salesperson had selected for her daughter] and said, [Charlotte snaps her fingers as she recalls the moment] "I'll take this, this, this, this, and this. Wrap 'em up." *She never looked at the price once!* The lady gave her 'bout five or six bags and she walked out the store. She said, "I *hate* to shop!" [Charlotte chuckles.] I said, "Yeah, I know what you mean!"

Shopping with her wealthy friend made Charlotte aware of her own middle-class status. Then and now, her budget demands that she constantly "look at prices, comparing, waiting on sales, using coupons." In comparison, she says, referring to Sarah, "My girl *never, ever looked* [at the prices]. She said, 'I'll take that, that, that, that, that. Okay, that'll do her for a while.' And she put it in the bag, paid her, and went on." Chortling, Charlotte remembers thinking at the time, " '*Dag*,' 'cause that's how you shop!" However, Charlotte's experience was sobering, too. It reminded her that middle-class blacks are "just all one paycheck away from poverty, because if you lose your job, you got nothing. You make these inflated salaries, you make, oh gosh, $150,000, something like that, but that's nothing if you lose your job."

Clearly, Riverton and Lakeview blacks are not *really* poor. They don't wonder where their next meal will come from or how they will be able to afford gas for their cars. Still, they are more likely than Sherwood Park blacks to worry about operating within a budget, rationing their paychecks until the next pay period, or living with mounting debt. Shelly, a thirty-eight-year-old Riverton resident and mother of a young boy and girl, stays within her budget by shopping for designer clothing at discount stores: "I choose to take my money and go to Marshalls [a discount department store]. A lot of people that shop at Saks [5th Avenue] and Neiman [Marcus] really can't afford it, but they want that name!

You can go to Marshalls, get a bargain, and find the same things." Operating within a budget is one way Riverton and Lakeview blacks hope to avoid dwindling finances and the possible erosion of their middle-class lifestyle. When I ask Jared if there are times when he feels concerned about maintaining his lifestyle, he responds immediately: "Well sure, that's the—that's my worry." "When does it happen?" I query. Laughing, he says, "When there's more month left than money!" Jared is not poor. He and his wife and two children live in a three-bedroom Riverton home that they have decorated attractively with African art and black history artifacts collected during their summer vacations. Their home is close to a members-only marina, a popular place to relax, especially in the summer. Jared is pleased with this location: "I don't have the big bucks, but yet I live by the water." He and his wife don't have the resources to do everything that they'd like to do, so they make careful spending decisions. Joining the marina's pool association is a five-hundred-dollar annual expense that Jared elects to forgo. He describes this as a "business decision": "The pool is expensive, and given that I'm an African American . . . I don't go swimming every day. . . . We don't swim every day. Therefore it's, relatively speaking, a lot more expensive for us to use the pool than it is for the Caucasians who would swim every day. If I swim once a week, or once every two weeks versus twice a day, you know, it's a lot more expensive." At first I misunderstand Jared. I think he is suggesting, circuitously, that he avoids the pool because he anticipates that blacks who join the predominantly white pool association will be mistreated by whites. When I ask, "Does this have anything to do with blacks not being welcome at the pool?" Jared demurs. He says:

> I don't think so. I've never experienced that type of thing down there. The first year here, I accepted what's called a "trial membership." And we patronized the pool, and I tried to keep count at the end of the year. And it was approximately twelve times for the entire summer. . . . I probably went eight times. We went twelve times [as a family]. . . . I came to the conclusion after the season when I was trying to decide whether to buy the membership. And I looked back, business decision, we only used the thing about twelve times for five hundred bucks! That's very expensive.

Jasmine and her husband Richard are also concerned about sustaining their middle-class status. They live with their two sons in a large, attractive, four-bedroom, split-foyer colonial in Lakeview. An Amway representative and a former real estate agent, Jasmine is charming, fashionable, and self-assured. "I come across to people extremely well, very confident," she declares. "I've been successful at everything that I've

done." Jasmine's grandfather was a prosperous man who became financially secure by acquiring property. She and her brother benefited from
his financial acumen and generosity. Jasmine recalls, "I didn't have a very
difficult childhood, so there were lots of things you didn't worry about.
I didn't worry about financial matters." At age forty-five, though, Jasmine does worry. She wonders whether she has stockpiled enough
money to maintain her current status position over the long run: "I'm
not comfortable at all. I wake up every morning nervous about that. I'm
not comfortable at all. I'm an entrepreneur, that's why. I don't have a
nine-to-five job. My husband does. . . . I worry about my children and
what I'll be able to leave them. Because what I have presently is not
enough. When my mother died, she left enough for me and my brother."

Terry, too, worries about money. She and her husband and two young
daughters have lived in their split-level Riverton home for the last three
years. Before that, they lived in an apartment and, briefly, with her
mother, who was recovering from a serious illness and needed Terry's
help. Despite enjoying the comfort of her mother's spacious home in an
established, upper-middle-class black D.C. neighborhood, Terry remembers yearning for "some place to lay your head to say, 'I'm in a neutral zone!'" When I ask, "Are there times when you feel concerned about
maintaining your lifestyle?" Terry responds:

> It's a constant; worrying about money is a constant. . . . It's just ever-
> present. When you haven't had a mortgage, [suddenly] you get a mortgage,
> and it's early on, like I said, third year. You write a check for fourteen hun-
> dred dollars, you gotta have this money no matter what—furnace goes out,
> car breaks down—you've gotta have that money. So yeah, it's a concern. I
> think ten years from now, it probably won't be as much of a [concern], in
> my mind, but right now, it remains a concern. And you want things for
> your kids. You have to budget. Will we always be able to maintain this?
> Some of my husband's friends [say], "You guys are livin' the life!" Every
> day somebody in one of these driveways drives out of here and goes to
> work. I don't see wealthy.

Terry and her husband bought a sturdy older home that had been on
the market for only three weeks. The house's interior was woefully outdated. Walls that now are a creamy, attractive beige previously were
what Terry describes as a hideous "turquoise blue, like the ocean." She
points to her daughters' miniature, sea-blue-colored barbells lying on the
floor in the den, where we sit talking. "See those barbells? Like that. The
walls, the ceiling—everything. And the carpet upstairs was that brown
shag carpet." Terry laughs as she remembers her husband's reaction to

the house in its original state. "You sure you like that house?" he asked her, clearly baffled, when they were discussing buying it. She is pleased with the changes they have made to the house's interior, but she wishes they had the resources to alter the exterior as well. The previous owners painted the bricks on the house's facade. Removing the paint is prohibitively expensive, so Terry has "learned to get used to it, because you can't afford the cost to take it off! It's a chemical treatment they do. It's like two hundred dollars per square foot. It's too much money; it's too much money to worry about taking it off." Restoring exterior brick to its natural red hue is a high priority for homeowners in upscale neighborhoods in the District. In Riverton's older subdivisions, where many of the suburban brick homes have been painted, such restoration work is rare.

Riverton resident Kevin shares Jared and Terry's worries about money, and about insurmountable debt in particular. The realization that he could take on a second job, if necessary, brings him peace of mind:

> If something happens, I ain't too proud to work two jobs. I got to provide. My wife and I joke everybody else got an *investment* portfolio, we got a *debt* portfolio. So we goin' be in debt. I worry about debt—you always worry about it, but you juggle stuff. You can't worry about stuff, you just got to let it happen. You put things in place for a real emergency. I worry, but I ain't goin' lose too much sleep on it. If all else fails, I'll just take another job somewhere.

The few Riverton and Lakeview blacks who report not worrying about money tend either to be religious people who believe God will provide or people who have only limited knowledge of their family's finances. Charlotte, for instance, says she does not worry, but she also leaves the task of paying the monthly bills to her husband. Indicating that she has no idea how much their monthly mortgage payment is, she suggests I ask her husband when I interview him. "I guess I'm not a person that worries about that," Charlotte says. "What can you do? God will work it out, I always think. I can't stay up nights worrying. But we do try to prepare." Isabelle, also a Lakeview resident and the mother of three children, perceives her life within a religious framework as well, as indicated by an e-mail she forwarded to me advocating prayer as a better solution to life's challenges than worrying or simply hoping for a favorable solution to a problem. "There's a certain amount of concern—I don't like to use the word 'worrying'—that all black people have, just in day-to-day operations," Isabelle confides, "but I think the ones who are living above their means would be the ones who would be concerned. . . .

What I'm saying is that material things come and go. So if you get your priorities straight and realize that *things* are not you, you'd be okay. You won't do a lot of worrying."

SHERWOOD PARK: PURCHASING COMFORT

"Regardless of how much money you make, you can always spend that amount of money," Michael warns. The upper classes in America have already absorbed this lesson, as they are socialized to live on the interest from sound investments, leaving the principal untouched. Of course, blacks in Sherwood Park are not the recipients of trust funds or other forms of inheritance that help to sustain the upper classes from one generation to the next. According to Philip, the difference between black and white middle-class people is that "in this town . . . you see all the black folks driving Mercedes, BMWs, and big cars, living in big houses," that they struggle to afford, while "a lot of white folks you see who are riding in these things have a trust fund. . . . They have this, that, and the other going for them. . . . We don't have those things. We don't have trust funds set up for us."[10] Still, like the American upper classes, Sherwood Park blacks are careful to strike a balance between enjoying a cushy lifestyle and cultivating a second generation of upper-middle-class blacks.

For the elite middle-class blacks in Sherwood Park, spending responsibly means thinking about what kinds of purchases will help make life more comfortable, a stark contrast both to spending wildly on shopping sprees and to adhering strictly to a budget. Some people, including Brad, stress the importance of ownership. He attributes his preference for ownership to what he learned from his mother and other members of his working-class family:

> It's important to me to own things—my house, own my car. Once you've been poor, there is something about being able to say, "This belongs to me." So, I drive an '88 Mitsubishi 3000, ten years old, 175,000 miles. Before that, I drove a '78. The luxury for me is being able to buy the kind of car I want, but to keep it for ten years until it drops. . . . I never wanted the Jag or the Cadillac. That was the hot car when I was growing up. I never cared about that. There are, unfortunately, some folks that pay more for their car then their apartment. That's a value judgment. I don't criticize it, it's just never been important to me. I think there's something in my own background, maybe from my grandfather or my mother, that to be responsible, you have to have ownership, which you do. It's not how flashy the car is, it's that it's yours.

Responsible spending doesn't mean doing without luxuries, though. In this context, while home ownership is an important signifier of middle-class status, buying a house is something Sherwood Park blacks assume that upwardly mobile people are conditioned to do, and something that they'll teach their children to do reflexively, like heading to college after high school. Whereas Riverton and Lakeview blacks associate renting with the lower classes, people whom they characterize as holding "low expectations" and engaging in financial mismanagement, Sherwood Park blacks associate renting with a state of bounded information, a lack of knowledge concerning the sometimes obscure benefits of home ownership and of reproducing wealth more generally. Michelle, Philip's wife, has no trouble understanding why even middle-class blacks may fail to grasp the importance of owning rather than renting. Now forty-four years old, she lives in a large home in Sherwood Park, but she grew up living in an apartment, and as a single black professional, she avoided purchasing a home:

> I was never a homeowner, so I was *way* out of my league. I had nothing to compare it to. . . . I had lived in other places, other places that I consider very nice, very exclusive, but they were not *homes*, and they were not anything I'd purchased. I would put so-o-o much money into having a fabulous apartment. I think, psychologically, I wasn't ready to buy property. I thought it was a waste of my money. I *should* have bought property—I should have bought a condo, I should have bought *something*. I just would throw money into a nice apartment. I had a *beautiful* apartment. . . . It had a pool, a clubhouse, two entrances. . . . Never once did it occur to us [Michelle shared her apartment with a girlfriend], "We should buy a house."

Michelle grew up in a working-class, urban neighborhood in New York City, where everyone was a renter and buying a home was a distant dream. "I remember my parents saying, 'We're gonna move, we're gonna move into a house,' and we never quite did." By the time her parents were able to purchase a home, Michelle had already left for college. Long before then, she had been socialized into becoming a renter:

> I didn't know any better. I didn't know anybody who owned a house. I knew people who had apartments. Plain old ignorance. My kids probably won't make that mistake. And that goes to a lot of concepts. Folks can end up having money, but without exposure and understanding—you know, I didn't buy any stocks or bonds, I didn't invest anything. It was just shop [and] have a nice place. . . . At this point, I realize that a lot of the things that you choose in life are based on your exposure and your knowledge,

and the more that my daughters can be exposed, the more they'll know what their choices are, as opposed to picking something 'cause it's the only thing on the list. You didn't know to pick something else.

The relationship between status and consumption Michelle advances is typical of Sherwood Park blacks. They perceive spending responsibly as purchasing luxuries that enhance the pleasure of daily life and at the same time expose their children to the many options life holds for them. In this way, Sherwood Park blacks' consumption patterns much more closely resemble those of the upper-middle class than they do those of Riverton and Lakeview residents. This difference across the black middle class in conceptions of status is compounded by Sherwood Park blacks' optimistic assessment of their economic situation.

None of the Sherwood Park blacks I interviewed have nagging concerns about a possible erosion of their current lifestyle. Instead, they report feeling certain of their ability to successfully rebuild their lives after an economic slump. As a result, the hypothetical threat of losing what they have accumulated does not worry them, with one exception. Focusing on their role as status producers, Sherwood Park parents do give thought to what a sudden plunge in class position might mean for their children. Greg, at forty-nine, is an experienced government official; his secure occupational status is part of the reason for his confidence. He, his wife Andrea, and their two children have lived in Sherwood Park for seven years. Greg feels he could weather an economic storm, especially if it hit him after his children had grown up. When I ask, "Are there times when you feel concerned about how you're going to maintain your lifestyle?" he responds this way:

> No, I guess, no. Because it wasn't always there, it's nice to have done that, and if I lose it all tomorrow, I'd go, "Okay, fine, been there, done that." And I'd press on and do something else. [He laughs lightheartedly.] My biggest concern would be the kids. As long as I can get the kids through college and they're out on their own, pssht. [He waves off the imaginary loss.] If somebody came and said, "Hey, your house, car, and everything else is gone," I'd tell them, "Okay, I can make it." I've reached that point.

Philip doesn't worry about maintaining his lifestyle either, though, like Greg, he would be concerned for his children if something were to happen that he hadn't anticipated:

> Naw, I don't, just because that's the nature of how I am. But in terms of my kids, yeah, because they've become accustomed to a certain way of life. But personally, I don't, because I can survive, you know, I can live with it. . . . Through the good graces of God, you accumulated what you did, but if you lose it, you just continue, I mean, just go on from there. You don't hang it

up and jump out of buildings and shoot yourself because you lost it. Hang in there and fight. That's why I say, if I lost all this, I could deal with it. Now whether or not my family could deal with it, I don't know. I think they would adjust to it eventually. My wife could. She's basically a fighter.

Brad's position is slightly different. His high-powered career has taken a physical toll. When we first meet, I am struck by how tired and worn-out this tall, slightly overweight man looks. I notice the gray liberally sprinkled through his dark, cropped hair. Brad, too, is aware of his prematurely old appearance. "I'm only forty-six years old, even though I probably look about sixty-five," he says, sighing. When I ask if he worries about maintaining his lifestyle, he focuses exclusively on what might happen to his family if he were to become seriously ill:

> [Sometimes] . . . I wonder about my own vulnerability. I've made provisions, through insurance and that type of thing, that if I die, my family will be provided for at this level. . . . But if I become really sick, and I'm not able to generate income, that's when I worry. . . . So long as I'm able to work, I'm not really concerned. My biggest concern would be if I'm not able to work. If I had some long-term illness that would drain my family, and drains my support of the family, that would worry me. But outside of that, no. And if it came down to selling this house to be able to provide ten or twenty years of apartment living, that's not a big deal.

Tammy's concerns are similar to Brad's. As she puts it, "Tomorrow is not promised." Periodically, she worries about her family's stability should her husband, the household's sole breadwinner, become disabled: "Yes, I think about it, but not to the point where I think that we'd ever be homeless, with the exception of, like, if my husband were to be disabled or killed, because we're basically a one-income family. I mean, even for me to get a job, I cannot generate the kind of income that he can. In that respect, I mean, things would change. We have life insurance, disability policies, and all that kind of stuff . . . but tomorrow is not promised."

As these comments indicate, while black adults in Sherwood Park acknowledge that "tomorrow is not promised," they do not worry constantly about money. This leaves them free to concentrate their efforts on exposing their children to a preferred lifestyle, one they anticipate the children will seek to reproduce when they are adults. This kind of exposure has its price, though. Sherwood Park children come to believe they are entitled to live at a heightened level of material comfort. They expect their parents will automatically provide them with material items considered luxuries in slightly less privileged families. These heightened expectations exasperate many parents; they grew up in working- and lower-middle-class families where no such attitude of entitlement existed. Michelle laments, "My kids, they think they're *supposed* to have a car when they're fifteen, [to take with them] to go to college and stuff. And I'm thinking, [when I was their age] I had a *bicycle*. And I was happy with that."

Still, there are only a few desires Sherwood Park parents deny their children—or themselves. Most of the material things these elite middle-class blacks want, they buy; their lives are not governed by the budgetary constraints that other middle-class families experience. Alluding to the usually unacknowledged boundary between her own group's lifestyle and that of the American lower classes, Lydia explains what she enjoys about her elite middle-class status: "You don't have the pressures of how you're gonna pay the rent, you know." I answered, "I don't know, actually!" Lydia said, "Well, you will!" We both laughed. She continued:

> It could be as simple as being able to go to the grocery store and buy whatever you want. I mean, I still watch prices. I still watch what I buy. But I ultimately know that if I didn't want to watch them, I could still buy whatever I wanted to. It's the kind of *mental security* that you can get things that you want. I mean, for a couple of months, you can get the things that you want. You can't get *everything*. I can't go out and buy a boat and have three Mercedes in the driveway. But generally, I can have the things that make my life comfortable.

Lydia's definition of her social status hinges on her ability to consume as she pleases, a characteristic that is decidedly upper-middle-class. But, as already noted, neither Lydia nor her husband Michael interprets their financial "mental security" as an indication of an *upper*-middle-class status. Like Lydia and Michael, Tammy does not consider herself upper-middle-class, although she neither needs to nor does work outside the home. Tammy's husband Franklin is an established surgeon, and Tammy knows how improbable a decline into the recesses of the lower classes is for her family. At the same time, she is also aware that in today's HMO-driven health care system, a doctor's occupational prestige often outpaces his or her earnings. "A lot of doctors' pockets are paycheck to paycheck, just like everybody else," Tammy points out.

The knowledge that some doctors struggle financially leads her to spend responsibly and live within her means, just as Lydia's awareness that she must work if she and her husband are to provide a comfortable lifestyle for their children motivates her to remain employed. Also like Lydia, however, Tammy understands sensible spending to include luxuries, not just essentials. When she and her husband relocated to the Washington, D.C., metropolitan area, they had hoped to purchase a large house on a vast plot of land. Tammy remembers that they were one of the first couples to view homes in Sherwood Park. The builder had barely broken ground, and potential homeowners had only the model home and one completed cul-de-sac on which to base their overall impression of the community:

> The Realtor showed us this development in 1987 and I didn't like it; my husband did. It was all woods then—it wasn't developed, and it wasn't five acres. The most you could get was an acre. And the largest house was about four thousand square feet, including the basement, and we were looking for five thousand square feet. So we didn't do it, and then ultimately ended up coming back here, because it *was* a lot of land, a big house, close to D.C., and the price was reasonable, so we bought here.

Standing in the family room, Tammy and I stare out through the French doors, taking in a view of the family's in-ground swimming pool and some of their two-acre plot. Part of the reason acreage was important, Tammy explains, was because "we knew we were going to put in a backyard pool. We were going to put in a pool *and* tennis courts, but then we realized there are courts in the area, so we didn't need to do that." The couple's willingness to incur the substantial cost of installing and maintaining a backyard pool so that family members and friends could swim at their home distinguishes their elite position in the status hierarchy from that of a core middle-class person like Jared, who isn't fully convinced that shelling out five hundred dollars annually to join his subdivision's pool association is the best use of his hard-earned money. Just as taking family vacations to exotic places and enrolling children in team sports that require frequent long-distance travel to invitational tournaments and playoffs are routine events for elite black middle-class parents, installing a backyard pool also is well within their reach. For members of the core black middle class, however, it is an unlikely undertaking.

Shopping, and in particular, which stores middle-class blacks frequent, is another area where study participants diverged. Most Sherwood Park residents prefer upscale stores, while most Riverton and Lakeview residents report shopping at discount stores such as Marshalls. There are exceptions to this general pattern, however. Both Riverton and Sherwood Park residents complain vehemently that there are no upscale stores in Prince George's County (see chapter 6 for a detailed discussion). Terry, a devoted shopper, is visibly irritated as she tells me, "They're developing everything in Fairfax [County, Virginia]. They're putting all that stuff out there, and *nothing* over here. . . . Depending on my mood, I either go to St. Charles [in Charles County, Maryland] or I go to Pentagon City [in Virginia]. Charles County [is] twenty minutes from here, . . . Pentagon City [is] across the Woodrow Wilson Bridge. But actually, I'm one of those people who no place is too far to go to go shopping!" Rather than basing her decision about where to shop on proximity to her home, Terry thinks about the quality of the mall's stores before she heads out. As a result, she shops at St. Charles infrequently: "St. Charles, I don't really go there that much, because I'm not . . . I might shop at *Penney's,* but I'm not really a Sears and Montgomery Ward shopper. And those are the kinds of stores that they put out there. But then when I look at the clientele—the blue-collar workers—that's what they want. They want a Kohl's. There's nothing in Kohl's I've ever seen that I want to buy . . . that's not my market. But I can understand why they have those stores out there. And they don't *want* a Macy's, they don't *want* a Bloomie's [Bloomingdale's]. They don't want it, because that would—" she sighs. "I guess they think they wouldn't be able to afford it. But you can catch anything on sale!" she says, her face brightening.

Forty-three-year-old Andrea, Greg's wife, is Terry's mirror opposite when it comes to shopping. Andrea doesn't seem to mind that the nearby St. Charles Mall does not include upscale stores. In her opinion, the mall has "all the [desirable] stores—Hecht's, Penney's, Sears, Kmart, and Montgomery Ward. And they've opened a Kohl's." Andrea was the only Sherwood Park resident to report shopping regularly at low-end stores like those in the St. Charles mall.[11] Still, her tendency to shop at discount stores (with the exception of Hecht's), and Terry's preference for high-end stores, suggests that where middle-class blacks choose to shop may not always align with their position in the status hierarchy. However, *how* individuals conceptualize the act of shopping does reveal differences in the status identities of middle-class blacks, differences that often go unnoticed in the literature. The experience of Brad's wife Crystal illustrates this point.

Crystal is a forty-five-year-old, heavyset woman. She is simultaneously laid-back and bubbly. Although she rarely wears makeup, on the day I visit to interview her, Crystal is wearing foundation, eye shadow, blush, and lipstick. She has just returned from the Olan Mills photo studio; she volunteers the information that her carefully crafted face was occasioned by the photo shoot.[12] The fact that she is rarely made up doesn't bother Crystal, and until fairly recently, the fact that her clothing was old and outdated didn't bother her either. She had gained weight during each of her pregnancies and for a long time had been reluctant to invest much money in new clothing. She had resolved to wait until she had lost the additional pounds. Eventually, Brad convinced her to shop for stylish clothing that would fit her at her current weight:

> My husband would keep telling me, because I'm a large size, he would say, "You just can't expect to go to Sears and pick something up and think it's gonna fit you exactly the way you want it to fit and look. It's not gonna happen." [She says this very deliberately and methodically, imitating her husband's voice.] And I said, "Well, I don't want to spend a lot of money until I lose weight." [He said,] "Crystal, I understand that"—you know, he's very intuitive, and he was right. He said, "But you've been saying this now for about twelve years, and I think you should go ahead [and buy clothing]." He said, "Have I ever bought a suit that I didn't have to have altered? *Ever?*" And I said, "No." [But] I never wanted to buy something and then pay to have it altered. It just didn't make sense to me. But then he said, "Most men have to do that when they buy a suit, so what's wrong with you doing it?"

Crystal finally agreed to go out to look for fashionable clothing. Brad went with her:

> So he took me shopping one day. He took me to Nordstrom, 'cause I, I am very cheap. [She smiles sheepishly.] Except for my children, and for him. If I like it, and I know they'll like it, I would buy it. But for me, I could not see spending the money. So he took me shopping this one day, about five or six months ago. I had never shopped at Nordstrom or no store like that. So we went into this department looking for large sizes, and I started finding things that I liked and that I thought looked nice. . . . Once I got past the thing that . . . I would put it on and I didn't look like a size ten—of course, I'm not a size ten—I started just feeling better about it. . . . So now, [she laughs] I've been shopping [there] since then. I don't shop no place else now! And I met a girl who works there, Jennifer, and she brings in things that she thinks I'll like.

Crystal's shopping experience at Nordstrom is reminiscent of what Charlotte observed when she and her upper-class friend Sarah went to Lord & Taylor. Just as for Sarah, shopping means having someone else go through the trouble of selecting items while she merely pays for them, Crystal also relies on a salesperson to sort through the racks of clothing to select items likely to appeal to her tastes. Thus, *how* Crystal shops— essentially through a personal shopper—is characteristic of the upper classes, not the middle class.

Riverton and Lakeview blacks have a different conception of the relationship between consumption and status. Characterizing themselves as people who spend responsibly, Riverton and Lakeview blacks distinguish themselves from the black working class (whose alleged materialism leads them to purchase luxury cars instead of homes), from the white middle class (whose alleged frugality leads them to deny themselves certain basic comforts), and from the white upper class (whose wealth leads them to pay no attention to either the number or cost of their purchases). Sherwood Park blacks believe they, too, spend responsibly, but their purchases include luxuries that help to make their lives more comfortable. They distinguish themselves from uninformed consumers, whether working-class or middle-class, and shop in ways that parallel those of the upper class.

Perceptions of economic dependency also shape middle-class blacks' understanding of what it means to spend responsibly. Riverton and Lakeview blacks feel more financially strapped than do blacks in Sherwood Park, leading the former to focus on maintaining their middle-class status, while the latter concentrate on exposing their children to the array of choices and opportunities available to members of the upper-middle class. The next section examines how middle-class blacks' views of their economic condition influence the degree to which they make sacrifices for the sake of their children.

"YOUR KIDS ARE IMPORTANT": SACRIFICING FOR CHILDREN

A third dimension of the definition of middle-class status among the three groups of blacks is their willingness to make sacrifices in order to provide their children with various advantages. In this regard, much as with their attitudes and behaviors with respect to work and spending, there are profound differences between blacks in Riverton and Lakeview and those in Sherwood Park. Riverton and Lakeview parents require their children to purchase luxury items with their own money; Sherwood Park parents willingly make these purchases for their children.

RIVERTON AND LAKEVIEW

Concerns about maintaining their own status position lead Riverton and Lakeview parents to spend cautiously, a sentiment which in turn prompts them to require their children to purchase desired luxuries with their own money. Riverton and Lakeview children receive many of the toys and material items they ask for, but parents find it difficult to justify buying them luxury items such as designer tennis shoes or, in the case of teenagers, cars. Parents perceive these items as too expensive and, perhaps more importantly, as nonessential for a middle-class lifestyle.

I first noticed this distinction between the two mind-sets—Riverton or Lakeview versus Sherwood Park parents—during an interview with Jasmine at her Lakeview home. After we had been talking for about an hour and forty-five minutes, her teenage son Brian, dressed in a fast-food worker's uniform, ambled silently into the room. Jasmine glanced up at him, and it was clear from her expression that she was irritated. When Brian politely informed his mother that he needed to be at work in about ten minutes, Jasmine erupted. In a voice shrill with anger, she asked him why he had waited until the last minute to announce that he needed a ride to work. Embarrassed, Brian slinked away as silently as he'd come into the room. His mother continued to fume, even as she stood up and began to gather her keys and purse.[13] Jasmine and her husband do not feel obligated to buy Brian a car, even though doing so would relieve them of some of the chauffeuring they are now required to do.

Isabelle and her husband also refrain from purchasing luxuries for their children. They bought their four-bedroom, colonial-style house in Lakeview five years ago. Prior to moving to Lakeview, they lived in a heavily black, working-class community in Fairfax County near Darby Town. Isabelle insists that the move did not change her: "I don't believe in being a snob and stuff," she tells me. But later, she suggests that her children have changed as a result of living in Lakeview, especially her son Ryan, who recently turned fourteen. Like Jasmine's son Brian, Ryan has a job—a paper route—that "he was motivated to get . . . to have his own money." Ryan wants to be able to buy things his parents refuse to purchase for him, such as designer tennis shoes. Isabelle says Ryan "used to wear Payless shoes and didn't have no problem wearing Payless shoes. In fact, he got a different pair just 'bout every week 'cause they were so cheap." But negative comments from his peers—teens from impoverished Darby Town as well as those from middle-class Lakeview—prompted Ryan to reject generic tennis shoes in favor of designer brands: "Once he got transferred to this school over here, and he was being in the class with kids from Darby Town, suddenly, oh, and also the kids in this neighborhood, suddenly they [the shoes] were making skid marks on the gym floor. *His* shoes were making skid marks. So that's when the transition started for him in terms of trying to make his status be with the neighborhood that he'd moved into." Isabelle pauses, laughs somewhat bitterly, and then continues: "I have resented those kids ever since. . . . We were quite capable of giving him the shoes, but we were not going to get them for him. I'm more tolerant now because he's getting older, but when he first started out, I wouldn't let him just take a whole paycheck and blow it on shoes." Wanda, Jared's wife, also expresses concerns about the lure of designer tennis shoes and clothing. She observes mockingly that some parents say, "Let's go shopping. Let's go shopping and I'll buy you the $150 shoes." She continues, "You know, [that] ain't goin' happen [in my household]. That's not what's important."

When asked if she would let her children, ages seven and eleven, get the shoes if they used their own money, Wanda responds:

> I had a big discussion with my nephew about that. He wants the $100 shoes. He went shopping with me and my older sister. We went to New York for spring break. He had the money, so no problem. We go into the store and he finds a shirt for $66! He was thirteen at the time; he's sixteen now. I said, "You know, that's very nice, put it back. Go over there, you can find a shirt that costs a whole lot less." He said, "I saw this shirt, I want it. This is the kind of shirt I've been lookin' for." I said, "Well, you find another one." He goes. He's on the men's side of the store, we're on the women's side. He comes running back over, he said, "I found another shirt, $9.99." I said, "Now we're talkin'!" [She laughs.] The shirt was 10 percent off. . . . He trips like that. You don't want to spend all your money in one place.

As the boys' longing for designer shoes and clothing suggests, middle-class children are as drawn to material forms of popular culture as their inner-city counterparts. The hip-hop culture of urban youth is so pervasive that children's desire to demonstrate their allegiance to it crosses both racial and class lines.[14] Nor is the longing for designer labels the exclusive provenance of teenagers. Eric, the seven-year-old son of Riverton resident Shelly, wants to wear the same kind of tennis shoes his peers wear. His five-year-old sister Amber is already an avid Spice Girls fan and proud owner of the group's first music video. When I arrive at their home, Amber is ensconced in an oversized beige leather couch, enjoying her Spice Girls video. As I stepped from the entryway into the living room, I recognized the refrain from the group's hit single, "Wannabe": "If you wanna be my lov-er, you gotta get with my friends-s-s / Make it last for-ev-er / Friendship never ends-s-s." As we make our way into Shelly's sunny kitchen, the Spice Girls waft behind us, "I'll tell ya what I want, what I really, really want." According to Shelley, Amber is "crazy about the Spice Girls. When I was growing up," she remembers, "it was the Jackson 5" that was the popular music group among young girls. "Now it's the Spice Girls."

Shelly is tolerant of her children's tastes, but she is unwilling to spend money to satisfy their every desire. She tells me that for many months Eric had begged her to get him a pair of Jordan sneakers. Shelly had refused to buy the shoes for him, but she was willing to let Eric spend his own money on this luxury item because he wanted it so badly:

> On his birthday, he got his money. The shoes were small, they were maybe fifty dollars. Fifty dollars is a lot, I think, to pay for children's shoes. I wanted him to understand that if you want 'em, *you* buy 'em. But once you give 'em that money, that money's gone. So don't say—he looked at the [sales]guy like, "Okay, I gave you my money, where is my change!" [She laughs.] "You don't have any more money. You spent your money on those shoes because that's what you wanted." He was disappointed for a few minutes, but then he realized what the lesson was. The lesson was if you want something that costs one hundred dollars or fifty dollars, *you* have to buy it.

SHERWOOD PARK

As the preceding sections have shown, despite their insistence that they are simply middle-class, Sherwood Park blacks make a concerted effort—from communicating a preference for financially rewarding work to engaging in calculated consumption—to construct an upper-middle-class status and to prepare their children to reproduce this status for themselves once they become adults. The significant degree to which these parents are willing to sacrifice their own desires for their children's benefit is a third aspect of Sherwood Park blacks' conception of status, one that distinguishes the elite black middle class from the core black middle class.

While their children are members of the household, Sherwood Park parents spend somewhat conservatively on themselves, choosing to allocate the bulk of their resources for their children's needs. This approach is especially clear in the case of Philip and his wife Michelle. They and their fifteen- and ten-year-old daughters live in a four-bedroom colonial home—the most extravagant of Sherwood Park's five models. Initially, they sent both daughters to Prince George's County public schools, but Philip and Michelle were disappointed in the quality of the schools. The girls now attend exclusive private schools in Virginia. Philip is explicit about the personal sacrifices he makes in order to assure that his children receive a top-tier education. "I'd like to have a bigger house," he tells me. "I'd like to have a Mercedes, I'd like to have a boat. I'd like to have a home in the Caribbean, a winter home in the Caribbean." He does not have these things at present because he has to prioritize. "What is important?" he asks and then supplies his own answer: "Your kids are important, so you give them priority over everything else."

Michelle's list of deferred pleasures is considerably shorter. She'd like to build an investment portfolio, a budding interest that she has decided to put on the back burner until her girls complete their educations: "I'm more interested in investing now because of my paranoia about being old and destitute and broke. I think I don't want to be that old woman alone in an apartment somewhere waiting for a social security check. Because I've spent most of my working years investing in their educations. We don't second-guess that, we just do it. I think that's what we're supposed to do. But once Samantha [the younger daughter] is done, I'll start investing that money."

Philip and Michelle curtail their individual desire for luxuries in order to finance their children's education, which they perceive as more important. Lydia also makes sacrifices. In order to provide her three children with luxuries, she keeps her full-time job. "[If I stopped working,] we'd probably have less expensive vacations. My [fifteen-year-old] son wouldn't be traveling around the world during the summer, a lot of their activities probably would be pared down, because for them to travel costs money. They go away for the weekend to tournaments—all that stuff costs money, things they do, that would change. We could *live*, we could pay the bills, that type of thing, but all the extras that I've gotten used to would be a stretch." Among the "extras" Lydia and her husband Michael anticipate giving all three of their children is an Ivy League education, a formidable expense.

By sacrificing their own desires, Sherwood Park parents help their children to develop a taste for the finer things in life, including foreign travel and elite private schooling, experiences rarely extended to the lower classes. The cultivation of taste is not a frivolous activity, nor one to be undertaken haphazardly: taste is the basis for the kind of cultural distinctiveness that underlies social privilege in American society. Thus, parents like John and Cassandra spend large sums of money on exclusive extracurricular activities and cultural enrichment for their daughter. According to John, supplying these opportunities requires that both he and his wife make sacrifices. "It's so much of a challenge to get her grown up. . . . I wish I didn't have to spend so much money," he sighs. "I wish I could save more money. I wish I could do other things with my money. But I can't. And the thought crosses my mind, and just as quickly as it comes, it goes, because that's just the way it is." Brad too willingly sacrifices for his sons. He confides, "There are people who say, 'Well, he's got this, he's done that . . . [he's] a recognized figure . . . so how come he doesn't live in a mansion?' Well . . . I don't care to live in a mansion. But I do care about making sure that my kids have what they're supposed to have." A quality education is something he feels his children are "supposed to have." Both sons attend elite private schools across the Potomac River in Virginia. Paying tuition rates set at well over ten thousand dollars per year for each child is a clear indication that Brad does not take status reproduction for granted. He spares no expense to ensure that his sons are well-positioned to sustain a middle-class lifestyle on their own.

In addition to financing private schooling and extracurricular activities, many Sherwood Park parents feel pressure to buy cars for their teenage children. In part, this is a response to the dictates of suburban culture. "Drive up to the high school sometime," Greg advises, "and see what the kids pull up in. I mean, the kids pull up in Lexuses, they pull up in BMWs, they pull up in Mercedes, oh yeah." "The kids?" I ask incredulously. "Not the teachers?" "No," he assures me, "the kids. Parking lot *full*. Parking lot *full*. . . . Once they get to a certain age, it's not cool to ride the bus anymore," he explains, with a tolerant grin. "Ride the bus!" He mocks his teenage daughter's indignation. "Oh, no, I'll have my friend pick me up." When I ask if he feels pressure to buy his kids a car, Greg responds, "Oh yeah! Geez, well, my daughter, she's a senior this year. She said, 'Aw, Dad, I can't catch the bus!' " When his daughter was accepted into a special program for high school students at the University of Maryland, she realized that she had also gained a persuasive pretext for demanding a car. "So," Greg continued, "she said, 'Dad, I need a car because I have to go to the University of Maryland.' Soon as school started, we had to buy her a car." His daughter was convinced that unless she could drive herself to the university, she was "gonna fail" the course. Greg indulged her, although what he bought was a new American-made compact car, not the foreign or luxury cars coveted by suburban teenagers. Brad also indulged his teenager. Although he buys a new car for himself only once every ten years, Brad bought a new Passat for his son Damien. He explained, "It's the car that when he was sixteen, we needed another car, so we first got a Honda. It wasn't doing well, so we traded it. . . . The only reason there's a Passat out there is because of the influence of my son."

Not all Sherwood Park parents provide their children with brandnew cars. After acknowledging that her oldest son would soon be sixteen and looking visibly distressed by my comment that he was about to drive, Lydia says, laughing, "I keep looking at my car [an older model Toyota Camry], waving goodbye to it." Although she and Michael own an older Jeep in addition to the two cars they drive every day, Lydia feels the Jeep is too dangerous for a new, young driver: "He'll probably take mine. He'll probably tell me to fix it up! . . . See that little raggedy Jeep outside?" I comment, "That's a *nice* car!" Lydia sighs in exasperation, throwing me a look that says she doesn't agree. "That's the car Michael *claims* he's going to give to him, but I think it's going to be too hard for him to handle. I don't know. We'll see. I think Michael wants the [Jeep] himself . . . so I would volunteer to give him my car. So I'll make the sacrifice," she chuckles, noting that once she has "sacrificed" her Camry, she will get a new car for herself.

A belief that parents should provide children with an abundance of material expressions of status—whether they request these items and opportunities or not—permeates Sherwood Park. In a slightly confessional tone, John admits that his eleven-year-old daughter has "a lot of toys that she's only played with once. She didn't ask for any of them. She should have never gotten many of 'em." John's own lower-middle-class upbringing did not include the kind of material abundance he routinely provides to his family. His parents supplied only the basics, and they were unconcerned that he and his brother might be negatively evaluated by peers on the basis of their generic clothing:

> I remember when I was in sixth grade and I wanted Converse tennis shoes 'cause that's what everybody wore, and I didn't get them, 'cause my Dad didn't see any reason to pay twelve dollars for a pair of shoes when he could pay three dollars at Kmart. And he was oblivious to what anybody might say, could care less. But I think, having come up that way, and now I've got a kid, I'd say, "Well, I don't want my kid to ever feel like I did when I was in sixth grade and had to wear those Joe Knuckle tennis shoes."

John attributes the general willingness to provide one's children with luxuries to the fact that middle-class black parents compare their lifestyles to those of the white middle class that they see portrayed on television:

> Black parents look out and they say, "Well, white people have it. Why shouldn't my kid have it?" If they're honest, that's what it will be reduced to. You look on television and you see all these happy, smiling white people with nice things and you say, "Well, why should they have that and I shouldn't?" Or "Why should their kid have hundred-fifty dollar tennis shoes and mine shouldn't?" . . . And now that I can do it, or struggle to do

it, I think a lot of people like me say, "Well, hell yeah! I'm gonna do it. I'm gonna give 'em everything that I can give 'em, because that's what they're supposed to get."

John implies that unless parents provide children with coveted material objects, they aren't really middle-class; after all, these advertised items are the products that middle-class people supposedly possess.

Sherwood Park parents' generosity toward their children is not unlimited, however. They give their children sufficient financial support to put them firmly on a path toward a successful and comfortable life. But once the children have completed college, most parents consider their work done; the children are on their own. Michael vividly expresses this widely shared mentality:

> They've got to be educated, they've got to be. I owe that much to them. So I know clearly in my heart that I've given them all that they've got. . . . They must become independent because I don't want to be—my dad is seventy-four. He used to introduce all four of us, and he would tell people that we'd all gone through school [college], all of us, we all got that piece of paper. You know older people, they see people and they just talk. But the surprising thing he talked about is that "ain't none of 'em living in my house!" Because he understood, you've got to push them out, let them go out on their own. . . . You don't want to have a grown man living in your house, or a grown woman! That's like you come to your mom's [house, begging], "Can I have some food out of the refrigerator?" "Don't you have a job? Get your own house!"

Michael, smiling as he reflects on this imaginary scenario, concludes, "It's okay occasionally, but they need to be able to become independent." Lydia concurs with her husband's sentiments. "I always try to impress upon my kids—and they may think it's cruel when I tell them—'This is *my* house.' They have to keep that mind-set that they've got to go out and make their way. That's what I really want them [to do]; it's like giving up their wings. . . . I want them to be able to take care of themselves and to live comfortable lives. I don't want them to be in a situation where they have to live in rough neighborhoods because they *have* to. I just want them to have an occupation that keeps them comfortable and happy. That's it." Like Michael and Lydia, Brad also conveys to his children that the financial support he extends to them is restricted to childhood: "My sons, I'd be surprised if they didn't—they know that their ability to be supported by this family is limited. At some point, they are on their own. . . . When they have families, they are responsible for that family, and whatever they need to do to prepare for that, they should do."

Once their children are on their own, Sherwood Park parents intend to shift their financial resources back to satisfying their own deferred desires. As Michelle puts it: "I want security, and I want [the girls] to have room to play, but then after they've moved on, a person needs to make an adjustment. The money that I'm dropping for private school and for this house, I want to be able to reel back in and put into my retirement, travel, I don't know, do something else." Thus, Sherwood Park parents make repeated financial sacrifices as a way of helping their children to reproduce for themselves the lifestyle to which they've grown accustomed. Free from the day-to-day financial worries that plague many middle-class adults, these parents are more concerned with status reproduction than status maintenance. Their ample incomes and career successes give them the assurance that there will be sufficient resources left over to attend to their needs and desires once their children have left their household. Michael lightheartedly captures this pattern of status construction: "I'm more concerned about getting out of this lifestyle—paying off my house, getting rid of these cars, getting these kids out of the house—so I can have a good quality of life for myself. That's my concern. And if my house is paid off, and I didn't have kids . . . I can go right down to McDonald's and fry hamburgers for eight hours a day."

Given Michael's earlier use of employment at McDonald's as the epitome of failure, I probe, "Now, would you [really] do that?" "Yeah," he replies, adding,

> I got no problem, I don't have a problem working. As long as I can have a little bit of cash. . . . See, you work to pay. We got bills to pay right now. We've got kids and we've got an obligation, not just to our kids, but also to society in general to get these kids out. If I educate my kids, then that's one less crew that's on the welfare rolls, or one less . . . you got to worry about robbing you. There's one less person to harm society. So my thing is, I'm not interested in maintaining this, but just get me out of this. Let me get out of here, and sit down and put my feet up.

CONCLUSION

None of the blacks living in Sherwood Park define themselves as upper-middle-class. But the status identities that these blacks construct differ in concrete ways from those constructed by Riverton and Lakeview blacks. Sherwood Park blacks' perceptions of work ethic, their definition of responsible spending, and their willingness to sacrifice their own desires for their children's benefit all point to a status identity more in sync with the upper-middle class than with the middle class. Hence, I define Sherwood Park blacks as members of the elite black middle class and Lakeview and Riverton blacks as members of the core black middle class. The very real differences between these groups form the basis of a status hierarchy that not only extends *across* classes in the black class structure, but also exists *within* a single class category ("middle class"). This growing intraclass heterogeneity matters, and so, too, does the fact that this diversity remains an under-studied aspect of the black middle class. Members of these within-class subgroups don't see themselves as the same; they don't believe they share similar material interests and life chances. Their understanding of themselves therefore is incongruent with most popular and scholarly conceptions of the black middle class. Moreover, these groups experience different degrees of economic dependency, and as a result, their children are exposed to markedly different representations of middle-class lifestyles. These status distinctions bear on the decisions these middle-class black parents make about how best to prepare their children further to make the transition to white mainstream society as adults. This transition involves parents socializing their children into both racial and class-based identities. I turn to these processes of identity construction in the next chapter.

5

Race- and Class-Based Identities
Strategic Assimilation in
Middle-Class Suburbia

Sociologists theorize that in the case of white ethnic immigrants in American society, the social status of the entire group improved as individual members ascended into the middle class. White ethnic groups once targeted for maltreatment, such as the Irish and Italians, face far less discrimination today than they did when they immigrated to the United States in the nineteenth century. Ethnic identity no longer determines where white ethnics may live or work, or whom they may marry. In the current period, white ethnicity becomes salient only when white ethnics make it so.[1] By contrast, blacks, even middle-class blacks, confront persistent structural discrimination—what Charles Tilly calls "durable inequality," referring to paths of separateness buttressed by a long history of racial exclusion and invidious distinctions.[2] For blacks, race is a liability, restricting blacks' access to settings commonly frequented by whites with power. Citing this evidence of the degree to which racism impedes blacks' assimilation into the white mainstream, some theorists argue that the classic assimilation path of white ethnics is not automatically available to immigrants of color and may not be available to native-born blacks at all.[3]

In contrast to this classic model, the theory of segmented assimilation advanced by Alejandro Portes and Min Zhou posits that three paths of adaptation are possible for immigrants of color. Ostensibly, one choice leads to the white middle class, but because immigrants of color grapple with racial discrimination when they enter the United States, this destination is not often achieved. The more likely scenario is that immigrants of color will pursue a second path, identifying with the black underclass, or will opt for a third form of assimilation by deliberately retaining the culture and values of their immigrant community. In following this third path, immigrants of color rely on their own ethnic communities for social capital, employment leads, and relief from discrimination.[4] In short, segmented assimilation theory characterizes an ethnic immigrant identity as a potentially invaluable resource.

In this chapter, I propose that middle-class black Americans' assimilation patterns—what I term *strategic assimilation*—are best understood as a variant of this third path. How middle-class blacks think about their integration into the American mainstream is a relatively neglected topic in the sociological literature on assimilation. Indeed, a central criticism of segmented assimilation theory is that it, too, characterizes a black racial identity as a liability (immigrants who adopt the second path and identify with the black underclass fare poorly). As Neckerman, Carter, and Lee have shown, segmented assimilation theory presents poor blacks (and their downward mobility trajectory) as representative of *all* black Americans, discounting the black middle class as a potential destination for immigrants.[5] Neckerman and colleagues outline an additional black middle-class path as a corrective, but their primary purpose in doing so is to demonstrate that the black middle class is a realistic destination for immigrants of color, not to assess, as I do here, the effect of class position on blacks' assimilation preferences.

Middle-class blacks travel back and forth regularly between the black and white worlds. They do not exist exclusively in one or the other. Existing models of assimilation do not, however, capture the processes required to successfully manage this ongoing duality. Strategic assimilation offers a theoretical framework for explaining how Riverton, Sherwood Park, and Lakeview blacks go about negotiating the racial dualism they believe is required of them in daily life. Like immigrants who follow the third path of segmented assimilation, many middle-class blacks with access to predominantly white colleges, workplaces, and neighborhoods continue to consciously retain the values and culture of the larger black community. Through their deliberate and frequent interactions in black spaces, members of the black middle class construct and maintain black racial identities. Here I focus on two aspects of these strategic assimilation processes: the boundaries middle-class blacks erect against the white world (race-based identities), and the boundaries middle-class blacks draw against lower classes in the black world (class-based identities).

The middle-class blacks in this study give considerable thought to nurturing black racial identities and to maintaining connections to the black world, which is intriguing because it involves reconciling a desire for racial integration with a perceived need for sustaining racially distinct spaces. On the one hand, these parents seek for themselves and their children the option of attending a white college or university, working in a predominantly white occupational category, or living in a majority-white neighborhood. On the other hand, they express concern that complete immersion in the white world will subject their children to racial discrimination, alienate them from the larger black community, and generate nagging doubts about their racial identity and black authenticity. For these reasons, retaining ties to the black world emerges as a central preoccupation among these blacks.

Middle-class blacks who spend much of their workday lives in white-dominated settings may seek access to and immersion in the black world for an additional and more positive reason than temporary refuge from discrimination and alienation, however. Few assimilation theorists have considered the possibility that there is something inherently pleasurable about being black and maintaining a connection to other blacks. Findings presented in this chapter help establish the missing link between an affinity for black spaces and the paths middle-class blacks pursue toward assimilation. Middle-class black suburbanites seek to combine participation in the political, educational, and economic mainstream with strong, ongoing ties to the black world, where they maintain and nurture racial identities and where they are free to simply enjoy interacting with other blacks. Thus, race matters for blacks because society says that it does. But race also matters for blacks because they relish their associations with other blacks and their connections to black culture. It is this latter explanatory factor that assimilation theorists have largely overlooked.

Scholars have also failed to acknowledge just how much work middle-class black parents put into nurturing and sustaining their children's racial identities. This work is compounded by the fact that in addition to teaching their children to negotiate the black-white boundary, these parents must also prepare their children to manage class-based boundaries between different groups of blacks. This chapter examines variations in how black middle-class parents attempt to monitor their children's interactions with lower-class blacks. Again, residential location plays a role, shaping the strategies parents employ to construct and maintain *class-based identities*. In predominantly black Sherwood Park, members of the elite black middle class highlight their distinctiveness from Riverton's core black middle class by creating gradations based on the relative status associated with the area's various housing subdivisions and on judgments about appropriate public behavior. Because the greater Riverton community is heavily black, members of the elite are motivated to mark themselves off as high-achieving blacks, relative to members of the core, who reside in less-prestigious subdivisions. In majority-white Lakeview, blacks are few in number, so middle-class black parents there define their own class-based identity, and that of their children, in relation to the black poor, rather than by amplifying distinctions among the members of the (admittedly small) black middle class in their area. This variation in parents' strategies points to the influence of residential location in dictating how black parents attempt to prepare their children to make their way through the black and white worlds. All parents undertake efforts of this sort, but as I show in this chapter, the racial and class composition of a family's suburban community provides a distinct set of opportunities and challenges that parents and children must confront as they take on the serious task of identity construction.

STRATEGIC ASSIMILATION THEORY: KEY TERMINOLOGY

I employ the term strategic assimilation to describe middle-class blacks' intentionally limited incorporation into the white mainstream, a process that privileges maintaining strong ties to the black community. In this section, I outline key terms essential to understanding strategic assimilation processes: perceptions of authentic blackness and operationalization of the black and white worlds. I then explain how parents' strategic assimilation strategies vary by suburban context.

AUTHENTIC BLACKNESS

"They can't forget they are black," Isabelle reasons when she reflects on whether her children will lose their racial identification growing up in majority-white Lakeview, "because we are black." Isabelle and her husband William, both from modest backgrounds, "married late"; they have three children: two girls, ages twelve and sixteen, and a boy, fourteen. It has been five years since the family moved to Lakeview from a lower-status, predominantly black, working-class community. William, who is a social worker, and Isabelle, who is an accountant, "never even dreamt" of living the kind of middle-class lifestyle they currently enjoy. Isabelle worries that her now-adolescent children may "forget about what-all has happened before for us to be able to live in this neighborhood," and that their commitment to their own racial identities could be undermined by living in a largely white, middle-class neighborhood. "I just don't want them to ever, *ever* think that they are something that they are not," she emphasizes, adding, "Sometimes you get caught up into— if you think that you 'made it,' then suddenly you forget where you came from."

Across the Potomac River from predominantly white Lakeview, in majority-black Riverton and Sherwood Park, parents are also concerned with nurturing their children's racial identities. "I want them to be proud that they are black," Terry explains, referring to her two daughters, ages seven and eight. Terry feels fortunate that she and her husband Rodney found a home in a desirable subdivision, where the children are free to play outside unsupervised and the parents "don't have to keep peeking out the window." Most of the children on Terry's block are black, but there are a small number of white students at the public elementary school her daughters attend, located just across the street from the house. Terry, who has white friends from college, is unperturbed that some of her daughters' friends are white. Still, like Isabelle, she wants her children to maintain a black racial identity: "I don't mind white friends, but do you know who *you* are? If they thought they had to change something about themselves to be with [a] group of white friends, then it would bother me. . . . Forgetting that you're black . . . I wouldn't like that."

Like both Isabelle and Terry, Sherwood Park resident Michael believes that a strong racial identity is important for his three children— two boys, ages fifteen and nine, and a girl, age eleven. Michael and his wife Lydia live comfortably, and Michael speculates that this kind of access to "the good life" (and to networks of wealthy whites) could create identity problems for most blacks: "I guess up at Harvard you can meet . . . [white] people whose families actually have *real* money," he speculates. "Yeah, and you get to know these people, some of them you know as friends, some as business partners down the line, but I think it can be to your benefit if you know who *you* are when you meet these people." No less for Sherwood Park's elite middle-class blacks than for core middle-class blacks in Riverton and Lakeview, "knowing who you are" requires acknowledging a specifically *racial* identity.

The parents I interviewed aim to help their children become skilled in

Figure 7. Street view from one of two entrances into the Lakeview community. Photo by Eric Shoaf.

Figure 8. Street view of the Riverton community. As in most middle-class suburbs, street activity is rare. Photo by Eric Shoaf.

Figure 9. Sherwood Park community. Each home sits on an acre or more. Photo by Eric Shoaf.

moving effortlessly across the black-white color line, but they also strive to help them forge meaningful connections to the black world, to a racial community where they can reconnect with other blacks after spending the bulk of their day in the white world. All the middle-class blacks in this study perceive black social spaces and residential places as *crucial sites for the construction of black racial identities.* Put simply, these parents believe blacks who do not have ongoing interactions with other black people are not authentically black. It is only through active participation in black spaces that black children learn what being black is all about.

The dilemma of authentic blackness is one that many black parents who have attained a middle-class status confront. Based on his interviews with black middle-class parents in Atlanta, Joel Garreau observed, "Because for so long it was the same thing to be black and poor, some first-generation middle-class black people are having trouble sorting out what it even means to be 'authentically' black in the absence of privation."[6] When these black parents say that they want their children to have a black racial identity, they mean that they want their children to understand the norms and values of the black world, they want their children to feel comfortable moving about in this world, and they want them to want to develop an affinity for other blacks. As this chapter shows, these parents have a firm sense of what they mean by "blackness" and they know they want their kids to have it and to be able to demonstrate it, even though they have a difficult time articulating exactly what black authenticity encompasses.

THE BLACK AND WHITE WORLDS

Parents like Isabelle, Terry, and Michael help their children to remember that they are black by providing them with access to black spaces. They also attempt to nurture the (middle) class component of their children's social identity. In their overt attention to racial identity, these middle-class black parents are engaged in a different socialization process than the parents depicted in Lareau's *Unequal Childhoods*. Lareau reports that a racial identity is important to the middle-class black parents in her study, but she does not expand on what the parents mean by the concept or depict in much detail how they manage to balance nurturing a positive black racial identity alongside the considerable effort required to instill a middle-class disposition in their children. The middle-class black parents in Lareau's study focus nearly exclusively on preparing their children for mainstream society. The parents in this study think differently about their children's assimilation trajectories. They want their children to fit in and succeed among whites while maintaining a strong connection to the black community, the community that will always accept them. The strategies parents use as they guide their children toward understanding themselves as simultaneously black and middle-class differ, and those differences are tied to where the family lives. For the parents in this study, helping their children to maintain a black racial identity requires as much thought and effort as nurturing a middle-class identity.

The black world is composed of spaces and places where these middle-class blacks reconnect with other blacks. To be sure, middle-class blacks have not always fit neatly into the black world. These physical and ideological black spaces are characterized by fairly rigid beliefs about what it means to be black. In *Acting Black*, sociologist Sarah Willie interviews black students who attended either Northwestern University or Howard University in the 1960s, 1970s, and 1980s. Some of the individuals who attended Northwestern grew up middle class, but because the prevailing view was that being black meant identifying with the black poor and working-class—indeed, coming from humble origins was a source of pride—some of the middle-class students pretended to

TABLE 4. RELATIONSHIP BETWEEN RACIAL
COMPOSITION OF SUBURBAN COMMUNITY AND
ASSIMILATION TASKS

Assimilation Task	Suburban Community		
	Sherwood Park (Majority-Black, Elite Black Middle Class)	*Riverton (Majority-Black, Core Black Middle Class)*	*Lakeview (Majority-White, Core Black Middle Class)*
Preparation for transition to the white world (racial identity)	Buffered from racism	Buffered from racism	Exposed to racism
Mechanism	Black neighborhood	Black neighborhood	Black social organizations
Negotiate connections to the black world (class-based identity)	Against lower-middle-class blacks in other subdivisions	Against the black poor	Against the black poor in nearby communities

be working-class in order to gain acceptance among the larger group of poor and working-class black students. The individuals who grew up in majority white neighborhoods and then went on to attend Howard University expressed a different concern: their anxiety about attending a historically black institution stemmed from fears that other black students would consider them culturally white. These data as well as my findings illustrate that the white world is not the only space where strategies of interaction are required; the black world must be negotiated too.

Thus, in addition to preparing their children to live and work in the white world, where mainstream norms and values prevail, middle-class black parents must also think about how to socialize their children to negotiate interactions with other black people, including lower-class blacks. In the larger white world of shopping malls, workplaces, and house-hunting excursions, middle-class blacks engage public identities in order to demonstrate their knowledge of mainstream cultural norms to white strangers, thereby smoothing interactions in these white spaces. (See chapter 3 for a discussion of public identities.) Class-based identities represent middle-class blacks' conception of their place within the black world. The strategies used to signal class identity, like those used to define racial identity, vary by residential context. Sherwood Park blacks seek to further distinguish themselves as members of the elite black middle class by erecting class boundaries against the core black middle class who live in Riverton's less desirable subdivisions. In contrast, blacks in Riverton and Lakeview erect class-based boundaries against the black lower classes. This diversity suggests that the particularities of the suburban context influence how members of the black middle class conceive of their integration into the American mainstream as well as their place in the black class structure. Differences in these decisions are documented in table 4.

THE IMPACT OF SUBURBAN CONTEXT

Why do middle-class blacks construct racial and class-based identities in different ways? Some theorists would account for these distinctions by pointing to variation in the racial attitudes of members of the black middle class. Fredrik Barth takes a different approach and focuses on regional variability instead. He contends that if members of the same ethnic group are concentrated in dissimilar environments, they will construct their ethnic identity differently: "The same group of people, with unchanged values and ideas, would surely pursue different patterns of life and institutionalize different forms of behaviour when faced with the different opportunities offered in different environments . . . [thus] we must expect to find that *one ethnic group,* spread over a territory with varying ecological circumstances, *will exhibit regional diversities of overt institutionalized behaviour which do not reflect differences in cultural orientation.*"[7]

Much as they do among individuals in Barth's study, the differences in how middle-class blacks conceive of their racial and class-based identities cannot be explained with attitudinal data. Indeed, differences in the nature and scope of boundary-work among the black suburbanites I studied exist despite a common cultural orientation governing their assimilation into the American mainstream, namely, that successful blacks should not relinquish their membership in the black world. In the next sections, I explore the ways Riverton, Sherwood Park, and Lakeview blacks articulate this common cultural orientation, beginning with attitudes toward integration and then turning to attitudes toward specifically black spaces.

THE DESIRE FOR RACIAL INTEGRATION

Assimilation theorists have paid little attention to the connection between middle-class blacks' attitudes toward integration and their ambiguous position within the racial hierarchy.[8] Middle-class blacks want integration, but they also recognize that race still matters, both in the white world and in the black world. In the white world, they often contend with discrimination in its various forms, as well as prejudice and stereotyping. In the black world, in order not to risk alienation or ostracism, they have to contend with identity and authenticity issues.

To properly understand the assimilation preferences of middle-class blacks and the significance of black racial identities, I examine my informants' perceptions of discrimination. Such perceptions reflect the broad racial backdrop against which identity construction processes are carried out. There is little agreement among social scientists over the nature and character of racial progress in the United States, despite many studies. One body of work paints a bleak picture, drawing attention to ongoing disparities between blacks and whites in wealth, access to housing, in the public sphere.[9] Another set of studies offers a different and more optimistic portrait, pointing to measures such as improved black educational attainment and a narrowing of the black-white wage gap as indications that racial discrimination is waning.[10] These disparate findings fan the flames of the debate on racial progress.

A potentially less contentious and more promising approach to gauging the level of discrimination in society is provided by attitudinal studies. As Lawrence Bobo and colleagues make clear, "race relations involve more than just external and material ingredients like housing patterns, incomes, or educational attainments. . . . There are also cultural, intrapersonal, and interpersonal aspects that affect the subjective experience of . . . Americans."[11] Thus, paying closer attention to black Americans' perceptions of and experiences with discrimination yields a clearer picture of the state of race relations in general and also reveals differences among subgroups within the black community. Using national samples, researchers report that the majority of blacks believe that racial discrimination has not diminished, but rather has increased, and that the pace of racial progress is painfully slow.[12] Moreover, this grim assessment is fairly pervasive among middle-class blacks. Wealthier blacks report more discrimination than poor blacks, are less optimistic about racial progress, and are less inclined to believe that whites positively type blacks.[13]

How does this assessment of ongoing racial discrimination expressed among national samples of middle-class blacks resonate with Riverton, Sherwood Park, and Lakeview blacks? Blacks in all three sites realize that the primary locus of interaction for their children will be the white world, where they will work, shop, and possibly live. Thus, all are concerned with preparing their children to function in predominantly white settings.[14] Indeed, all three groups report support (albeit sometimes lukewarm) for indicators of assimilation, such as allowing their children to marry interracially or not trying to prevent them from joining a white fraternity or sorority. They know they won't be able to prevent their adult children from living their own lives. However, this general support is undercut by parents' awareness of ongoing racial discrimination. Often citing their own experiences, respondents say they fear that their children will endure unnecessary hardship in these kinds of intimate interactions with whites. Philip, a Sherwood Park resident, typifies this perspective. In explaining how he would react if his young daughters wanted to marry white men when they grew up, Philip tells me in a voice thick with resignation:

> I'd talk to them about how interracial couples fare in this society, some of the drawbacks about being married to a white person, how you're not going to be able to relate to that family like you'd like to. Going to family functions is going to be real tough . . . when you meet rednecks in your [husband's] family. And regardless of what their economic status is, you're still going to have that. And again, once all these things are made clear to them, if they still want to do it . . . after I've painted that picture for them, then hey, it's on them.

Philip's neighbor Lydia also seems unhappy over the prospect of any of her children marrying a white person: "I wouldn't encourage it, but I would accept it." Given her pained expression, I ask, "What would concern you?" Lydia hesitates, then responds, "I guess psychologically, I would want little black grandkids. I'm not sure how to explain it. I just would prefer that. It's a personal preference." Lakeview resident Isabelle expresses similar concerns—and a similar resignation. "I would not rule out that all three of [her children] at some point in their lives will date someone white," she concedes. "And I'm not gonna sit here and lie and say that that thrills me, because it doesn't."

Riverton residents, too, are unenthusiastic about interracial marriage. Wanda, married to Jared, doesn't really want her children to marry interracially, though she doesn't intend to prevent them from doing so. "I'd prefer not, that's my personal opinion. I would rather that they didn't," she declared. "But whoever it is that they choose, that they bring home, we would [deal with it]." Wanda's reservation stems in part from her mother's pleading that she not marry a white man: "Before I even met Jared, in fact when I was leaving home, packing my bags and getting ready to walk out the door, that was the last words that my mother said to me—'*Please* [don't get involved with a white man].'" She laughs, and continues, "She said that! . . . It stuck with me. I just didn't. I had [white male] friends, not anyone that I dated, but I had friends. I wasn't connected to them in any other way."

Wanda's reservation is also tied to her belief that there are many available black men for black women to marry:

> In general, it's not for me. I'm more relaxed as the years have gone by. I used to be totally opposed to it. I asked this young lady that was sharing an office with me once, "Why? Why are you marrying this white man?" I mean, you didn't find a black person that you felt the same way about as you do this guy? He does something for you, the heart thing, that no black man could do? Or have you not given yourself enough chance? . . . I kept saying, "You're young and you're gonna get married," 'cause she was younger than I was and I wasn't married at the time either. But she went to a predominately white college, and she was like, "I mean, we have a lot in common" I just had to know. I'm not trying to be mean, just tell me so that I can understand. I guess I got done now because my brother married a white woman. [She laughs nervously.]

Only Wanda's husband Jared maintains that he would actively prohibit his son and daughter, now seven and eleven years old, from engaging in black-white unions later in life. "I ain't havin' it!" he declares with force. After some prodding, Jared grounds his resistance in the fact that, historically, white people have seen themselves as superior to black people:

> I will say this: I happen to feel that most European women feel that they have—that they are special. We all feel we are special, but they have this 'nother level of feeling special. . . . I think it's part of the[ir] culture. That's what's been embedded in their minds from the beginning. I'll go back this far. For instance, in this country, we all read the history books, and we know that white men, of course they had a white wife, and that wife was put on a pedestal and made to feel really, really special. In fact, so special that they— [He pauses.] Can I speak freely? [I assured him he could.] So special that they didn't—how can I say this [longer pause]—open up sexually and things like that. They saved that for the mistress or the "bedwarmer." [White women] were that special.

Sherwood Park, Riverton, and Lakeview blacks also are resistant to their children joining a white fraternity or sorority, although just as nearly all would not intervene to prevent their child from marrying a person of another race, they also would not preclude a child, once adult, from seeking membership in a white organization. Their concerns range from their own negative experience with fraternities to suspicions about the ulterior motives of whites to the greater importance of black social spaces. Greg, a Sherwood Park resident, points to his own negative experience with a fraternity as a motivation for keeping his children away from such organizations:

> I went to my majority-white school and I was being pledged in a certain fraternity. . . . Went through all the hell week and the whole nine yards. I find out they were about to lose their charter because they didn't want to accept any black kids. . . . Whoever the founding fathers were, they said, "No, we can't have any black folks in this fraternity." I'd have been the first . . . so I was joining *until* my pledge brothers . . . were putting on this event the day that Martin Luther King got shot. I had to be down at the fraternity house. . . . One of the guys walked in and said, "Oh, they shot that nigger." . . . I leaped up and hit him upside the head. [I asked if Greg knew that he was talking about King.] Well, no, I just heard the word "nigger," and that just set me off . . . and I was fighting everybody. So they pulled me off and then later they said, "Aw, Greg, he didn't mean it." So [after that] I didn't want to join their fraternity, so I didn't.

That Greg's pledge brothers recruited him at least in part because the fraternity needed black members in order to maintain their charter would not surprise William, Isabelle's husband. He is frankly skeptical of the sincerity of the outreach efforts of previously all-white institutions, including fraternities:

> I would tell [the children] to . . . find out the real reason why they want them to join. . . . One of my friends . . . is from Hollins College . . . and when he was growing up, the only black people there was custodians. Now they recruiting blacks. But when you look at the reason *why* they recruiting blacks, is it because they want 'em there, or is it because of the aid they get from the federal government? . . . Is there a quota that you must have to survive? Because if you know what you're dealing with, you can deal with it. But if it's under the table, then later you find out the real reason, it might do more harm to you mentally than if they'd just laid it out on the table.

Another Lakeview resident, Richard, a member of a black fraternity, is visibly upset by the thought that one of his sons might join a white fraternity. He bristles when I pose the question. "I would probably throw up," he says when I ask him what he would do. Then, tempering his feelings, he continues, "I don't know if I would be supportive of it. But in the final analysis, if that's what they wanted to do, I would not block it. . . . I just don't think that's fair."

Although most respondents oppose white fraternities and sororities, few object to their children attending a majority-white college. Most attended majority-white colleges themselves. Laughing, Terry, a Riverton resident and graduate of a white college, exclaims, "I went to one! What's the difference?" Michael jokes that his child could go to a white college "if he got the money!" Then, turning serious, Michael explains that he favors white colleges because of the access these institutions provide to influential social networks.

> My wife went to [a white college]; she says she missed some of the black experience. . . . I went to [a historically black college]; I probably had too much of the black experience! . . . I don't see it negative. I think they're equal. You go to an all-white school, you're rubbin' . . . elbows with some of the next day's leaders. . . . Not that black people can't be leaders, but [my wife] was telling me . . . she was talking to people who had maids and servants, and stuff. Now, I didn't know anybody like that.

Richard believes attending a historically black college is a good thing to do before going on to a predominantly white graduate school: "I think at an undergraduate level, it's good to experience that black college university environment. I think it's nothing like it. Best four years of my life. Now, when you think about going to graduate school, then I think that might be the time to get to the best school. I kind of took that path myself. I went to graduate school at [a white university]. And undergraduate, I went to [a black college]." Michelle's position is the strongest of all. She insists that she would compel her children to attend a white college, because that is the "real" world. "I expect my kids to go to white colleges," she says emphatically. "Because you need to know what real life is like. I don't think black colleges give you that experience. I went to a predominantly white college." When her ten-year-old daughter, who is sitting in on the interview, asks, "Are you saying that if I wanted to go to Spelman, you wouldn't let me?" Michelle responds without hesitation, "Not gonna happen."

These comments, offered by residents of Riverton, Sherwood Park, and Lakeview, indicate that all three groups of blacks share a cultural orientation with respect to the degree of social integration they desire with whites. All sense a palpable current of racial discrimination underlying blacks' interactions with whites. Consequently, respondents are "not thrilled" about the possibility of their children entering into interracial marriages. They want their children to marry blacks and to socialize with blacks. Using these measures of social integration, residents draw sharp boundaries around the black world. Yet respondents are open to their children attending white colleges. Members of all three groups perceive this form of integration as an important step on the path to economic success. Moreover, attendance at a white college or university may facilitate blacks' ability to move to and from the black and white worlds as they pursue their post-academic lives.

In the next section, I turn to attitudes toward black spaces. Riverton, Sherwood Park, and Lakeview blacks all emphasize the value and importance of their ties to the black world. Similarly, they agree on the limits of social integration. Where they differ concerns how best to prepare for interactions in the white world. Much as Barth predicted, this difference is associated with the patterns of race relations that residents encounter in their respective suburban communities.

THE DESIRE FOR RACIALLY DISTINCT SPACES

The role of black spaces as a crucial construction site for black identity formation among the black middle class has an important historical component. During segregation, middle-class blacks were compelled to develop strategies, such as rejecting segregated sections of public spaces that had been designated for black use, in order to ease the pain of their marginalized existence. In the process, as sociologist Bart Landry explains, middle-class blacks turned private, black spaces into places of refuge: "While blacks of all classes kept to themselves . . . middle-class blacks especially were diligent in avoiding situations that reminded them of the dilemma of their status. . . . They eschewed . . . the segregated balconies of white theaters and the substandard black theaters, preferring parties . . . at home. . . . Behind closed doors, middle-class blacks could act as though the outside world that rejected them did not exist or at least could feel a little sheltered from it."[15]

Growth in the percentage of the black population that is middle-class and the introduction of civil rights legislation in 1964 and 1965 have contributed to a shift in the social meaning of black spaces. Today, the legal barriers to most white spaces have been dismantled, but many informal barriers remain. In the face of this ongoing condition of social marginality, a middle-class black affinity for black spaces is not surprising. As many classic sociological studies and more recent memoirs penned by middle-and upper-middle-class blacks emphasize, the black community offers a psychological and emotional refuge from the demands of the white world, a place where, as Lawrence Graham, author of *Our Kind of People,* puts it, "there is a comfort—and a sanctity—that makes it almost possible to forget that there is a white power structure touching [black] lives at all."[16] In such an environment, racial identity is nurtured with little or no conscious effort—being black becomes something that you *are,* rather than something that you *do.*

Middle-class blacks' frequent references to black spaces as places where people can be "who they are" offer a telling reminder of the modern dilemma of identity negotiation these blacks undertake every day. As a middle-class black in Sarah Willie's *Acting Black* put it, interacting in the white world is "a game that gets played from nine to five," but after five, "you can click this shit off" and return to the black world. W. E. B. DuBois called this condition *double consciousness,* highlighting the idea that black identity is bound by external *and* internal determinants.[17] Theorists who insist that black identity is entirely or almost entirely defined by non-blacks inappropriately give more weight to the way in which blacks are perceived by others than to how blacks perceive themselves.[18] In this chapter, study participants from both predominantly black Riverton and Sherwood Park and predominantly white Lakeview make clear the importance of within-group factors in shaping identity.[19]

GROWING UP AROUND BLACKS: RIVERTON AND SHERWOOD PARK

Michael, a corporate manager and ten-year resident of Sherwood Park, maintains, in a confident tone, that he "can tell black people that didn't grow up around other black people, 'cause they act different. . . . I haven't been able to put my finger on it. It's either the expression, the way they give five, I mean it's just *something.* They missed something. Well, I shouldn't say *missing,* but they are *lacking* something. And that's not positive or negative, they just don't have an ingredient. Not that they aren't black, but . . . they're just missing something."

The view that blacks who did not "grow up around other black people" are missing something compared to those who did grow up around blacks is shared by all blacks in the study, regardless of the racial composition of their suburban community. All believe that racial identity is constructed primarily through social interaction in the black world, and that blacks who grow up outside the larger black community miss many important aspects of the experience, such as learning black slang, childhood games, and other formal and informal norms and cues of black culture. As a result, these blacks are reduced to the status of "outsiders."[20] The key distinction among informants involves not just how they define what constitutes growing up around other black people, but how they ensure their children's access to the community. Some do it through their neighborhoods; others do it through social organizations, because their neighborhoods do not provide access to other black families. In Riverton and Sherwood Park, the neighborhood serves as the construction site for black racial identity. The children in these areas develop an insider's sense of what it means to be black as they learn cultural cues through interaction with black neighbors. Thus, their parents believe that they do not have to actively nurture and build that identity in an overt way.

Because Riverton and Sherwood Park families are immersed in a mostly black environment, parents tend not to discuss racial identity with their children outright. Most assume, as Greg explains, that their children "learn on their own." Laughing, he recounts his daughter Amara's first experience in a majority-black school:

> My daughter had . . . gone for her first day of school. [She] . . . came home and asked, "Are we black?" [I replied,] "What do you mean?" She says, "Well, we don't *talk* black." [I said,] "What do you mean?" "Well, we don't say 'honey chile.'" [Greg drags this out, using an exaggerated Southern accent.] And I said, "Well, you know, we just don't talk that way." . . . It was the first time that she had been to a majority-black school. . . . It *was* a culture shock.

Greg is currently a supervisor with the State Department's foreign services branch. Back when he was an officer in the military, he and his family spent three years in Taiwan. There, "because of where we lived, because of where we lived in the military, where we were stationed," Amara "would be maybe the only black child, or maybe one of two others, so that's what she was sort of used to." Thus, when the family returned to the United States, Amara and her younger brother were outsiders, unfamiliar with the boundaries blacks erect to establish the parameters of blackness. This dilemma was resolved by the family's permanent residence in Sherwood Park, where Greg feels they "live more in tune with black folks." "Basically, we encourage our children to be black . . . just by living here, the experience," Greg says, adding the clarification, "We're in a black neighborhood, so . . . all her friends will be black, and she can live that black experience [for] herself."

Like Greg, Riverton resident Jared believes that living in a majority-black suburb, where he and his family are in close proximity to other blacks, structures his son and daughter's racial identity. "I choose to have them grow up around blacks," Jared declares, "so they can experience culture, their *own* culture." Expanding on this idea, he continues, "I think that culture and history are very important, because if you don't have that, you tend to get a distorted picture of the world. That's the bottom line. I think [it] is a good thing to help you understand who you are."

Michael, too, allows his children to develop their racial identity through their experiences with other blacks in the neighborhood. In the black world, blacks can be simply "who they are," because there the social construction of their racial identity occurs more or less by osmosis:

> It's really hard sometimes for them [my children] to get a conscious under-standing of what black is. . . . It's not so much "we doing this, we doing that," but they know that [their neighbor Brad] is a judge, and they can see the different types of interactions, and the people that come to the house. So . . . I feel that they will just grow up being who they are. . . . It's not so much they're wearing blackness on their chest . . . walking around talkin' 'bout "I'm black and I'm proud." . . . If we lived in an all-white neighbor-hood, we'd probably have to do that, you know. But we don't, because they just see it.

Lydia echoes her husband Michael when I ask her, separately, if she talks to her kids about what it means to be black. "No," she says, "because I think partially that that's part of living out here. They know what it is."

For Riverton and Sherwood Park blacks, blackness—"the black ex-perience"—is synonymous with just "being who [you] are." But despite the similarity in language, this perspective differs significantly from the essentialist platform used by gender theorists to describe the motivation for gender-based social movements such as feminism.[21] Rather than per-ceiving the essence of blackness in terms of a socially constructed bio-logical component, Riverton and Sherwood Park blacks argue that when they are ensconced in their heavily black suburban neighborhoods, race is a given, and that therefore it can be set aside. What remains is the iden-tity they or their children construct in neighborhood interactions. John, a college professor and Sherwood Park father, has little patience with the view that parents should teach their children "how to be black." He complains:

> You know, I hear people talking about, "That little girl don't know she's black." To me, that's the most ridiculous thing you could ever say! How am I, I mean, should I teach [my daughter] about being a woman? Should I teach her about being an earthling? No. I don't see any point in that. Now, I know a lot of people would criticize me for that. She is going to be black. There is nothing that I can teach her that's going to prevent her from being black. Or help her to be black.

For Riverton and Sherwood Park blacks, blackness is actualized as a natural outcome of socializing in a black environment. During their everyday immersion in a black community, children in these suburban areas prepare for their transition into the wider world. "I want my children to be able to leave my house strong enough to make it in the [real] world," Lydia tells me. Lydia and Michael perceive their residence in predominantly black Sherwood Park as a significant part of their children's training.

Riverton and Sherwood Park parents believe that to "make it" in the "real world," their children must learn how to travel back and forth between the black and white worlds. Yet the term "black world" does not refer solely to a *spatial* community of black residents. The black world is also an "interpretive community," with boundaries defined by a cultural repertoire that middle-class blacks rely on to define the black experience. It is this interpretive community that black middle-class residents of Lakeview access as they construct their racial identity.[22]

PREPARING FOR THE "REAL WORLD": LAKEVIEW

At first glance, it might appear that Lakeview blacks have chosen to sacrifice their ties to the black community in order to live in a white suburb, but this is not the case. "When I moved here, it wasn't one of those things that I tried to move away from blacks," William informs me. "It was one of those things where I tried to move to a place where the kids could get the best of what the county had to offer." In other words, William chose the suburb where he believed his children would have access to the greatest amount of resources. Lakeview blacks reason that, given today's highly mobile society, they need not live near blacks in order to socialize with them. "I wasn't as concerned about how many blacks were gonna be living out there [in Lakeview]," explains Alana, a corporate attorney and resident of Lakeview for twenty-two years, "because I used to say that would be my job, to supplement my kids with exposure to other blacks. So that was not a factor, and is still not, because there are a lot of other ways that they can interact with blacks."

What does concern middle-class blacks in Lakeview is the same as what troubles Riverton and Sherwood Park blacks: how best to prepare their kids for the "real world." Riverton and Sherwood Park blacks focus on how they see themselves in relation to their black neighbors, who are in the majority in their neighborhood. Lakeview blacks, whose children spend much more time negotiating interactions with whites than do children in predominantly black suburbs, stress how others—whites in particular—perceive them. Charlotte, whose son and white daughter-in-law intend to raise their biracial daughter to believe that she is "human," insists, "It's not important how *you* define yourself; it's how *other people* define you. Because if I told my child that they were white, or half-black, and they went to school thinking that, and then when they got in school, the kid called them a 'nigga,' then they're gonna say, 'Well, I don't understand, I'm not really that, I'm this.' You have to prepare your children for the world." Lakeview residents like Charlotte admonish their children to recognize and value their black identity in part because they believe their children will confront racial discrimination, and likely sooner rather than later. Alana's fifteen-year-old daughter attends a public school where admittance is based on a competitive exam. Since blacks constitute about 5 percent of the school's student body, many of her daughter's friends are white. Alana reports that she occasionally reminds her daughter of her racial identity: "I say it just like this: 'Remember, you are black.'" I ask if Alana thinks her daughter has forgotten. Her "no" is quick, almost reflexive. After a pensive moment, she amends her answer:

> Sometimes, to be truthful, yes. And I'll just say, "Remember." We haven't had any incidents, but I just want her to realize that there could come a time, so that when and if it does happen, she is not devastated by it. . . . Sometimes *kids* can be fair, but when they get home, [the parents are appalled]: "What? You invited *who* over here?" . . . She hasn't shared where she knows that everybody in this little circle of friends were invited someplace and she wasn't. But you gotta be honest, everybody doesn't treat everybody the same, and I don't want her to say, "What?" And that's just my way of telling her, "Remember, you black," and there could potentially be a time when that will determine something.

Despite the greater potential for racist encounters, Lakeview residents believe that raising their children in the "real world"—meaning one where whites dominate—is the best way to prepare them for negotiating the boundary between the black and white worlds when they are adults. Alana expresses concern for black children who grow up in a predominantly black environment, and for black adults who never master the art of traversing the boundary between worlds: "Some kids have a difficult time because they are not as comfortable in all types of settings. And they have to get used to that, because that's the *real* world. When you go on a job, if you go to Harvard, clearly you are not going to be in the majority, and a lot of kids—not even just kids, a lot of *people*—can't deal with it. They've got to be around their own element." When they are not at work or at school, though, Lakeview blacks socialize in the black world. They actively seek this contact by participating in black religious and social organizations. Lakeview residents are more likely than Riverton and Sherwood Park residents to attend a black church; to be an active member of a black sorority, fraternity, or social group; or to participate in Jack and Jill, an exclusive black social organization.

Founded by a group of upper-middle-class mothers in 1938, Jack and Jill's original mission was to provide upper-middle-class black children with the educational, cultural, and social experiences traditionally reserved for upper-middle-class white children. Membership in Jack and Jill was, and continues to be, by invitation only (anyone whose mother was or is a member is automatically eligible for "legacy" membership, however). This screening process is far less restrictive now, though, than it was at the organization's founding. Early on, Jack and Jill acquired a reputation for snobbery. "Some people don't like it [even now]," Charlotte admits, "because they say in the beginning it just had a lot of—you know how you had the black people who are lighter-skinned, they were like the doctors and lawyers. It was an exclusive group. . . . But then, like a lot of groups, it changed."[23] Today, the majority of the membership base consists of black suburban mothers and their children. According to Lakeview resident Jasmine, "Now Jack and Jill is more for people in suburbia, like we are, when there are not enough African American kids, and [that way] your kids have someone to bond with." Still, Charlotte points out, "Some of the chapters are real sticky. They only have a certain number to come in each year. This woman told me—she's from Jamaica—she said,"—Charlotte imitates a Jamaican accent—" 'Gettin' into Jack and Jill . . . is like gettin' into heaven!' " Charlotte dissolves into peals of laughter. "I was rollin'! But our chapter is real down to earth."

Most mothers who join Jack and Jill do not do so to make friends for themselves. The invitation to join is premised on the fact that the prospective member already has established friendships with other mothers. Instead, membership in Jack and Jill provides mothers in majority-white suburbs like Lakeview with a creative way to expose their children to other blacks, and specifically to ones with class backgrounds similar to their own. Alana, for example, notes that through their participation in Jack and Jill, her children "have African American friends; [they] see that there are other people who are like them, who have interests like them." Providing her children with opportunities to spend time with black peers is important to Alana because she believes contact with other blacks is essential to the development of racial identity. Lakeview's predominantly white racial composition precludes neighborhood-based friendships with other black children, so over the years, Alana has sought alternative avenues, including Jack and Jill, for fostering her son and daughter's intraracial friendships.

Jack and Jill is an identity construction site in Lakeview just as in Riverton and Sherwood Park the suburbs themselves are construction sites. In all three locations, black parents hope to prepare their children to live successfully in the white world while retaining their connections to the black world. Riverton and Sherwood Park blacks find that their children figure out how to be black on their own, through their interactions with others in their majority-black community. Lakeview blacks find that developing a strong racial identity in a white environment requires intervention; learning "who you are" needs to be reinforced through participation in black social organizations—the interpretive community. Traditionally, middle-class blacks have used social clubs and organizations to "express and reinforce the middle-class ideals of restrained public deportment and 'respectability.' "[24] In the segregated black community, these kinds of social organizations were an integral part of life. Now, unlike their counterparts in mostly white Lakeview, the few Riverton and Sherwood Park blacks who participate in Jack and Jill see their membership as just one social activity among a host of others. Jack and Jill may reinforce racial identity and values important to the family, but in majority-black middle-class settings, these are not the primary reasons for membership. Sherwood Park resident John characterizes his daughter's involvement this way: "She's in 'em 'cause it's something fun for her to do, meet kids and learn stuff. . . . I don't see her whole life as organizing it around teaching values or reinforcing blackness. She gets enough of that at home. These things, she wouldn't do any of these things if she didn't want to do them. These are just opportunities for her to get out of the house."

In sum, regardless of their place of residence, study participants report seeking spaces where black identity is nurtured, a community where they can socialize and reconnect with other blacks after spending the bulk of their day in the white world. The key difference in respondents' affinity for black spaces lies in their access to these settings. Riverton and Sherwood Park families are immersed in a black residential community, and parents therefore assume that their children will have ample opportunities to interact with other blacks. Lakeview blacks live in a suburban community where blacks are rare. Parents thus take additional steps to expose their children to black spaces. Study participants' stated preference for socializing in the black world but pursuing post–secondary school education in the white world constitutes a pattern of *strategic assimilation.* Middle-class blacks expect to spend their lives transitioning back and forth between the black and white worlds. They prioritize black culture and cultivate social ties in the black world to preserve their connections with other blacks and to benefit from the resources and social networks exclusive to their group.

DEFINING CLASS POSITION IN THE VARIEGATED BLACK WORLD

My middle-class black informants extol the virtues of interacting with other blacks, and they speak reverentially of black spaces and places. But like most people, they prefer to interact with others much like themselves, blacks who share their values and lifestyle. Thus, the black community that parents are at pains to expose their children to—the world adults look forward to reconnecting with at the end of the day—is one carefully bounded by class. Defining themselves in class terms through their interactions with likeminded people allows middle-class blacks to signal their exclusive place in the black class structure and to regulate which individuals gain entry to the black middle class.

Just as residential location structures the construction of racial identities, proximity to the black lower classes influences the kinds of class-based boundaries that middle-class blacks erect against their poorer counterparts. Majority-black Riverton hosts a hodgepodge of subdivisions whose residents range from middle to upper-middle class. Residents of tony Sherwood Park reinforce their standing as members of the elite black middle class by establishing their distinctiveness from blacks living in Riverton's less exclusive subdivisions. In mostly white Lakeview and in the middle-class subdivisions of Riverton, residents maintain their position as members of the core black middle class by drawing boundaries against the black poor. All of the blacks in this study, through their residential location, successfully buffer themselves from the black poor.[25] Sherwood Park blacks achieve an additional level of class exclusion by isolating themselves from the black lower-middle class as well.

Regulating membership into the black middle class through the maintenance of class-based boundaries is complicated by a pattern of behavior Mary Pattillo-McCoy terms "the ghetto trance" and Alex Kotlowitz calls "the romanticization of urban poverty." Pattillo-McCoy's term refers not simply to an impoverished geographical space but also to a "mood," a form of cultural expression in which black and white middle-class children attempt to adopt the language, clothing, and gait associated with poor black children in a dramatic show of symbolic allegiance to the poor. Kotlowitz's goal is to reveal what motivates suburban *white* teens to embrace black popular culture, but he could be speaking about middle-class black adolescents when he states, "By purchasing, in complete safety, all the accouterments . . . they can believe that they've been there, that they've experienced the horrors and pains of growing up black and poor. Nothing, of course, could be further from the truth. They know nothing of the struggles their neighbors endure."[26]

The romanticization of poverty resonates with many middle-class black teenagers because, in the larger black community, racial identity is predicated on a demonstrable awareness of the culture of the black lower class. In a provocative article, Orlando Patterson theorizes that while the one-drop rule classified anyone with a single drop of black blood as black, native-born blacks are characterized by a broad range of skin colors and physical characteristics; therefore, the basis for their unification "could not be purely physical, it had to be cultural and social. . . . For this cultural nationalism to be meaningful . . . it had to emphasize precisely the life style which was peculiar to the black community; and the traditional cradle of this peculiar life style has always been the black lower class."[27] The pervasive image of black popular culture as the legitimate culture of all American blacks renders those who lack knowledge of this lifestyle as outsiders to the black world.[28] Since teenagers are most susceptible to the lure of black popular culture, black middle-class parents must think not only about how to orient their children to the black middle class but about how they will manage their children's interactions with lower-class blacks who live on the margins of their suburban communities.

CLASS-BASED BOUNDARIES WITHIN THE BLACK MIDDLE CLASS

RIVERTON AND SHERWOOD PARK

Katherine Newman's study of responses to economic downturn in a typical American suburb draws attention to the importance white residents attach to the intraclass distinctions among them. While the suburb she studied was as a whole decidedly middle-class, the class continuum ranged from lower to upper-middle. Thus, some residents occupied "approved social position[s]," while others were relegated to a less enviable status.[29] Although Riverton differs from the suburb Newman studied in many ways, a similar intraclass distribution is present, and these distinctions are exacerbated by residents, particularly those from upper-middle-class Sherwood Park.

Blacks in Sherwood Park, the most exclusive of the Riverton subdivisions, draw marked symbolic boundaries between their immediate neighbors and residents of the less exclusive subdivisions located close by. They situate themselves as blacks of high accomplishment and social status relative to the mid-level blacks (the core black middle class) living in Riverton's other subdivisions. Just as middle-class blacks on Chicago's segregated South Side erected boundaries between themselves and the community's impoverished residents during the Depression, upper-middle-class blacks in Sherwood Park emphasize differences associated with social class—the status of the subdivision, lifestyle distinctions, and appropriate public behavior.[30]

Sherwood Park residents believe that their choice of residence says something significant about who they are. Greg notices that when people learn he lives in Sherwood Park, "It's like, 'Oh [he lets his voice rise, as if impressed], you must be a nice guy' or something." The subdivision looks expensive and it is. When the development opened in 1989, sales prices ranged from $275,000 to $350,000. Now, as then, the price of the homes constitutes an important social boundary, one that marks residents as successful, hardworking, and deserving. "The price of the houses encourages a certain type of person to come in," asserts Philip, a corporate administrator. "You're not going to get a person who basically isn't responsible. . . . The cost of the houses will result in people moving in who have similar tastes, background, advantages, values, as the people who are already here." For most residents of Sherwood Park, the home "becomes an extension of who [they] are," as John put it. John confirms this with the remark that he chose his Sherwood Park home because he wanted "a house that would show well" when he entertains. Only Brad seems inclined to downplay his residence. Noting that some people seem surprised that he and his family live in one of the more modest of the subdivision's homes, Brad says dismissively that he does not need to live in a "mansion." It may be that as a well-known judge, he derives ample status from his high-profile occupation and fine reputation, and thus is content with a home that is elegant but not lavish.

Boundary-work among Sherwood Park residents reinforces the view that they do not share the same social category as blacks from other

Riverton subdivisions. That blacks of considerably weaker financial standing have been able to obtain adjustable rate mortgages that allow them to purchase homes in Riverton subdivisions is a sore point among Sherwood Park blacks. "The mortgage institution was very liberal in its lending," says Philip, with the result that "people who ordinarily wouldn't have qualified for mortgages elsewhere were getting mortgages [in Riverton]." Robert, who moved to Sherwood Park from Nottingham Hills, a less exclusive Riverton subdivision, remembers being appalled by the turnover the banks' liberal lending policies induced in his former neighborhood: "One of the problems I had with [Nottingham Hills] was that a lot of people were buying that land with a flexible mortgage. They would come in at a low rate, then after that period of time, the mortgage go up, and a lot of those folks didn't count on that. 'For Sale' signs went up all over the place! I said, 'Good Lord, these people just got out here and they selling already.' That was just one of the problems they had over there."

Sherwood Park residents believe these newcomers embrace a different set of values and therefore create social problems in the Riverton community. Philip expands on this shared perspective:

> You had people who weren't able to afford other places coming in . . . and you can almost pinpoint where the parents live. Because I used to go to my daughter's class, and I could see the little knucklehead kids, and I could just imagine the sections where they came from. . . . They were a part of Riverton, but there's the cheaper section, and there's the more expensive section. Every once in a while, you'd have someone from the more expensive section who was a knucklehead, but it was more likely that that knucklehead came from the cheaper section.

Not only do Riverton's less costly sections shelter "knucklehead" children, but according to my informants, they are home to boorish adults. Robert's immediate neighbors in Nottingham Hills refused to keep their lawn neatly cut. On those occasions when the neighbor finally did mow, "he would never clear up the cut grass," Robert recalls. "It just looked bad. That was one thing that prompted me to move [to Sherwood Park]. It just looked bad." Unmown grass in Nottingham Hills is not the only eyesore to mar Riverton's middle-class subdivisions. Philip reminisces about when his family lived for a short time in Nottingham Hills, prior to their move to Sherwood Park. He remembers a Nottingham Hills family that "had a couch that they used, not an outdoor couch, a *living room* couch that they put in front of the house. I thought they were going to throw it away." Instead, "they ended up putting it out in front of their house, they were *sitting* on it," Philip exclaims, still astonished by this unseemly behavior.

In earlier studies conducted by W. E. B. DuBois, St. Clair Drake and Horace Cayton, and Elijah Anderson, middle-class blacks associate inappropriate behavior in public spaces with blacks of a lower social class status.[31] Similarly, Sherwood Park residents believe that reprehensible public behavior is a trait that separates residents of the other Riverton subdivisions from themselves and others in their subdivision. Lydia notices that, although the children from the middle-class subdivisions on the right side of Riverton's main road don't "hang out" in the streets, "you find a lot of kids that live over in [Nottingham Hills] by the retail area, you do see kids, teenagers, hanging out by the stores." As a result, Lydia began to feel unsafe there after dark, and she imagines other shoppers did as well. "I'm sure that's affected people coming and going. . . . I see they've put in a security guard. I'm a little more cautious now about going to the store at night, which I used to do all the time. Never gave it a second thought. But I don't do it anymore."

In addition to adjusting their shopping routines, Sherwood Park residents attempt to limit their children's association with children from the "cheaper" sections. Philip's ten-year-old daughter Samantha attended the neighborhood elementary school for one year. The following year, he and his wife enrolled her in a private school, in part to steer Samantha away from a group of children they considered a bad influence:

> [I remember] going to pick her up one day, and the coordinator of the aftercare program told me, she said, "Mr. Henderson, I wanted to let you know that Samantha is changing from the sweet little girl who came in," and they said it's mainly because of who she's hanging around with. And I immediately put into that, and I said, "I don't want her with those, with that group of kids." My wife and I took care of that; we don't want that. We asked the coordinator to separate her if she saw her playing with them.

Although when asked directly, all respondents maintain they would be unconcerned if their children had friends from a lower social class background, comments many Sherwood Park parents made in other contexts suggest that they worry over the possibility that such friendships might lead to their children picking up bad habits. Philip articulates this common concern. Describing other aspects of Samantha's year in the local public school, he notes that his daughter was "pickin' up traits." The school coordinators "said that, you know, she was getting into these habits. You know, like an attitude [he changes to a gruff, abrasive tone]: 'You talkin' to me?' or that shakin' of the head, that 'Sapphire attitude,' I call it."[32]

Sherwood Park parents face a dual challenge: they aim to raise children who can succeed in both the black and the white worlds *and* who understand that the black world is composed of a diverse group of blacks with a range of resources and values. Given the proximity of blacks from less exclusive neighborhoods, Sherwood Park parents have to prepare their children to negotiate this boundary as well. These elite black middle-class adults are well aware that as their children grow older, they will increasingly discover that a significant aspect of participating in the "real world" is managing relationships with blacks from lower-middle-class backgrounds. The strategies Sherwood Park parents rely on to guide their children are unique to the sheltered circumstances of their neighborhood. They bear little resemblance to the approach core middle-class and lower-middle-class black parents take to managing their children's relations with poor, urban blacks. In these less exclusive communities, the structure of the neighborhood precludes effective, consistent parental control over children's social networks. Some Sherwood Park parents count on the development's exclusive nature and secluded location to reinforce their efforts to completely exclude black lower-class children from their children's lives, but others, particularly those with teenagers, seek to establish a balance. For instance, Brad and Crystal's teenage sons attend a prestigious, predominantly white private school. Crystal readily concedes that their school environment is "absolutely culturally different from being in the inner city." Although she and Brad do not want their boys "to be"— she pauses for a long while before continuing—"the word that comes to mind—it's not a good word—but the word is 'street,'" neither do they want them to be outsiders in the larger black world:

> We wanted them to be able to go into the city and talk. So we chose to let them listen to the music, watch the videos, so that when they get out into the real world—because where they are [attending school] isn't. It is and isn't. It's the real *business* world, but not necessarily the world that they would be social and participate in. We recognized that when they get ready to go to go-gos [parties] out in the city, they have to be able to know how to talk the talk, and be, to be able to do this stuff. That's why we decided not to make their world antiseptic.

Boundary-work, whether undertaken on behalf of one's own children or on behalf of one's whole social class, requires ongoing (though not always conscious) effort. Sherwood Park residents, whose upscale, predominantly black enclave sits hidden amid an assortment of subdivisions that are home to blacks from a host of social class categories, work hard to distinguish themselves as members of the upper crust, highlighting differences that signify their elite social status. In doing so, they impose symbolic boundaries that are far more complex than the middle-class/ underclass dichotomy proposed in recent sociological literature on class stratification.[33] These studies reveal ongoing polarization between middle-class and impoverished blacks.[34] Sherwood Park blacks, though, do not contrast themselves with working-class or poor blacks. Instead, they define and sustain gradations *within* the black middle-class population. Like the upper-middle-class black respondents in *Black Metropolis,* who held lower-middle-class blacks in contempt because of their allegedly spendthrift ways, frivolous attitudes, and dubious public behavior, Sherwood Park blacks use boundary markers such as the status of their subdivision, residents' resources, and judgments about appropriate public behavior to define their own position as members of the elite black middle class. Those blacks who live in less desirable Riverton subdivisions are stereotyped as people to be avoided, and Sherwood Park residents struggle to cordon them off.

LAKEVIEW

Unlike the upper-middle-class blacks in Sherwood Park, Lakeview's black residents do not stratify the black middle-class population by occupation or housing subdivision. The distinctions these residents draw between themselves and the black poor are consistent with the "middle-mass" model, where "middle-class" is defined broadly as including anyone who holds a white-collar job. Within this framework, middle-class would include professionals and managers, but also clerical workers, sales clerks, and small business owners. In Lakeview, the primary boundary between groups also has a physical component. Before Congress authorized the construction of an interstate highway in the area, people traveled north to south along a two-lane road, now expanded to a four-lane highway. On one side of this road is Lakeview, its long-established, heavily white conglomerate of exclusive neighborhoods interspersed with newer (ten- to fifteen-year-old) subdivisions. On the other side of the road are smaller, less appealing neighborhoods, collectively known as Darby Town. Because the road was heavily trafficked before the interstate was completed, it has all the hallmarks of having once catered to large populations of travelers. Lakeview resident Charlotte's description nicely captures the general flavor of the thoroughfare: "The whole strip has a lot of rinky-dink hotels, motels, and fast food places." Middle- and upper-middle-class whites and some blacks live on the Lakeview side of the main road, and low-income blacks, whites, and Latinos live on the other side. Until the mid-1980s, the road acted as a physical barrier as well as a symbolic boundary. Residents kept so strictly to their own sides of the road that very little cross-contact ever occurred.

Major changes followed in the wake of a 1980s decision to institute busing in the local schools. An immediate casualty was the area's enormously popular public high school, Lakeview High School. Children who otherwise would have attended Lakeview High were shifted to a newly built school that also included children from Darby Town. Black and white Lakeview residents agree that the plan "didn't go over very well at all." In fact, the now decades-old decision to close Lakeview High is still a point of contention in the community. According to Matt, a white structural engineer who is from one of the first families to settle in Lakeview, "In the wisdom of the county," (his voice is laced with sarcasm) "they took a great high school and they closed it." Isabelle jokes that, "Just like the Civil War, you got people who still mad about that. Well, it's the same with Lakeview High. It still lives on in the heart of people that they wish they could turn [the new school] back to Lakeview High." Remembering Lakeview residents' initial reactions to the busing plan, Audrey says, "The area that they were going to bus them from was a low-income area, and [had] more blacks. But [white Lakeview residents] didn't want those children to come over here. And some of 'em, I didn't either, because of, you know, the backgrounds that they were coming from." Charlotte emphasizes how negative those "backgrounds" are when she confides, for my benefit as a nonlocal, that Darby Town is commonly known as "the 'low-class' part of [the] county." She tells me about a newspaper article she read in which a real estate agent was quoted as saying, "Move out of the [Darby Town] housing. You don't want inferior schools." The agent was later sued for his insensitive remarks, "but it was like he was saying what everybody was feeling. If you live out here, you'd be exposed to inferior schools, or your house wouldn't sell as well."

Once busing began, Lakeview children started to have more contact with Darby Town children. Audrey recalls her son's initial delight at having black playmates in his community:

> I remember when the [Darby Town] children first came over here, [my son] was in elementary school, and I was working full-time, so we used to have a sitter to come and stay until we got home. And he always had several black children around. I guess he was happy to see them. And he thought that [Darby Town] was another *state* almost! The area is *low*-income, like

drugs, that's when drugs was just starting, and a lot of other things were going on over there. Well, he thought . . . why couldn't we move to Darby Town? [She laughs.] He wanted to move to [Darby Town]! He had never been over there, but just, these children coming here, sometimes seven o'clock at night, these kids still haven't gone home from school, and the parents not even interested [in where their children were], it seemed. These were elementary school kids, fourth graders! So anyway, he wanted to know why we couldn't move to [Darby Town]!

By the time Audrey's son was ready to start high school, however, he was well aware of the stigma associated with Darby Town and no longer socialized with children who lived there.

In Lakeview, a neighborhood's status is correlated with its racial composition. The descriptor "majority white" is taken very seriously in this community. Typically, there is only one middle-class black family, and certainly never more than a few black families, per subdivision. Jasmine, who has lived in Lakeview with her family for many years, casts this limited integration in positive terms. When her brother-in-law drops in while she and I are talking, Jasmine introduces him, adding with an air of disapproval that he lives in "an all-black neighborhood" in Prince George's County. Later, again referring to her brother-in-law's community, Jasmine leaves no room for doubt about her estimation of all-black neighborhoods, "I know that if I bought a house in [his community] that the majority of the people in my neighborhood would be African American. There are no neighborhoods like that in [Lakeview]. There are some neighborhoods where you would have public housing. Maybe you can count on some African Americans living there."

Because the status of the neighborhood is tied to its racial composition in predominantly white Lakeview, living in one of the community's less exclusive subdivisions (so long as it is not in Darby Town) does not diminish one's social status as it does in Riverton. Alana points out that her subdivision "has professional as well as blue-collars, as well as—I mean, it's just an array. And the reason I can say that is that you can see in some driveways where people have driven their [commercial] vehicle home. So there might be a plumber."[35] Alana, like other black residents of Lakeview, draws the boundary between a broadly defined middle-class group (including nonprofessionals) and those who appear not to subscribe to middle-class values such as home ownership. But Alana, unlike most other study participants, finds this boundary difficult to defend. Recall Alana's comment: "I wouldn't call my neighborhood upper-middle-class. I think it's a mixture of people. And I'm basing this clearly on occupation."

Lakeview residents set boundaries between themselves and impoverished blacks, with whom they associate illicit behaviors. But Lakeview blacks struggle with how to relate to a group of blacks they come into contact with only infrequently. Their physical and social distance from blacks of a lower social class status leads to a perception of the poor's value system that differs from that held by blacks in Riverton and Sherwood Park. Lakeview residents tend to advocate judging people as individuals rather than as members of a denigrated social class. "I think that's where people really get off on the wrong foot, when they start classifying people," declares William, Isabelle's husband. He explains his opinion this way:

> Because then everything become a dog tag, or a different ethnic group, or what have you. I just think people should just start looking at people as individuals, and judging people on that, rather than saying, "This person make thirty thousand [dollars], this person make eighty thousand [dollars], and I don't want to bother with him because he only making twenty thousand [dollars]." You know, that person who make twenty thousand might have more character than the person making three hundred thousand. So I just look at people as people. I just put the blinders on when I'm dealing wit' people, and just judge them for what is at hand in front of me.

Alana, too, seems to realize, when she stops to think about it, that good values are not the exclusive domain of the middle and upper classes. "You can have people who are wealthy whose values are less than someone who's not. So maybe [the association between home ownership and values] was a poor choice of words, and I do know that." The criteria Lakeview blacks employ as they draw boundaries against impoverished blacks is composed of a different set of signifiers than those Riverton and Sherwood Park residents use. With few exceptions, Lakeview blacks concentrate less on the kinds of social and economic resources their neighbors have at their disposal and focus more on specific values, which they do not necessarily believe are unique to the middle class.

The class-based identity that middle-class blacks assert while in their suburban neighborhoods is linked to the boundaries they draw as they construct their racial identities. In the black suburb, the presence of blacks from an array of social class backgrounds impels Sherwood Park residents to distinguish themselves from the pack in some meaningful way. Some researchers argue that middle-class blacks worry about being mistaken for members of the black working class or underclass, and avoid associations with these groups on that basis. But that does not explain why Sherwood Park blacks draw boundaries between themselves and Riverton's core black middle class. Moreover, the majority of informants deny ever having been mistaken for members of a lower social class. (For more on this type of boundary-work, see chapter 3.)

When it comes to asserting their identity as blacks, Sherwood Park residents are not proactive; they feel little need to explicitly address racial identity issues because nearly everyone living in both their immediate neighborhood and in the surrounding communities is black. As John points out, the residents are "going to be black. . . . Nothing [is] . . . going to prevent [them] from being black." However, not all blacks who live in the greater Riverton area have or will attain the same level of social mobility. Some high-status jobs are more strongly associated with upward mobility and greater prestige, and it is this distinction that Sherwood Park residents are motivated to highlight. While researchers tend to target specific *areas* as undesirable, usually based on census tracts or zip codes, Sherwood Park residents focus on groupings of people within these communities, distinguishing the elite black middle class from the core through the class-based boundaries they impose.

Thus, for Riverton blacks, the term "real world" is intended to describe not only the white-dominated world, but also the peculiarities of the variegated black world, what Crystal refers to as "the world that they would be social and participate in." In Riverton, blacks construct their class-based identity in relation to whites *and* to a diverse black community. By contrast, Lakeview residents use the term "real world" to refer exclusively to the white world. For them, constructing a class-based identity involves erecting symbolic boundaries against the black poor, as opposed to their middle-class neighbors. These two very different understandings of the "real world" are consistent with Barth's claim that members of the same social group who live in dissimilar environments will express their social identities differently.

CONCLUSION

The middle-class blacks in this study maintain their ties to the black world not only as a refuge from discrimination, but also because they enjoy interacting with certain other blacks. Their pleasure in being black and their affinity for black spaces and places stems in part from their belief that the construction of an authentic black racial identity is incomplete in the absence of meaningful interactions with other blacks.

But middle-class blacks do not embrace the larger black world uncritically. Indeed, they prefer to interact with certain kinds of blacks, and they actively exclude others. Since racial identity is bound with a working knowledge of black popular culture, however, black middle-class parents must balance their desire for ongoing interactions with blacks with active monitoring of their children's exposure to blacks from the lower classes. Residents of predominantly black Riverton are more likely to confront lower-class blacks in their everyday routines than are blacks in Lakeview. Still, within Riverton, a form of class stratification unexplored in existing literature is present. Members of the elite black middle class draw boundaries against their most immediate neighbors—the core black middle class who live in less exclusive Riverton subdivisions— rather than against the black poor, who live well on the margins of the Sherwood Park subdivision. By contrast, middle-class blacks in Lakeview, separated from the poor by a formidable physical boundary—a four-lane highway—draw fairly weak boundaries against the black poor, whom they rarely confront.

In much of this chapter, I have demonstrated the importance of distinctly black middle-class spaces and places for identity construction among the black middle classes. The middle-class blacks in this study move back and forth from the black to the white world. I have proposed the theory of strategic assimilation to capture this element of deliberate, limited incorporation into white mainstream American life. Strategic assimilation theory represents an alternative to the classic assimilation model. Like segmented assimilation theory, this model suggests that retaining a connection to one's ethnic or racial origins is an invaluable resource. It is something that middle-class blacks may not be willing to give up in order to fit in in America.

In their residential choices and in their selection of social organizations, middle-class blacks set themselves apart, literally, from lower-class blacks and from the white middle class. There are, however, also instances in which middle-class blacks align themselves with their white counterparts. In the next chapter, I consider examples of actual alliances between black and white suburbanites, focusing specifically on the opportunities and constraints that members of the middle class confront in their suburban communities. When such alliances are successfully forged, they constitute suburban identities.

6

Suburban Identities
Building Alliances with Neighbors

onventional studies of suburban life focus on a single community, most often one undergoing profound racial transformation, and chronicle ongoing tensions between residents. A much less tense and more cooperative pattern of race relations may occur, however, in middle-class suburban communities where blacks either constitute an appreciable racial majority or do not perceive *overt* racial hostility. I spoke to a black woman, Julia, now in her sixties, who had moved with her husband and three children to a predominantly white subdivision in Prince George's County in the 1970s (not to the subdivisions included in this study). She told me angrily that once her family had settled in, odd things started to happen. They found a dead rat decaying in their mailbox, and the light bulbs illuminating the colorful Christmas lights strung along the roof of their bungalow disappeared slowly over the course of the holiday season, one by one. Eventually, she learned that a white teenage neighbor was responsible for these and other racially motivated pranks.

Today, middle-class black suburbanites in the Washington, D.C., area are more likely to experience a different pattern of interaction with their white neighbors. On the one hand, black suburbanites may experience indifference from their white neighbors or be ignored by them. Michael avoided moving his family into desirable, predominantly white subdivisions in Montgomery County, Maryland, because he simply didn't feel comfortable there. No one accosted them during their housing search, but Michael explains, "We sort of got that [negative] feel. We didn't feel a warmth in any of the communities." And Jasmine calmly relates that in her majority-white community, "There are people on this block that I don't speak to, who don't speak to me. I waved enough times to be able to determine that they are not going to wave back."

At the same time, there are also instances where black and white suburban neighbors come together, most notably to organize around shared community interests. This chapter examines the conditions under which middle-class blacks in Riverton, Sherwood Park, and Lakeview establish alliances across racial lines. To the extent that they share community interests and objectives with their white neighbors, middle-class blacks signal their investment in the collective life of their subdivisions and demonstrate their commitment to maintaining or improving their community's status and reputation. These shared interests among black and white suburbanites are the basis for the construction of *suburban identities.*

This formulation builds on existing understandings of the effect of place on suburban identity construction, including M. P. Baumgartner's assertion, in *The Moral Order of a Suburb,* that suburbanites negotiate grievances with one another largely through avoidance. Baumgartner terms this preference for as little combative interaction as possible *moral minimalism.* Since only the middle-class suburbanites in Baumgartner's study appear to embrace moral minimalism, and since her sample does not include nonwhites, it is unclear whether moral minimalism is a uniquely suburban form of conflict negotiation or a white middle-class pattern of behavior that happens to find expression in suburbia, where most middle-class people live. By identifying the shared interests suburban blacks rely on in the formation of alliances with their white neighbors, we gain a better understanding of the relationship between place and the construction of suburban identities.

In Riverton, Sherwood Park, and Lakeview, local development and school quality are two community issues especially important to residents, regardless of race. Riverton and Sherwood Park are both located in Prince George's County, where the tax burden is high but county services are nevertheless underfunded. Some residents favor construction of a proposed large-scale tourist resort and office complex, in hopes that the project will lower their taxes and increase their property values. Others object to the development, citing increased costs for county residents (officials estimate a tab of $137 million to cover the construction of new roads, parking structures, etc.) and quality-of-life issues, such as traffic congestion, noise, pollution, and the possible introduction of casino gambling. There are cross-racial alliances in both camps. Cleavages emerge not along racial lines but in relation to how close to the proposed project the residents live.

In Fairfax County, where Lakeview is located, black and white residents also grapple with the pros and cons of development. The issues there are different, however. Fairfax County is financially sound, owing in large part to the tax base provided by long-established high-end retail stores, restaurants, and businesses. This broad commercial presence, combined with existing residential areas, means that only relatively small parcels of land remain undeveloped. Proximity to a proposed development is thus a less decisive determinant of who favors and who opposes development in this county. Instead, age separates the two camps. Elderly residents, including those in Lakeview, tend to strongly favor the status quo; development is viewed negatively and as a threat to tradition.

School quality is a major concern for black and white residents in both counties. This is hardly surprising. Securing the best possible education for their children is a defining feature of the suburban middle class. Aware that a good education ultimately opens the right doors, parents often go to extraordinary lengths to give their children an edge. In *The Two-Income Trap: Why Middle-Class Mothers and Fathers Are Going Broke,* Elizabeth Warren and Amelia Warren Tyagi argue that middle-class families give top priority to buying a home in the best neighborhood possible so that their children will have access to superior schools.[1] But getting into the best school is only the first step in parents' efforts to manage their children's educational experience. Fairfax County's school system is ranked among the very best in the nation, but black parents report having to intervene to discourage poor treatment of their children by teachers and counselors. In contrast, Prince George's County residents live in a community with a troubled school system (state takeover was pending at the time of this research). Both black and white Sherwood Park parents avoid traditional classrooms, opting for either private schooling or prestigious magnet programs within the public school system. Riverton parents tend to enroll their children in the public schools, believing that the way to improve the system is to work from the inside.

In addition to articulating shared interests concerning development and schools, suburbanites in this study are vocal boosters of their respective communities. The middle-class residents of each county are

strongly attached to their own area. These loyalties color their perceptions and reinforce convictions concerning the unique character of each
locality. Prince Georgians and Fairfaxians firmly believe that they are different from each other, that the suburban communities in each county
have a separate, defining cultural framework, and that residents gain a
different set of advantages as a result of their respective suburban locations. The next section describes salient characteristics of the social landscape that contribute to residents' sense of place and thus help shape
their suburban identities.

THE VIRGINIA-MARYLAND RIVALRY

Just as athletes, siblings, and educational institutions compete against
one another for status and recognition, suburbanites compete in both
subtle and explicit ways. In referring to their suburb's reputation or status as superior to another's, suburbanites communicate important information not only about the suburb itself but also about the kind of
people who choose to call a particular community home.

In the unofficial but highly influential ranking of Washington, D.C.,
metropolitan area suburbs, Fairfax County vies with Maryland's Montgomery County for top billing. Fairfax County's status is derived principally from its enviable public school system, which consistently ranks
among the top-performing districts in the nation. However, as Prince
Georgians make clear, this glowing portrait is tarnished by northern Virginia's steely reputation for racial exclusion. For its part, Prince George's
County consistently comes in near the bottom of the suburban ranking
system, just ahead of the District of Columbia itself. The county's negative image arises mainly from its troubled school system and heavily
black population. Prince George's County residents argue that this un-
complimentary portrait obscures the area's significant advantages, including affordable homes and racially diverse neighborhoods.

In Prince George's County, where financial woes have resulted in a
curtailment of some county services, suburban identities are constructed
in the context of general dissatisfaction with officials' management of the
county, their development-centered approach to increasing the tax base,
and their futile attempts to reform the school system. "The schools are
terrible," complains Andrea, a Sherwood Park mother of two. Fellow
resident Crystal, whose teenage sons attend prestigious private schools,
concurs, though in more temperate language. "The schools are not
good," she tells me. Poor schools and other negative characteristics dis-

courage white home-seekers. For example, Andrew and his wife, who moved to Sherwood Park from Fairfax County, initially dismissed the idea of house-hunting in Prince George's County. Andrew explains: "We had never really considered Prince George's County because of the fact . . . " he pauses, looking uncomfortable. "I lived in Old Town, for, as a bachelor, for years. And we realized that this was over here, but we were half afraid to come over." I ask why they were afraid.

"Well, because . . . " he seems concerned with how I will interpret his comments.

I assure him, "You don't have to use euphemisms with me."

"All right, all right. Well, you hear all the stories of the, the gunshots, plus the school system was abominable, and it still hasn't made a whole lot of strides. Matter of fact, the state has threatened to take it over."

Many black home buyers, particularly those who grew up in or near Washington, D.C., prefer Prince George's County, where they can live comfortably among middle-class blacks much like themselves, to majority-white communities where they could be ignored by their white neighbors. For people like Sherwood Park residents Lydia and Michael, remnants of the Old South make Virginia's suburban communities, including those in Fairfax County, unappealing. In the early 1980s, when they were looking to buy their first home, they avoided northern Virginia altogether. Lydia recalls, "We didn't look in Virginia because, I guess—Michael and I both grew up in D.C.—and so for many reasons, it's kind of like a mental block that Virginia is someplace else." Michael says bluntly:

> I wasn't going to Virginia. Virginia to me has always been the heart of the Confederacy. I mean, growing up in D.C., we never partied in Virginia—I mean, you know, *never*. I may have went to *one* party out in Virginia. I mean . . . you know, running around the home city, running into people, there might be a party in Virginia or a party up in Montgomery County or Prince George's County . . . but *never* did we go to Virginia. Probably has to do with the water barrier. You know, we were separated because you have the river. . . [I] didn't know anybody who lived in Virginia, didn't have any friends lived in Virginia. This was just not the place to go to.

"Now, Virginia, I think has a personality all its own. It really doesn't blend with mine," explains Lisa, who also lives in Sherwood Park. "They just have a different culture over there," she adds, trying to clarify her assessment of Virginia. Lisa grew up in southeastern Virginia, about an hour and a half from northern Virginia. She had been the first black child in her hometown to integrate into the local white elementary school in the aftermath of *Brown v. the Board of Education.* Her daily experience with institutional discrimination began before she even got to school. Every morning, "I got on the bus, the bus driver closed the door, and for a whole year, this white woman [bus driver] came, picked me up, I got on the bus by myself at the end of the day, silence, for a whole year," Lisa recalls. "I would say, 'Good morning,' 'cause that's how I was raised, and she wouldn't say anything."

Prince Georgians who did not grow up in or near Virginia are aware of what Sherwood Park resident Pierre terms a "preconceived Virginia-Maryland rivalry . . . a big difference . . . in attitude" between Maryland and Virginia residents. He attributes this difference to the racial composition of the counties: "Obviously, now, . . . there is much more of a racial difference between them. And it's interesting to see how that still affects people." But he tends to emphasize other aspects of their county's merits. Pierre, who is French and white, portrays Prince George's County as a well-kept secret. He and his wife Natalie, who is Taiwanese, immigrated to the United States as adults. They now live with their two children in Sherwood Park. Pierre enjoys seeing the surprised reactions of Fairfaxians who come to his community for the first time: "We'll be inviting kids over [for playdates] . . . and it's interesting to see the reaction. . . . [The parents] come across the bridge. They've been astounded to find what it is like over here." Michelle, another newcomer to the Washington, D.C., area, who settled in Sherwood Park with her family after a brief stint in Nottingham Hills, describes a similar reaction among some of her children's friends. "My kids have white friends who come and visit them . . . and they come here and go, 'Wow!'. . . . One little girl [in my daughter's class] . . . told the whole class, 'Oh, you should see the forest that's in [Samantha's] backyard!' "

Michelle first learned about the Virginia-Maryland rivalry from discussions with her white colleagues about where to begin concentrating her housing search. "I was hearing feedback from my co-workers, and they knew that I was new to the area. [I'd say,] 'Hey, we're looking for a place to move. What would be a good place to move?' And from their point of view, you definitely move to Virginia." Michelle's boss, who is white, lives in a house "probably about half the size" of hers, but, she explains, "it's in *Lakeview.* And there's a difference, living in his town. . . . You're in *Virginia,* it's on the Potomac River. . . . All the senior staff live in [Lakeview] or nearby." But when Michelle queried black Washingtonians, she received a different response: "As I spoke to friends that I met in the area that were African American, they'd say, 'Black folks don't move to Virginia; they move to Maryland.' So you listen to people, you try to figure out which way is up. Being new to the area, Tysons [Corner], Vienna, Annandale, none of that meant anything to us, it was just another name. But my colleagues at work urged, 'Virginia, Virginia, Virginia is the *nice* place to live.' "

Residents of Fairfax County concur: Virginia is indeed a "nice place to live." Suburban identities there are constructed in the context of abundant amenities and overall satisfaction with elected officials, particularly with respect to their role in preserving reliable and familiar county services. Charlotte, who has lived in Lakeview for twenty-three years, explains the county's broad appeal: "People move [to Fairfax County] for two reasons. They move for the schools and they move for the area, in terms of what the potential for that house is to go up [in value]. . . . It's *lo-ca-tion*." Helen echoes this sentiment. She and her husband were one of the first black families to move into Lakeview. They bought their colonial-style house in Lakeview in the early 1970s for less than a hundred thousand dollars. Helen estimates the current market value of her home "in the four hundred [thousand dollar] range." Heather, a white mother of two, says her home, purchased twelve years ago, has doubled in value. The house had been "on the market for two or three weeks when we bought it." Today, homes in Lakeview "don't even last that long," Heather reports. "They're basically sold before they go on the market."

Like property values, school quality has risen steadily. Richard, who is black and an eight-year resident of Lakeview, points to Fairfax County's public schools' excellent reputation as his suburb's key advantage over other communities: "Having two young boys at the time [we moved here], the educational offerings were extremely important. And, of course, with the track record that Fairfax County has, that was a no-brainer. Having access to community services, like the fire department. The hospital is very close. So education and other supporting services were important. Education was probably number one."

School quality figures in Heather's calculations of county services as well. Noting that the superintendent of schools had just announced that "all the high schools in Fairfax County rank in the top best schools in the country," she remarks gleefully that she sent the press release to her brother. He spends large sums of money to send his children to private school because the quality of the public schools in his distant hometown is so poor. "I hate to brag, but . . . " says Heather, her voice trailing off as she laughs.

Most Washingtonians consider homes in Fairfax County a good value compared to more risky ventures in Prince George's County. Stephanie's husband, Stewart, a Riverton resident for almost six years, sums up the prevailing view this way: "The perception of Prince George's County [is] we don't get a lot of bang for our tax dollar compared to other counties around the beltway. Fairfax, the perception is good schools, good value. When I say 'good value,' [I mean] more facilities, better libraries, good recreation centers, more businesses close by."

The attachment to place evident in the entrenched Virginia-Maryland rivalry is expressed in other ways as well. The next section describes residents' awareness of and concern for their respective community's thorniest problems and examines how theses issues and responses shape alliances blacks form with their white neighbors in each suburb.

DEFINING SHARED INTERESTS: RESPONSES TO DEVELOPMENT

Suburban identities find expression in black and white neighbors' ability to define shared interests and to mobilize to resolve their community's problems. On a broad scale, Riverton and Lakeview blacks, like suburbanites elsewhere, oppose dramatic tax increases and excessive or distasteful development, a recipe incompatible with the ambitious growth agendas of elected officials, who perceive development as a reasonable way to offset the rising cost of municipal services such as water, sewer, roadways, and school construction. Describing what may well be Disney's most embarrassing public failure, the wildly successful campaign carried out in Prince William County, Virginia, to bar the proposed amusement park called Disney's America, Richard Moe and Carter Wilkie explain why elected officials embraced Disney's plan, despite its growing unpopularity among Prince William County residents. "Most county officials, who represented the densely populated I-95 corridor in the eastern end of the county, felt that the only realistic solution to their fiscal woes was to attract high-value development and build their way out of it, even at the risk of angering residents in the county's sparsely populated western end along I-66. . . . When the Disney company proposed its $650 million project, the company seemed to offer county officials everything they had hoped for and more, all in a single package."[2]

And they did anger residents. While the park itself would sit on only three acres, concerned residents needed only to look to Anaheim as an example of the kind of traffic congestion, motel strips, and endless restaurant chains the amusement park would engender, sprawl spanning miles and miles beyond the actual Disney's America site. In addition to residents, preservationists and prominent historians across the nation weighed in, alarmed that the proposed amusement park would destroy the tranquility of the historic Piedmont region. These groups were joined by black residents, who objected to the thematic tone of the park. The Disney corporation pledged to "show the Civil War with all its racial conflict. . . . We want to make you a Civil War soldier. We want to make you feel what it was like to be a slave or what it was like to escape through the underground railroad." In the case of Disney's America, economic, historical, cultural, and racial concerns hurled a disparate group of concerned citizens together, united against the establishment of the controversial amusement park. In the end, Disney relented, and the park was never built.[3]

In this section, I compare the cross-racial alliances forged in Prince George's County and in Fairfax County in response to impending development. Like their counterparts in Prince William County, these alliances are not formed along racial lines. In financially strapped Prince George's County, where residents have consistently voted to cap property taxes, elected officials court developers to offset near-deficits in the budget. There, attitudes toward proposed development have more to do with residents' proximity to the development site than with race. Alliances in Prince George's County reflect suburbanites' residential location. In fiscally sound Fairfax County, where most of the land is already built up and there is little to attract large-scale development, support for smaller development projects is influenced by age cohorts. Older residents, steeped in tradition, prefer preservation of open spaces over development. They want their neighborhood to stay the same, while younger residents welcome change.

PRINCE GEORGE'S COUNTY: TAXES AND DEVELOPMENT

A popular policy known as Tax Reform Initiative by Marylanders (TRIM) has created an economic quandary that can be found in many suburban communities: suburbanites insist that property taxes be kept as low as possible, but they also want superior county services—an enviable school system, timely police and fire response, and well-maintained roadways—all of which are funded largely through local tax revenue. Overwhelming support for TRIM is a unifying factor in Prince George's County; however, a low property tax base leaves the county vulnerable to potentially divisive development.

Back in 1978, Prince George's County residents voted by an overwhelming majority to impose limits on property tax increases. Reacting against a steady rise in property tax rates imposed to cover the costs of new roads, schools, sewers, and other services that the county was compelled to provide following a dramatic rise in the county's population, 70 percent of voters embraced TRIM as an immediate way to reduce their tax burden. TRIM restricted the total amount that Prince George's County could collect annually in property taxes to no more than the amount collected in 1979—$143.9 million. In voting for TRIM, Prince George's County homeowners believed they would improve their quality of life by reducing the amount they shell out each year in property taxes. At the same time, voters hoped to force the county government, whom many perceived as fiscally irresponsible, to operate within a strict budget. They were wrong on both counts.[4]

While homeowners supported TRIM in large numbers precisely because it was touted as a remedy for relentless tax increases, in reality, most homeowners paid more under TRIM than they did previously. TRIM did not impose a ceiling on property assessments, which are based exclusively on market appraisals (typically 40 to 45 percent of the home's full value). Therefore, just as they had done before TRIM, the state tax assessors continued to assess the total value of homes along with the average rate of growth in the past year for Prince George's County. Then, county officials had to construct a tax rate that would not exceed the $143.9 million cap—the maximum amount allowed by TRIM. Under this system, homeowners whose homes lost value, neither gained nor lost value, or gained value more slowly than the county average of 6.6 percent paid less in property taxes than they had prior to TRIM. Homeowners whose property value increased at a higher rate than the county average paid more in taxes than they had before TRIM. This was the case for most homeowners.[5] In addition, county council members, determined to attract new construction projects to the county, resisted taxing developers at rates high enough to support the installation of new infrastructures, resulting in tax increases for homeowners in Prince George's County, as Andrew, one of the first white residents in Sherwood Park, discovered. He counts off the houses as he tells his story:

> One, two, three people here that had—they all happened to be Caucasian, but they moved over here because they got a price break. I paid . . .
> *$19,000* in *taxes* that the county imposed on you. [His voice rises angrily as

he recalls this tax payment.] Transfer taxes—the builders got all those taxes transferred from themselves that included front foot-development, that the builders normally pay. We got that! . . . I got something like $700 to $800 in utility. What it does is it covers the installation of utilities for the county. [He is practically shouting now.] Normally, the builders, developers would pay that. Then they would pass that along to the buyers. Well, we discovered after we bought the house that *oh no,* that this was legal. . . . My next-door neighbor hired an attorney . . . who charged him $1,500 . . . to inform him that the state legislature had passed a law, at least one year, two years before that, taking those developmental costs and permitting the developers to pass them on to the unsuspecting buyer. . . . So, in essence, by the time you financed it over the years, and we pay about $700 or $800 a year, uh, I'm gonna end up paying back about $12[,000] or $13,000 more for this property than I ever thought I was paying to begin with.

A related problem was that the county's fiscal needs far exceeded $143.9 million. Forced to work with an inadequate budget, Prince George's County laid off thousands of teachers, scaled back plans to build new schools in heavily populated neighborhoods where these structures were desperately needed, and cut back the total number of hours that libraries were open to the public.[6] Any hopes of a subway system in the Riverton vicinity were also dashed, much to the chagrin of Riverton residents like Terry, who attributed the lack of available money to mismanagement: "I have to drive to the subway station. . . . That is the only drawback [to living out in Riverton]: there's no subway line. The closest subway, like I say, is Anacostia, and that's all the way in southeast." When I asked why she thought Prince George's County would not build one closer, Terry responded, "Money. Prince George's County isn't willing to put up the money. Prince George's County doesn't have the money to put up to match the funds from Metro [Washington, D.C.'s public subway system]. Their development money, they're not willing to put it up. Not saying they don't *have* it; they're not willing to *put up* the money." In any case, before long, it was clear that the county could not maintain basic services if TRIM was not repealed or modified.

A debate ensued over whether to modify TRIM or to let it stand. Opposition groups emerged, comprised mostly of Prince George's County residents whose children attended the public schools. With funding from the Maryland State Teachers Association and the National Education Association, a group known as Citizens for Yes on K spent nearly twenty thousand dollars in a 1982 campaign, urging voters to reform TRIM. According to Citizens for Yes on K, the county could easily raise eight million dollars by modifying TRIM to include revenue from new housing construction and an annual 4 percent increase in the general tax base. Prince George's County residents voted by a 3–2 margin to reject Question K. Then, in 1983, two city council members proposed the Cicoria-Mills bill. Its passage would have allowed the county to increase property taxes on new developments annually; it, too, was rejected by voters. And in 1984, a group called Fairness for All County Taxpayers (FACT) emerged, promising to educate voters about the insidious effects of TRIM, namely, underperforming public schools and classrooms filled well beyond capacity.[7] But since 60 percent of Prince George's County residents had no children enrolled in the public school system, these arguments fell on deaf ears.[8]

In the fall of 1984, Prince George's County voters finally agreed to modify TRIM, eliminating the five-year-old $143.9 million cap and replacing it with a property tax rate of $2.40 per $100 of assessed value, a move that allowed the county to operate with a less restricted revenue base. Voters refused to repeal TRIM in its entirety. As Doug, a black resident of Sherwood Park, hinted during a discussion of the pros and cons of TRIM at the annual block party, services will diminish if the tax base is not increased: "We don't want to raise taxes, we don't want to get rid of TRIM." Either way, a sacrifice is required. Yet even with TRIM firmly in place, Prince George's County has an astonishingly high property tax rate, second only to Baltimore in the state of Maryland. Residents' unwillingness to shoulder a steeper tax burden has meant that basic services in the county are underfunded, their survival subject to incessant, contentious debate.[9]

One such debate occurred at a town meeting of all the Riverton subdivisions, held on a humid summer night. Elected county officials and state representatives invited by the Riverton subdivisions' neighborhood associations attended the mass meeting along with more than a hundred concerned Riverton residents. Early in the question-and-answer period, a middle-age black man rose from his seat near the back of the room, and, speaking with great emotion, asked why so few new schools had been built in the county. He implied that the real problem was the county's fiscal irresponsibility: "When will the mismanagement of funds stop?" he demanded. "When will we start to care about our kids' education, because it is very poor." The state senator attending the meeting responded, "Let me say this: we have built nine schools. I think two others will open soon—out of twenty-six [that were promised during the last statewide election]." "Where?" the man countered, eyeing the senator dubiously. She replied:

> They are not down here. Prince George's has to pay a share of the cost of new schools, and you don't have the money. The state puts you on a formula. . . . We don't have the local dollars to put up our share of the deal. So, no, we will not build those [proposed] schools until local dollars will be able to match the state formula. That's number one. So we have a responsibility right here at home to raise the local dollars to match the state formula to build the schools. Without it, we will not build them.

The senator's comments met with loud groans from the audience. She continued:

> How are we gonna fund [the schools]? Slots, or casinos, and/or state sales tax. You elected me, so whatever you want to do. But we've got to come up with a funding stream. Don't let people tell you, "We don't have the money, we [simply] can't do it." I'm willing to pay my fair share of additional taxes because it's gonna help build the schools and pay the teachers and get the curriculum in order and make our schools equal to Montgomery and Fairfax, the two leading school systems in the nation. Too bad we're next door to them, but we are. That's a fact of life. Were we anywhere else, we'd be much better off. But we are in comparison with those two districts. Fairfax, they have the right sales taxes. Montgomery has already raised their taxes. But we don't want to raise our taxes. And yet our taxes are the thing that pays for our public schools. You've got to understand where the money comes from.

The shortages attributed to TRIM led the county's elected officials to solicit controversial economic development in order to expand the tax base. Prince Georgians' stance on TRIM also bleeds into discussions of the kind of community development appropriate for the county. Suburbanites' proximity to the proposed development dictates the kinds of political alliances that arise in Prince George's County with respect to a proposed large-scale development called National Harbor. In 1986, James Lewis, a Washington-area developer, planned to build a residential community on the undeveloped waterfront in Prince George's County. He named the proposed development Port America. Martha, a white resident of Riverton, remembers that she and many of her neighbors were excited to learn of this development. They were nearing retirement, and the group of condominiums and time-shares Lewis had proposed sounded like good alternatives for them to remain in the area without having to maintain a large home. Unfortunately, Lewis's company went under before he could complete his vision, and the 534-acre plot was first taken over by the county, then sold to a different developer, Milton Peterson, for $10.3 million in 1997. Peterson planned a much grander *commercial* development, one that would include upscale shopping, an office complex, four thousand hotel rooms, and an amusement park. According to a Peterson representative,

> The thought was that you've got this great water, you've got Washington, D.C., which is the third most-visited area in the country behind Las Vegas or Orlando. It's always going to be an area that people visit because it's the nation's capital. . . . Even if they come here for something else, they're always gonna take an extra day or two [to sightsee]. And you've got this burgeoning Prince George's that wants retail, entertainment, and wants to spend their money. Then you've got Washington, D.C., people that are already there. So the market is already there. You don't have to establish it. So they decided to move from making it a residential kind of thing to more of an entertainment/tourism destination.

Initially, Prince Georgians supported Peterson's plan for National Harbor, because its construction would mean they would no longer be compelled to drive across the river to Virginia in order to shop at high-end stores like Nordstrom or Bloomingdale's. At the time of the study, there was not a single upscale department store in Prince George's County. But as Peterson's actual plan for the waterfront property unfolded, support for the development splintered into two factions. Local politicians, newcomers to Riverton, and residents living farthest from the National Harbor site are more likely to support the project, while long-time residents and those in close proximity to the site tend to oppose the development or support it with serious reservations.

Because Peterson's plans for the site have changed dramatically over time, nearly everyone questions what kinds of stores will eventually go into National Harbor. Lydia, who doesn't favor the development, doubts the stores will be the kinds of places where people like her would want to shop:

> The problem I see is that they're not gonna—I don't think they're gonna attract the kind of, I guess, retail activities that I would spend my money on. . . . I think that what's gonna happen, you'll end up having like little boutiques, you know, places you walk through and look around but you can't spend your money. It'll be like, "Okay, I walked here, but I can't find [something to buy]"—it's not that you *can't* buy, you don't *want* to buy anything. So that's how I envision this kind of little chic-type thing, and not really a vital retail area.

Jeff, a white Sherwood Park resident who moved to the area two and a half years ago, looks forward to National Harbor, though like Lydia, he's not quite certain about what will be there. "From the plans I've seen, it looks like it could be a marina, hotels, Nordstrom, nice restaurants. That's what they're talking about. The only thing that's for sure is the hotel, which is . . . it's a chain. Now, what else is gonna be there is open. It's still all open."

And Pierre, a white real estate attorney who moved to Prince George's County nine years ago in part because he had learned that the precursor to National Harbor, Port America, was going to be developed, says, "It was happening, and . . . values were going to . . . skyrocket. . . . It was going to be a great investment." But now, he allows, "I don't think anyone really knows exactly what's going to be there." He continues:

> Well, you know that they have . . . a plan of what they want to build. It's sort of a Main Street type of thing with the waterfront, . . . with shops and entertainment and . . . . sort of convention center and a couple of hotels, but, you know, again . . . having come from inside the profession, . . . the way the developer will work, he'll put the package together, . . . do pretty drawings, and then you go out and look for tenants who are going to sign up for it. . . . You say, "Well, we're going to put a hotel here and a hotel there and a hotel there," and you work out the maximum you can put on there, so, let's say, a ten-story hotel—"We can have five hundred rooms. That's the maximum I can fit on there." And you'll do sort of a pretty picture of a nice hotel at this stage. This is what it may look like. But then you don't know whether it will be a Marriot, a Holiday Inn, or a Hyatt, or who's gonna be there. . . . The thing that they are looking for here in the county are . . . *decent* shops. . . . Not T. J. Maxx type shops, but a Nordstrom and that type of thing, 'cause otherwise you know you have to sort of head off somewhere to find it.

But when National Harbor is completed, Prince Georgians will still have to drive to northern Virginia for upscale shopping. Though she supported National Harbor at the outset, Martha, who has lived in Riverton for more than thirty years, now questions the usefulness of the development after learning from attending a series of early community meetings that National Harbor will be a "family vacation destination." Martha concludes with visible disappointment that National Harbor will contain "the kinds of stores that you're going to get when you go to Vegas." Peterson's spokesperson confirmed that National Harbor will be "much more of a specialty retail, [like] what you'd find around Baltimore's Inner Harbor. . . . It's unlikely that we would put a department store in National Harbor. Because when you're walking, . . . you're window shopping, you see a cigar store, you go in and spend two hundred bucks. You see a jewelry store and you're not even looking [specifically] for jewelry, you're just window shopping down at the water. When you're near the water, money gets out of your pocket. There's a psychology [to it]."

While National Harbor representatives justify their decision to orient the site to tourists' tastes as an economically sound judgment, some Prince Georgians feel the decision is racially motivated. Years ago, longtime residents watched as developers allowed Landover Mall, the main mall in Prince George's County, to deteriorate as the county's black population grew. "It started deteriorating something awful," Martha remembers. "I used to shop there all the time. There was Garfinkel's, there was Woody's, there was Hecht's." Nowadays, "Hecht's doesn't carry the same stuff that you can get across the river [in Virginia]," she observes. Known as "Black Flint" among black Prince Georgians (an oblique reference to a popular upscale mall, White Flint, located in Montgomery County), the only anchor store left in Landover Mall is the poorly stocked Hecht's, which infuriates Terry, an avid shopper:

> I refuse to go to Landover Mall. I refuse. . . . Just based on the neighborhood that it's in. When Woody's went out of business, which is one of the largest stores out there, . . . JCPenney's bought Woody's out and it was between JCPenney's or Macy's to put into the mall. They were going to replace Woody's. They wouldn't put Macy's in there based on the theft ratio . . . 'cause, you know, "you're gonna lose something." I promise you, a thief will come in and take no matter what you do. Color has nothing to do with it either, the thief is gonna steal from me. . . . I think they wouldn't put a Penney's in there, either, because there's already a Penney's close by. So they just left those people who live out there—there's a Hecht's and that's it. There's a Sears, and they left those people [with vacant stores]. And the quality of materials they put in these, I think that is truly racially biased. It's a predominantly black neighborhood. And I think it is racially motivated. So I said I wouldn't give them any business, I'd rather see the mall go out of business, uh-huh, than give business to them.

Like Terry, Lydia feels retail developers engage in racial redlining in Prince George's County and that the developers at National Harbor are following an established practice. "They won't get a really good anchor store. There will be no Nordstrom, there will be no Saks [5th Avenue], there will be no Neiman Marcus over there, which is what the county needs. And what else can it be besides racism? I mean, Virginia complains because if a decent retail store goes up here, [we're] going to stop fleeing across the river [to shop]."

Philip also believes that the kinds of stores that retailers promote in Prince George's County are a function of the racial composition of the community. That is to say, retailers will only put upscale stores in communities with high percentages of whites.

> In Washington, D.C., in certain neighborhoods, whites are moving back into the community and taking it over. That hasn't happened here. Until that happens, you're gonna have a predominantly black community and you're gonna have a lack of major shopping centers here. You know, no Nordstrom, Macy's—that's a problem. And it's going to be a problem trying to get these places. You have these strip malls [in Prince George's County], but you have the income, I mean Riverton and Mitchellville, you have the income to maintain a store of that level. But it's in Virginia [not Prince George's County].

Still other Prince Georgians turn to economic explanations to explain the dearth of upscale stores in the county. For example, Martha explains, "one of the reasons that we don't have more shopping and restaurants here is because we don't have the density." And Michael supports National Harbor because "they're trying to get National Harbor . . . right around the corner from me, which would raise my property value," adding that exclusive, national retailers will only locate in malls that can guarantee a specified level of foot traffic:

> I read an article about [how] they want . . . a major mall out in Mitchellville. They want nice shops out in Mitchellville, Nordstrom and stuff. Well, from the business that I'm in, it doesn't make sense to put a mall down in that area of PG County. . . . because if you look at the mall, let's say Pentagon City [in Virginia]. It's right across from an office development, which means that during the course of the day, you gonna have a massive number of people shopping because there's an office development around it. All the major malls have—even Silver Springs [Maryland] has—like a major office population as well as the residential. . . . Mitchellville, what do you have? You have a lot of nice residential units. Who's gonna go to that mall between nine and five? [At National Harbor,] there's an office building, but it'll be more of an entertainment complex, more on the scale of, let's say, what the Inner Harbor looks like over in Baltimore. But it has high visibility. [A] lot of people go across the Woodrow Wilson bridge on a daily basis. So something like that could work because of its location.

Indeed, National Harbor developers argue it is the only formula that works for upscale chains. According to their representative:

There's a misunderstanding or a lack of understanding about demographics and money and race. I'd never fault it solely as race, but . . . the people that live in the county, they don't understand that to get the kind of retail they want, you'd have to have a much more dense population. . . . A retailer gets somebody to do the demographics. If you're Nordstrom, you're looking for income, homes, education, disposable income. You've got a number that helps you figure out, "This is an area where customers come twice a year, this is an area where customers come twelve times a year." . . . So if you're Nordstrom, you say, "I'm only taking 'A' locations. Don't show me any 'B' locations, don't show me any 'C' locations." Then you'd make the cut from the "A" locations. You'd throw your darts. . . . Prince George's had three major regional shopping centers approved in the late [19]80s. None of them got built. So when Nordstrom was ready to build a new store, they went to Columbia and Annapolis. Prince George's lost out.

Many Prince Georgians also question the wisdom of footing the $137 million bill, the amount the county council agreed to divert over a seven-year period to constructing roads, parking decks, and other structural innovations that would facilitate the opening of National Harbor. Some believe, as Martha does, that their local politicians agreed to advance Peterson such a large sum because they felt certain that the tax revenue generated from National Harbor will cover the cost of this expenditure. "Taxes," she declares. "They think it'll be an economic boom. They figure they will get the tourist dollars, we'll get the sales tax from the hotels, some kind of a room tax. They've talked about it being the crown jewel of Prince George's County for economic development. . . . They figure it'll be enough to pay for the infrastructure and also do a lot for the schools. Maybe. The way they spend money, though, I don't know."

Jeff feels strongly that revenue from National Harbor will revive the county's sluggish economic base: "I think, done right, it's gonna be great for the county, because, hopefully, what it's going to bring . . . [is] commercial revenue to the county, which we desperately need. I mean, our schools are a joke, and the reason is the property values. Obviously, down here and in Bowie, they're great, but in the rest of the county, they are terrible, and they don't support the school system. So how are you gonna do that?"

Jeff's query brings to mind the state senator's challenge to Riverton residents gathered at the town meeting: "How are we going to fund [the schools]? Slots, or casinos, and/or state sales tax. You elected me, so whatever you want." Regardless of how it's done, from Jeff's perspective, it is critical to lure commercial development into the county:

> You have to attract commercial companies to come in and spend money and have a big tax base. That's another way to get it in. So that's why most

of the local politicians feel so strongly that this project is one of the big ways to do that. And if they're correct, and it's done right, you know, now they're talking about maybe putting a casino in, and 'course, there are issues about that. Is it going to be an upscale casino, like Mirage, or is it gonna be the slot machines and attract, the quote "undesirables"—you know, surrounding people?

Don, a middle-aged black man who has lived in Riverton for eleven years, is a little more suspicious than Martha of the county council's unbridled enthusiasm for National Harbor, and far more suspicious than Jeff:

> When the community learned of National Harbor, we began to request meetings with the developer, request plans be presented and all. And what we found out was that the developer had intended to build what he called an office and recreational complex on the riverfront. We asked ourselves, why does anybody want to build additional office space in Prince George's County when we have office space by the hundreds of thousands of square feet that are vacant? . . . And we asked ourselves, what attraction does Prince George's County have on the riverfront that could compete with the attractions the District of Columbia provides to visitors? And it became very apparent at that time that the developer had a long-range plan for National Harbor and that plan exceeded what he was reporting to the public. His plan for the public was an office and commercial complex and recreational, but the long-range plan was an infrastructure for gambling, and I daresay *casino* gambling at that.

In connection with casino gambling, National Harbor developers have petitioned for permission to widen a two-lane road that passes through a residential area into a four-lane road. The road would allow National Harbor visitors, including gamblers, to travel by shuttle bus from a designated parking area to the site. Conservative predictions estimate that up to twenty-eight thousand cars per day will make use of the road. Many of Don's neighbors live along this road and will lose their homes if National Harbor's petition is granted. One of these neighbors, Joan, a sixty-year-old white Riverton resident, still lives in the childhood home that her father built, a home that lies in the path of the proposed widened road and is slated for demolition. She is furious that she will likely lose her home to a casino:

> If they were mowing down my house to put up something better, I'd feel *totally* differently about it, 'cause I'm not against progress. . . . The truth of the matter is, I understand change is constant. And what I say about that is, I like my change to be positive. [She laughs.] So if we were having something, if it were something that was going to transform this area into a more affluent, better place, I'd be *very* supportive. But the developers swore, they promised us that it wasn't going to be gambling. . . . I'm not against gambling. The rich, if they want to dump millions, let 'em. . . . But

essentially it's a tax on the most vulnerable people. And they want to put it in African American neighborhoods. I mean, I'm just *sick* about it.

Just as some Prince Georgians feel retail redlining lives on in the county, Joan and many of her neighbors worry that when searching for sites for new casinos, developers target minority communities exclusively. Don lamented:

> The blacks who have struggled to be able to afford housing in this commu- nity, [who] have mortgaged themselves to the hilt just to be able to live de- cently, are the ones that it's gonna affect, and it is going to be affecting very negatively. Taxes are gonna go up, pollution is gonna go up, noise is gonna go up, crime's gonna go up, traffic, garbage, crimes against people, every- thing that gambling brings is gonna be impacted in this black community. Nowhere—nowhere—where they proposed gambling casinos have they ever done it in a white community. It's always been black and Indian. Think about that. When you go across the nation, look at where the gambling communities have sprung up (except for Las Vegas; it sprung up in the mid- dle of the desert). But everywhere else . . . black and Indian. It's as if black people don't have any hope to train for a future because developers can come and wipe that out in one fatal swoop using [blacks'] own elected offi- cials to do it.

Martha, Don, Joan, and Jeff are all residents of Prince George's County; however, they will each be affected differently by National Har- bor. Longtime residents of Prince George's County, Martha and her neighbors once supported National Harbor, but are now ambivalent about the development. "We all want economic development," she con- cludes, "and we want to have businesses bring tax base into the county, but we want development that's *reasonable*." She and her immediate neighbors raise questions about the noise level at a development that will be larger than Tysons Corner Center and Potomac Mills Mall combined. They also worry about floodlighting and traffic congestion. Living in close proximity to the site, Don and his immediate neighbors fear that life as they know it will change with the expansion of their main road- way. By contrast, for Jeff and most of his neighbors, National Harbor is an experiment with much promise. Blacks in Sherwood Park live close enough to the site to envision their property values increasing and far enough away to avoid the headaches associated with having a major tourist site in your backyard. As Jeff reasons:

> Of course, for me, living down here, it's not going to affect us, in the sense of my traffic's not going to change. I'm three miles away. Nobody's going to

affect things here. If the roads go in there, it's gonna be great for me. Now if I lived on [the main] road, and my house was gonna be taken away from me, I mean, I can see those people's point, too. For the county overall, it's going to be a good thing. For the people up in that neighborhood, it's not going to be a good thing. And that's why people are very vocal about being against it, because they're affected in a negative way. They're concerned about it, and rightly so. But for us down here, the attractiveness of having shops and restaurants and upscale things is very good. So from that perspective, I hope it happens, and I hope they do it right.

FAIRFAX COUNTY: TRADITION AND DEVELOPMENT

"You gotta consider who benefits from the increased development, and the ultimate beneficiary is the county administration," explains Neil, a white Lakeview resident. He and his wife and two children have lived in Lakeview for fourteen years. He is a serious, thoughtful man who has become a somewhat reluctant fixture in community politics in Fairfax County. "So," he continues, "I would be very surprised. It's an unusual event that a county administration is other than pro development." Neil is pro development too; many of his neighbors are not. Neil wants the county to make improvements in his subdivision; many of his neighbors are content with their subdivision just as it is. In contrast to Prince George's County, Fairfax County does not have vast plots of undeveloped land. The county is blanketed with upscale stores, office buildings, and restaurants, businesses that support the county's tax base. Consequently, Fairfax can afford to be more selective in terms of the small development projects the county accepts. Among older residents, a balanced county budget translates into opposition to *any* new development, as Neil observes:

> It comes back to "I don't want anything to change." We have this [fictitious group], we call it the CAVE group: Citizens Against Virtually Everything. There's a [sentiment that] "everything oughta be a park"—if it's an open space, it oughta be a park. I went to a meeting one time and proposed that we should not convert open space to parkland because it's available to be developed [if it is not already tagged parkland]. The real issue is funding the county's responsibility for continuing operations. And the more development we have, the less each of us individually has to pay of the burden. And the same people that got up and complained about their property taxes were willing to say, "Well, I want to have this park in my neighborhood because it now limits the amount of development." "Anywhere but my neighborhood"—that's kinda the way it goes.

Neil sees a direct connection between development and reduction in property taxes. Some of his neighbors overlook this relationship. Whereas in Prince George's County, cross-racial alliances form based on residential location, in Fairfax County, cross-racial alliances form based on age cohorts. In this section, I explore how an adherence to tradition among older residents affects the kinds of political alliances that form in Lakeview.

The Garden Club provides an example of the tension between tradition and change in the Lakeview community. Though it began as a series of "classes on flower arranging, now it's turned into more of a social club," says Blanche, a retired white Lakeview resident who has held a membership in the Garden Club for "twenty-five or thirty years." She continues in her thick, southern accent: "We tour gardens, we go to the theater, we go to lunches, we have lunches." The signature event of the club is the flower arranging contest, in which each contestant brings in a flower arrangement for judging. During the summer competitions, members arrange flowers from their personal gardens. In winter, contestants arrange flowers purchased from a greenhouse. "Basically . . . you make an arrangement every other month, and you have judges come in and judge you, and you win and you receive points for your arrangement and your horticulture. . . . It's *extremely* competitive," Blanche exclaims proudly, adding that she has received three such awards for her exquisite arrangements. Despite Blanche's overwhelming enthusiasm for the organization, the Garden Club's membership has declined over the years, from more than twenty members to fewer than sixteen, nearly all of them elderly. Steve, the president of the neighborhood association, believes changing demographics explain why membership in the Garden Club has fallen off:

> We have a bunch of women in the area who had organized a Garden Club, and they are all getting too old, and they've done like an annual judging of yards. That's another thing, we have an annual judging of yards, the best front yard, back yard, and also the best holiday decorations. [He smirks, appearing amused.] And they've done this contest every year, and they actually put sticks in the lawns of the winners. But they are retiring, so one of the big things that they worry about is that someone would carry on in doing these contests. So I don't know, it may die. A lot of these things were started in the [19]60s where, you know, the women were home and they would put some real effort into it. Now, the neighborhood is turning over. We have a lot of dual-career couples, and actually, surprisingly, a lot of stay-at-home moms. On this block, we have three stay-at-home moms, but the dominant thing is two-career couples.

Though she insists that the Garden Club remains "a very, very *active* garden club," Blanche also concedes, "We had a kind of transitioning period. . . . We have a whole lot of mothers, people twenty, thirty years old with young children, and many of [these homes] have two working parents. So it's very, very hard to get new members in the club, and the people who've been here for twenty-five or thirty years are tired. . . . We don't have enough people to really keep it going."

No one can deny that Lakeview today is a different place than it was forty years ago. That the Garden Club has fallen out of favor is but one indication of the neighborhood's response to demographic changes in the suburb. A central concern, then, is balancing the interests of older residents with those of young newcomers to the community. Neil observes:

> When the neighborhood was formed, it was very homogeneous—same price range, same group of people, generally same professions, younger, have children—so that's created a character for the neighborhood at that time. You often hear from the old-timers, "We've been doing that for years; this is the way we've always done it." And you have to balance that with the way the neighborhood is now. And the way the neighborhood is now is drawing a new character, as defined by the new generation of people coming in and their set of interests, activities, and goals. And they don't necessarily remain the same. The problem is, how do you define a set of common interests? Because for community activities, volunteerism, you have to have a set of common goals and interests in order to generate enthusiasm, willingness to participate. And, of course, you would expect that the older generation, which feels, "Oh, we've got our groove here"—they want it to be the same and never change. And the younger folks come in and they see things that are changing. So you're caught between trying to balance the needs of the generation that's emerging, and those that want to sit on what was there and compete with the other varied interests.

Occasional clashes over the need for minor structural improvements to the neighborhood reflect generational alliances in Lakeview. For instance, a number of young couples with small children who live at or near the intersection of two busy entryway streets brought to the attention of their more distant neighbors the fact that people were speeding through the subdivision and losing control of their cars as they rounded the corner. Several of these reckless rides have resulted in one-car accidents, with a number of these drivers either crashing into the curb or coming to a dramatic stop in the front yards of the young families who occupy corner homes at this intersection. Calling for a stop sign at the intersection, concerned Lakeview residents set out to secure the requisite number of signatures necessary to secure the sign. Community leaders and affected parents launched a campaign to educate residents about the dire need for a stop sign: they photocopied flyers and eventually circulated a petition to gauge whether community members favored the sign. They needed 75 percent approval from residents, but only 57 percent of community members favored the installation of the sign; the bulk of those in favor were younger residents. Neil recalls, "We were stymied from going forward not because we didn't have a majority, but because we didn't have the required sort of a 'supra majority.'"

The tension between tradition and change emerged again in response to a proposal for the installation of continuous sidewalks in Lakeview. Admittedly, it is unlikely that the county will ever install continuous sidewalks in Lakeview, as the community's request rests at the bottom of the county's endless list of various subdivisions targeted for neighborhood improvement. More decisive than the county in diminishing residents' hopes for additional sidewalks, however, were the reactions of the long-term community members to the proposal. Neil perceived a division across age cohorts in support for sidewalks:

> When we polled the dozen or so folks directly involved, they were not willing to grant easement for the county to do the sidewalks. It breaks down along clear demographic lines. Most of the younger people want the sidewalk; they're willing to sign up to grant it. The older folks don't want anybody walking by their house. [They say,] "We've lived without sidewalks to this point; why should we have them now?" And it doesn't matter to them when you point out to them, "Well, the reason why we should have them now is because when you moved into this community, your road was a dead-end road. Now it's connected to [two main roads] and there's cut-through traffic. . . . But that doesn't register 'cause they don't have kids [any more] and they don't think about it day to day.

Because Lakeview residents are divided as to how many improvements they want to see in their community, the suburb doesn't have as much leverage or political relevance as some other, more unified suburbs in Fairfax County. For instance, Cedar Heights, a community just west of Lakeview, muscled the county into purchasing an eighteen-acre plot of land bordering their community, *then* convinced the county to convert the property to parkland so that no developer could build on it. According to Neil:

> The property was an eighteen-acre parcel, and that particular property came up for sale and was actually purchased by a developer. The Cedar

Heights community galvanized to try to force the county to buy the property and turn it into a park. And they *did.* And they did. There was a big debate—it was going to cost the community two and a half million dollars—but the community and others put pressure on the county to do it. It turns out that once the political support for approval to go forward with the park purchase happened, the price actually increased to *four and a half million dollars,* but that never was publicly evaluated. And the reason why is because the Cedar Heights community is a well-to-do community. It's basically an older community. We talked about "who are the voters." The voters are retired people. This is exactly where it came down. . . . [This area] has a higher acreage per resident metric than any other district in Fairfax County, so we really don't need any more parkland, . . . [yet] the plan for the park was to leave it unimproved, which means *nothing* happens, and it gets overgrown and can't be used for anything useful.

The defining feature in the Cedar Heights community's campaign to prevent development of the parcel was that they had achieved political relevance. They had the ear of the county's elected officials. Neil continues:

They had political clout, they organized. I went to one meeting. There were probably fifty people there from Cedar Heights, none of them under the age of fifty-five. There was one woman that particularly impressed me because she was on an oxygen tank who spoke on behalf of wanting an unimproved park with a few hiking pathways, and that was the limit. . . . I was thinking to myself, "That woman hasn't seen a hiking pathway in thirty years." But the whole gist of this was this was the camouflage language. Not only did the purchase get made at a higher price than was included in the public debate—which was probably the public's fault—I spoke, saying that I didn't think we needed the park. The fact that we would acquire it and then make it an undeveloped park when we already had plenty of undeveloped parkland in the river valleys that was already becoming useless because it was being overtaken by vines and vegetation that made it impossible for use and the county didn't have enough manpower to maintain it properly anyhow for public use all added in my mind to the sense it would be better utilized if it were developed and then contributed to the property tax base. I got booed. And it was because the adjacent property owners in Cedar Heights decided they did not want to have that land developed and they were going to go ahead and leverage their political clout to get the county to go ahead and buy it. So the county spent four and a half million dollars to buy this property.

By contrast, Neil feels the county supervisor ignores more reasonable requests from Lakeview residents.

Now when we went to [the county supervisor] to try to get improvements to [the main road] and the sidewalks, it comes down to no one in our community, I think it comes down to, no one in our community contributes to his campaign fund . . . There were substantial contributions from Cedar Heights. . . . They probably spent ten thousand dollars to do it, but the fact is that ten thousand dollars tapped them into four and a half million dollars of public funds. . . . It all came out of bonds, a parks bond that the county bought. . . . And they've got time to do it. See, if I went around our community, and tried to find ten people willing to drop a thousand dollars for improvements to [the main road], I don't think I would be able to get it. And it's because of the priorities that they have to set. I mean, we're a middle-income community. . . . We're an affordable enclave, but even though we're affordable, the folks who are there are still pretty strapped.

Despite the county administration's desire for rapid growth, the pace of development in Fairfax County is tempered by older suburbanites' conservative preferences regarding land usage and new construction. Just as they do in Riverton, Lakeview residents disagree as to what sorts of development constitute progress; however, wealthier Fairfax County residents have far more influence on county officials than others.

DEFINING COMMON INTERESTS: ASSESSMENTS OF PUBLIC SCHOOLING

Suburban identities also find expression in residents' assessment of their respective school systems. In financially strapped Prince George's County, black and white residents agree that the schools generally are "terrible." Alliances form with respect to what should be done about the system. Sherwood Park residents resolve the problem by enrolling their children in either private schools or the public school system's competitive magnet schools, while most Riverton residents enroll their children in the public schools, concentrating their efforts on improving the system from within. Here, again, within Prince George's County residential location influences the kinds of alliances blacks make with whites. In Fairfax County, where many of the schools are nationally ranked, black and white suburbanites are generally pleased with the school system, but black residents report maltreatment of black children in the public schools and position themselves to advocate for their children.

PRINCE GEORGE'S COUNTY   One consequence of the passage of TRIM is that the public schools in Prince George's County are sorely underfunded. Indeed, the school system suffers more than other county services do from a restricted property tax base, because over 50 percent of the county's dwindling budget is earmarked for education.[10] The school system's financial problems are compounded by the surge in the county's population, placing greater demands on roadways, sewage, and the school system itself, as it scrambles to incorporate the expanding population of students. While Sherwood Park residents are hopeful that the system will eventually improve, they are not willing to expose their children to the standard public school classrooms until it does. For instance, Jeff feels concerned about the schools—after all, his taxes help to sustain them—but he won't risk his young daughter's education by sending her to public school:

> She's in Montessori school. She's been in Montessori school for two years now. Would I like her to go to public school? Yes, if it were an ideal world. We're paying a lot of taxes here, you know? So we don't get the benefit of it. And that's a shame. It's not the way it's meant to be. But at the same time, the schools are uniformly dogged here, and people that have the money to send their kids to private school do in Prince George's County. One of the things that attracted us is that we couldn't live in this house on the other side [of the river] for what we paid to get in here. So there was a trade-off, understanding that, "Hey, we're going to send Lauren [our daughter] to private school."

Philip's daughters attended public school for one year, but he and his wife decided to switch back to private schools once they realized that their children were not learning as much as they should:

> The school system is *horrendous*. My kids, we took them out of private school one year and put them in public school, and it was a *disaster.* . . . They weren't being challenged. We put 'em in private school because they weren't being challenged. My daughter . . . was in third grade at the time, and her mother was a teacher at the school. We had her at the school that her mother taught at. And it was one of the better schools in PG County. Well, she could do all her homework in ten minutes. After she got out of class and went to her mother's homeroom and waited for her to finish up, she'd do her work. And she was always finished in ten minutes. She was making the principal's honor roll, which is all As. Not the *regular* honor roll, but the *principal's* honor roll. You know, we realized that she was smart, but she wasn't *that* smart that she could do her homework in *ten minutes* a day and make all As. For fourth grade, we took her out of there and put her into a private school . . . in Virginia, which is a very private institution, one of the better schools in the area. It's on the par of Georgetown Prep and Georgetown Day School and National Cathedral. Well, we put her in there and she struggled. And she eventually adjusted and got back to the point where she was making the honor roll, but it was a struggle for her. So she needed the challenge. But the school systems here don't measure up. They don't measure up to the schools in the other counties.

When they lived in the District of Columbia, Lydia's oldest son, now fifteen, attended a private school, and when they first moved to Sherwood Park, he was enrolled briefly at the neighborhood elementary school, but now all three children attend prestigious talented and gifted (TAG) schools within the public school system—the two youngest attend a math and science TAG, while the oldest attends the competitive university high school, where students who pass the entry exam go on to take Advanced Placement (AP) courses and earn college credit. Magnet schools are the county's response to a flawed, court-induced 1971 desegregation mandate, one that included mandatory busing and, in a county plagued by white flight and neighborhood succession, simply resulted in black children being bussed from their own predominantly black community to another majority-black one. Black parents were enraged by this policy. As John, a Sherwood Park resident, explains, "Because Prince George's is more affluent than it used to be, and blacker than it used to be, it does stand to reason that many black parents wouldn't want to bus their kids out of the neighborhood to maintain racial balance that they're not maintaining. That's just ludicrous."

Magnet schools were touted as the mechanism for achieving actual school integration. The first magnet schools were housed in majority-black neighborhoods as a way of drawing white students back into the public school system. Later, magnet schools were established in predominantly white neighborhoods in order to encourage blacks to integrate into those schools. Younger students may attend magnet programs centered around the performing arts, foreign languages, the Montessori model, science and math, TAG, international studies, or traditional academics. High school students choose from magnet schools devoted to the natural sciences, technology, visual or performing arts, or programs linked to the University of Maryland.[11] In some neighborhoods, an entire school is a magnet; in others, the magnet program is housed within the traditional school.

Lydia feels that in the magnet schools, her children receive the quality of education that she grew accustomed to when her son attended the private school. As she explains, the education that her son received at the neighborhood public school did not compare favorably to his private school education:

> They weren't challenging him enough. He was in their talented and gifted program. He was just not getting enough challenge. He came home the first semester and he had straight As. He's just not a straight-A student. So, I went up to the school to see his teacher, and I said, "He is *not* a straight-A student. . . . What's going on here?" She seemed kind of taken aback. I

know he was an A/B student, more Bs than As. And I knew he wasn't working at home. I mean he would come home, do homework, that was it. There was no studying, nothing. Then, to come home with straight As—something was wrong. It's not just about getting grades, it's about learning. That's my focus. Bring home a C if that's your best and you've learned the material. I'm not impressed by grades if I don't think you've learned the material. . . . I want to be sure that you've learned the material. [The teacher] said, "Well, that's what he earned." Well, what happened after that is that the next two weeks I sat in the classroom, on and off, for two weeks to see what was being taught. And ultimately I found that the curriculum they were teaching was not challenging at all.

Lydia withdrew her son from the school after six weeks.

Other parents of children in the neighborhood public school were concerned as well. Middle-class parents fear that if their children are not properly educated, they won't be able to successfully compete in the world as adults. Lydia recalls, "A group of parents got together and we kind of started talking, like, 'What is going on here?' And we had the school come in and do an evaluation of [the teacher], and I guess she was under so much pressure that she just resigned. . . . But before they did all that, I knew that my son couldn't wait for them to figure out what they were going to do. So I moved him."

Lydia's son entered a TAG magnet school, but even there, she has had to monitor his educational experience. When her son was in seventh grade, Lydia learned that not only was he relegated to a less challenging math class—which she describes as "a waste of time"—languishing there even though he "scored high on all the aptitude tests," he also had not been offered the opportunity to take algebra in sixth grade, as many of his white classmates had done. Lydia was furious as she recalled how the teachers had tracked him. "See, what I found, which really makes me very unhappy . . . they have . . . white kids taking geometry in seventh grade! . . . And they took algebra in sixth grade!" I ask her how she discovered this. Lydia responds:

I went to the school, talking to parents, going to the classroom. I found out. . . . I was in the hall one day with my son. He tries to avoid me when we're in public, so I just stand away from him, and I heard the teacher say to one of the kids, who I knew was in the seventh grade, something about geometry class. I thought, "Wait a minute, this kid's in the seventh grade. How is she taking geometry?" So first I went to that class with that child. I went to her class to make sure. I've found that you need to go to the classroom, because they will tell you one thing, and that's not really true. So [if I go to the classroom,] I can say, "This child with this name in this class. How did she get there?" I wasn't going to ask, "If you can." These are the facts. Now, explain to me how this happened. . . . [In the geometry class,] they weren't all seventh graders; some were. But the seventh graders who were taking the class were all *white* kids. . . . They brought an algebra teacher into the school in the sixth grade for these kids to take algebra.

What Lydia had discovered was that white children enrolled in the program at a TAG magnet school in a predominantly black neighborhood were receiving a completely different education than the black TAG children at the school. "They go for racial balance," Lydia explains. "The idea is that they want to bring white kids into black schools to [help achieve] a racial balance. But what they were clearly doing, the resources were following these white students."

Riverton parents argue that magnet programs are unfair to the children who *don't* get in. Terry explains why her two daughters attend the neighborhood elementary school, not the magnet schools:

> Well, I don't like the magnet school. I don't like the way they have the program set up for the gifted and talented. I think every school should have every one of those programs at every school. . . . How can you tell somebody their child's not *capable?* She just wants to try. And some of the school systems are not giving kids the opportunity; they're limiting, they're closing off the classrooms. You can't do that. . . . I noticed when they were in, my children attended a nursery school that went through kindergarten. And they would allow the kindergartners to assist with the two-year-olds. It only helped everybody along the process. And one year they got a new director and she cut that out. [She believed] the classrooms needed to be separate. And you could just tell the difference in the kids. She ended up going back to the old way. But you could just tell. They can only help each other. If you pull all your gifted people and you put them in a classroom and it's nothing but gifted students, are you telling me that the rest of the kids are not special enough?

Terry's perspective can't be attributed to sour grapes. Her oldest daughter is in the TAG program at the neighborhood school. Gifted students are pulled out of the traditional classroom two days a week for special sessions. Terry's eight-year-old daughter participates in TAG even though she didn't quite test high enough to get in.

> Well, I really don't know too many third graders who do well on a timed test. They panic, they rush. But now they've come out and said, well, my oldest didn't score high enough. I was like, "Now I know she should pass this test. I know my child." Now they say—they tacked it on since then—

"The *teacher* can recommend for her to be in talented and gifted" [recited in a sing-song voice]. Well, why not just be under teacher recommendation? What's taking the test gonna do? She got in based on her teacher's recommendation, not on the score from her test.

Despite her support for the public schools, like Lydia, Terry questions whether the neighborhood elementary school's TAG program is rigorous enough:

What has she had to do? You ask your child, your child will say, "Oh, we go on Tuesday and Thursday." "Well, what do you do?" [She'll say,] "Oh, we read, we write." For homework, they had to write three stories, and she wrote the stories; we didn't hear anything [back]. Is she doing well, are you doing math with them, what are they doing? You see, I don't see homework on a regular basis, which I think if you're in this program, you'd be giving them somethin' to do on a regular basis.

I ask if her daughter would reveal that she had additional homework, if she did. She answers, "Oh, she would tell me. *This* one would tell me. Now the youngest one probably wouldn't tell me." She laughs. "But the oldest one is a school *fanatic*. She's a school person."

Jared, another Riverton resident, echoes Terry as he explains why he won't enroll his children in private school: "I don't believe in it. I don't want my kids to feel special; I don't want them to feel like prima donnas. And God knows, there are problems in the school system, but I say, 'Let's fix them. Let's not run from them.' I know I'm probably paying for it with my children's education, but somebody's got to do it."

FAIRFAX COUNTY   While nearly all the white Fairfaxians spoke in glowing terms about their children's experiences with the Fairfax County public school system, black Fairfaxians tempered their praise for the system overall with criticisms of the system's treatment of black students. Specifically, black parents perceive that the school system's ideological framework encourages teachers to hold lower expectations for black children than they do for white students. Consequently, black parents feel compelled to monitor their children's teachers and counselors. Isabelle is visibly angry that a school counselor encouraged her daughter to "take cream puff subjects so that she'd be an A student rather than more challenging AP courses" that would better prepare her for college:

As far as the school system is concerned, I still see that there are different standards for the different races. Although I mentioned that being up in here, my kids have more opportunities and all this, that, and the other, there is still room for a lot of improvement, especially with the teachers. Some of them do not have the sensitivity to recognize cultural differences. Some of them, especially counselors—and they can be black, I make no distinction based on race—they do not push our kids or encourage them to be in different activities. I'm constantly trying to stay on top of that. If you look at the yearbook . . . you don't really see the diversity. It's as if only one or two minorities actually attend the school, and that's a very unfair picture.

I am conducting this interview on a Friday evening, and Isabelle tells me that she will get to the bottom of it when school resumes: "I'm livin' and breathin' for Monday morning so that I can go out there [to the school] and get things started." The thought of this confrontation with the school counselor amuses Isabelle, and she manages a laugh.

Helen, one of the first black homeowners to move to Lakeview, also reports that school representatives—in this case, teachers—respond to black children differently:

> We had researched schools when we found out that we were going to move here [from out of town,] and we knew that Lakeview had one of the best school systems, and we wanted to be in that. . . . The school system was just awesome; we loved it. [But] being a black parent, I had to really stay on top of it to make sure that they got the quality education that was out there for them. Because so many of the black kids—I remember [my son] Ronald, in the third grade, his teacher at that time, her name was Mrs. Clay. And Ron was getting into all kinds of trouble at school. So I went over and had a conference with her. She said of his little friend that he was associating with at the time, she said, "Well, I have just given up on Tony." He was also a little black kid. And I said, "Well, you just better not give up on Ronald." So this is the kind of thing that I had to go through the whole time with the kids. When [younger son] Nelson got over here to Lakeview High School, I had to go over there because the courses that they had put him in, it was really for a trade. And I said, "No, no. I don't want him—we are not just goin' have a trade."

Black parents realize that living in a county with a quality school system doesn't absolve them of the difficult work of advocating for their child. Alana also expresses concern about how black children fare in the Fairfax County school system:

> I could send my child to Langley [a competitive high school north of Lakeview]. But as a *black* child, if there are some teachers over there that don't have a good attitude about black kids, then putting them over there at Langley did me absolutely *no* good. Even though I moved to that neighborhood because I think the schools are better. Well, yes, they may be [better] overall, but not necessarily for *my* child. Again, looking on paper, you don't know—you *never* know—whether this school is really for your child. And you don't learn until you get there.

A few white parents are critical of the school as well. However, they object not to the organizational structure of the institution, which they believe is sound, but to the behavior of a few students and teachers. Heather's oldest daughter, Megan, tested into the gifted and talented (GT) track, a program that Heather believes some teachers at the school feel is divisive:

> The current principal is not a real pro-GT person. . . . We had a couple of I don't want to say confrontations, but *issues* last year, where I thought it was just coming across way too strongly that it was a "we/they" situation between general education [gen ed] and gifted education in the school. And that hadn't been the case [in previous years]. . . . What was happening was some of the teachers . . . the gifted kids last year where hearing these gen ed teachers put them down. . . . They were hearing, and . . . again, last year I was working from home, so I would do things like drive the carpool for the Girl Scouts. So I would have a whole vanload of Girl Scouts, and then you learn a lot, if you're quiet. . . . They forget you're there and driving, and they're just yammering, yammering, yammering, and I started hearing stuff that really bothered me. . . . Teachers in the gen ed program . . . were saying things like, "Well, the only thing they teach in GT is how to misbehave" or "how to act better than other people." This is what I was hearing the girls say. . . . Okay, so I went in and confronted the particular teachers that the kids were talking about. I went in to the principal and said, "I want to talk to these teachers."

Heather was aware that some of the children in the general education program resented children in the GT program. She knew that "the kids have always made a distinction. And it has always been an issue—'Oh, well, you're so smart,' or 'You're in the *greatly talented* program.'" There wasn't much she could do about this, even though she believed these taunts tainted her daughter's experience in the GT program. However, Heather did feel that she should speak out about the teachers:

> The teachers had said [these things] in front of other kids and in front of other teachers, and so I confronted it. You know, I said, "You know, this is—it is bad enough when the kids do it, but if the kids are being reinforced by the teachers, it's not acceptable." And so the teachers came in, the gifted teachers and the gen eds, and it's all sixth grade stuff. And so I sat down and talked to them, and I became convinced if it had been said, it had been heard out of context, but the point that I was making was, "Okay, and I can understand that appearance can often be worse than actuality, but this is what the kids are hearing and this is how they feel that other teachers are perceiving them," and one reason was because there were absolutely no activities that crossed the boundaries. They weren't taking lunch at the same time, they weren't having recess at the same time, they weren't having music at the same time—so all these things that could cross those boundaries aren't happening and they used to. They used to go on field trips to-

gether. Like when my daughter was in third, fourth, fifth grade, there was a lot of integration of activities, but last year it was too much of a scheduling burden.

CONCLUSION

The alliances that black suburbanites form with their white neighbors reflect their concerns about the most urgent problems in their suburban communities. Cross-racial alliances are most prevalent in Prince George's County, where the county's dismal fiscal condition unites black and white residents on key issues, namely, development and schools. The central factor in these cross-racial alliances is residential location. Black and white residents in Sherwood Park live far enough away from the site of a controversial development that they are buffered from the negative consequences that accompany a major tourist attraction. They are united in the belief that the new development will increase their property value, and they have achieved a high level of political relevance. By contrast, black and white residents of Riverton who live closer to the site worry that their peaceful neighborhoods will become noisy transit routes for tourists traveling to and from the site. Assessments of the troubled public school system follows a similar pattern, with Sherwood Park residents opting out of the system (or into the prestigious programs within it) and Riverton residents enrolling their children in the public schools as a way to improve the system.

Across the river in Fairfax County, residents are unlikely to grapple with any proposal for large-scale developments, but residents disagree about the best use of smaller plots of land. Cross-racial alliances form there on the basis of age cohorts, with elderly, wealthier communities uniquely positioned to employ political relevance in order to stave off small-scale development. Still, racial differences are evident in Fairfax County residents' assessments of the school system. Black parents believe the system is racially biased, while white parents feel some teachers are not as sensitive to the needs of gifted and talented children as they should be.

Race is not always the factor that unifies or divides suburban residents. I have shown here that the particularities of residential location, coupled with class position, shape cross-racial alliances and help to determine whether a community will achieve political relevance.

Conclusion

Scholars disagree about what it means to be black and "make it" in America. One group suggests that racial boundaries are *not* porous: that blacks experience life one way and whites another way, even when the individuals are middle-class. These scholars argue that society is stratified primarily by race to such an extent that people who are black and middle-class are not necessarily rewarded with the material objects that we would expect to come along with their status position, such as attractive housing in a desirable neighborhood or competitive neighborhood schools. Thus, the middle-class component of their identity is virtually invisible to others. In short, proponents of this view believe that middle-class blacks' daily experiences don't differ significantly from those of blacks below them on the class ladder. This dominant perspective has gained momentum in part because researchers have studied *lower-middle-class* black communities, not middle-class black communities. Indeed, the urban and suburban communities depicted in existing studies are characterized by many of the thorny problems that haunt inner-city poor and heavily black communities. Because the disparities between the middle-class blacks portrayed in these existing studies and middle-class whites are so great, scholars advocating this position imply that they cannot be said to occupy the same class category.

A different group of scholars determine that middle-class blacks may share more in common with middle-class whites than they do with the black lower classes. These scholars believe that racial boundaries are permeable and that class is increasing in importance in terms of its impact on the everyday lives of middle-class blacks. In contrast with the dominant view outlined above, these scholars imply that middle-class whites and blacks are members of the same class and that their life experiences overlap in important ways that are not immediately obvious. Proponents of this view argue society is stratified primarily by class and that people who are middle-class are in a better position than those in the lower classes to negotiate mainstream institutions such as the school and the workplace. These social advantages, they argue, accrue to members of the middle class regardless of their race.

This study merges components of these two perspectives to show that being black and middle-class is a distinct but fluid identity, one that overlaps in some ways with the white middle class, in others with the black lower classes. Consistent with the class perspective, I show that certain aspects of everyday life are similar for middle-class people whether they are black or white, and that race isn't the only dimension of their identity that middle-class blacks care about. But the class perspective alone cannot explain what it means to be *black* and middle-class, not merely because it does not devote sufficient attention to the racial discrimination middle-class blacks report experiencing, but also because the class perspective cannot explain why the middle-class blacks in this study are so intent on nurturing and maintaining black identities, even as they ascend the class ladder. In explaining middle-class blacks' affinity for the black world, I challenge a popular standpoint held by some proponents of the race perspective, namely, that black identities are a liability in a racialized society. Instead, I argue that the middle-class blacks in this study believe there is something enjoyable about being black and participating in a community of blacks, and are motivated to maintain black racial identities for this reason.

At the same time, I argue that the way social scientists operationalize "middle class" in existing studies is too broad and imprecise. I believe that we should conceive of the black middle class in terms of two groups: the elite black middle class and the core black middle class. When we do, we see that not all middle-class blacks reap the same benefits from their seemingly enviable class position. This book demonstrates there are middle-class blacks for whom class matters a great deal, but it matters differently depending on one's place of residence. All the middle-class blacks in this study live in attractive, middle-class subdivisions, but the upper-middle-class blacks who reside in Sherwood Park enjoy a subdivision more imposing than either Lakeview or Riverton. These distinctions seep all the way down to the children. Both middle-class and upper-middle-class parents want to provide their children with class advantages, but while Sherwood Park parents are free from the burden of financial constraints and may therefore lavish their children with luxuries, parents in Lakeview and Riverton, feeling financially constrained, spend more conservatively on their children.

To conclude this study, I begin by reviewing the dimensions of middle-class blacks' boundary-work that are distinctive by class, focusing specifically on differences among the suburban groups. Then I discuss the dimensions of their boundary-work that are distinctive with regard to race.

BOUNDARY-WORK BASED ON SOCIAL CLASS

Living in particular kinds of suburban communities results in different effects on the kinds of social identities middle-class blacks construct to highlight their status. On the one hand, residents of upper-middle-class Sherwood Park erect boundaries that establish their group as members of the *elite* black middle class. In terms of the construction of *status identities,* Sherwood Park blacks are concerned principally with status reproduction. They admire rich people who don't have to work, and direct the bulk of their resources to educating their children and enriching their lives culturally, even when this means deferring their own material desires. The Sherwood Park parents use their considerable assets to ensure their children will be able to reproduce the class position to which the children have grown accustomed once they reach adulthood. The parents' behavior mirrors the patterns of reproduction embraced by the white upper class. As Oliver and Shapiro explain, people who have wealth use it judiciously to "create opportunities . . . or pass class status along to [their] children."[1] Sherwood Park blacks reinforce their elite middle class status through the kinds of *class-based* boundaries they erect against the black poor. All of the blacks in this study, through their residential location, successfully buffer themselves from the black lower classes. But Sherwood Park residents achieve an additional level of class exclusion by creating gradations between their group and the core black middle class. They rely on moral distinctions as well as socioeconomic differences to locate themselves higher than the core black middle class on the class ladder. Sherwood Park's location, set back from the main

roadway and cloistered by dense rows of trees and shrubbery, contributes to the notion that the upscale subdivision is distinct from the rest
of the Riverton community. Shared interests among black and white
neighbors are expressed through the construction of *suburban* identities.
The most pressing community issues for both blacks and whites in all
three suburban communities are local development and school quality.
On both these community issues, Sherwood Park residents' attitudes are
more closely aligned with those of their white Sherwood Park neighbors
than they are with white or core middle-class black Riverton residents.
Their considerable distance from the proposed large-scale tourist resort
encourages black and white Sherwood Park residents to favor its construction. Black and white Sherwood Park parents are also united in their
avoidance of traditional schooling. Most Sherwood Park children either
attend private schools or are enrolled in prestigious magnet programs
within the public school system.

On the other hand, black residents of Lakeview and Riverton erect
boundaries that establish them as members of the *core* black middle
class. They differ from blacks in Sherwood Park in that they conceive of
status identities in terms of protecting what they have. Lakeview and
Riverton blacks speak disparagingly of people who don't work, and believe directing (comparatively fewer) resources away from necessities and
toward luxuries for their children will threaten their social standing.
They encourage their children to assume some of the financial burden of
a middle-class lifestyle. Lakeview and Riverton blacks make no distinction between upper- and middle-class blacks, but the racial composition
of their communities leads the two groups of blacks to think differently
about how they construct *class-based* identities. There are no poor black
communities *in* Riverton, but there are low-income communities in close
proximity. As a result, Riverton residents attempt to cordon themselves
off from the less desirable poor elements living on the margins of their
communities through the erection of moral boundaries. Lakeview blacks
come into contact with poor blacks infrequently. The nearest low-
income black community, Darby Town, is accessible only by crossing a
four-lane highway. With little threat of actual contact with the black
poor (apart from in the schools, which contain a proportion of Darby
Town students), Lakeview residents concentrate less on socioeconomic
markers and focus more on character, believing moral rectitude is not
unique to the middle class. In Riverton, black and white residents oppose
the construction of the tourist resort, citing concerns about increased
traffic, crime, and accelerated noise levels in their community as the

source of their opposition. They live nearest to the proposed development and will therefore pay the steepest price when the development is constructed. Moreover, Riverton residents believe the best way to improve the schools is by working within the system. Most Riverton children attend the public schools. In Lakeview, race is not a factor in alliances related to development. Instead, alliances form on the basis of age. Older residents are generally resistant to the status quo, see development as a threat to the community's tradition, and seek to limit it. Race does factor into Lakeview residents' perceptions of the school system. Both black and white residents believe the Lakeview schools are among the best in the nation (this perception is corroborated by national rankings); however, black parents complain that they have to maintain a constant presence in their children's schools to ensure that the children are not the targets of discriminatory treatment.

When we consider the boundary-work made possible by class position, the upper-middle-class blacks in this study do partially resemble the upper-middle-class white American men depicted in Michele Lamont's *Money, Morals, and Manners*. Like Lamont's sample, the elite black middle-class men and women in this study rely on socioeconomic indicators—money and all the advantages that money buys—to define their group relative to those above and below them in the class hierarchy. This social standing is buttressed by moral indicators—in particular the notion that working hard early on is a springboard to financial independence later in life. But what about the core black middle class? We now know they don't draw class- or status-based boundaries in the same way that the elite middle-class blacks do. But would middle-class whites or other middle-class racial minorities engage in the kind of boundary-work that Lakeview and Riverton residents perform? Would elite members of these groups rely on socioeconomic and moral boundaries to construct class- and status-based identities?

My sample of whites is too small to make this claim with certainty, and, of course, I have no Latinos in my sample. But the reports from the few whites who are included here suggest that questions of status maintenance, social distance from the poor, and shared community interests are generally concerns of the middle class, not simply issues relevant to middle-class black people. Few middle-class individuals seek to live proximate to the poor; still, on average, blacks must look longer and more fervently than whites to find an acceptable middle-class community. I have argued that the black middle-class tool kit reflects black middle-class experiences; however, some of these experiences may not be distinctive by race, and are therefore potentially available to other middle-class people. Future research should explore the extent to which middle-class whites and middle-class Latinos make use of the kinds of class-distinctive and status-based identities I identify.

BOUNDARY-WORK BASED ON RACE

While core middle-class and elite middle-class blacks differ in their construction and use of class-based, status-based, and suburban identities, the three groups of middle-class blacks perform similar kinds of boundary-work in reaction to discrimination in the public sphere. Blacks from all three suburban communities employ *public identities* to manage their interactions with white strangers in the public sphere. When these blacks are moving about in the public sphere, they are at risk of being mistaken for the black poor. The notion that to be black is to be poor is pervasive in the public imagination, and both elite and core middle-class blacks may confront this stereotype as they move about in public spaces. In this study, I have focused on three public spaces commonly frequented by middle-class blacks in order to understand how the same individuals characterize their actions in a variety of public spaces: stores, the workplace, and the housing search.

Racial dynamics in each of the three sites influence how the middle-class blacks in this study use public identities. While shopping, these middle-class blacks perform *exclusionary boundary-work* in an effort to signal that they are not members of the black lower class. When they are able to go into a store, buy what they want to buy, and emerge from the store without experiencing a confrontation, these middle-class blacks believe they have successfully signaled their class position to the store clerk through their use of public identities. In simple terms, this would mean that they are not "dressed down" and that their credit card and zip code serve as additional indicators of their class position. *Exclusionary boundary-work* is readily apparent in the workplace as well. Some scholars suggest pressure to conform to mainstream standards is greatest in the corporate world. To manage subordinates and diffuse racial conflicts, these middle-class blacks rely on public identities to highlight their job title and professional status. In doing so, they remind others of their role as authority figures who hold considerable power in the corporate arena. The housing market has long occupied the attention of social scientists as one social arena in which racial inequities have persisted over time. As home-seekers, these middle-class blacks feel compelled to draw *inclusionary boundaries*, that is, they employ public identities to erase the distinctions between their group and the white middle class. They do so by emphasizing areas of consensus and shared experience as defined by upscale clothing, strong language, and an expertise about the housing market of interest. These expressions of public identity suggest that middle-class blacks engage a broader set of reactions to racial stigmatization in public exchanges than previous studies have acknowledged.

Of course, impression management is a human universal. All people must think about how to alternatively fit in or set themselves apart. However, because of their ambiguous position in the racial hierarchy, middle-class blacks must work harder at pulling off a convincing middle-class presentation of self than middle-class whites who are also concerned with exhibiting their status. In this sense, the blacks in this study differed from their white middle-class counterparts. Thus, I have outlined the black middle-class version of this process, with special attention to documenting how this sample of largely first-generation middle-class blacks acquired cultural capital in the first place. The middle-class blacks in this study make choices about when to attempt to reshape the encounter and when to let it go, investing their energy and valuable time elsewhere. Others have described this kind of impression management for other racial and class groupings.[2]

Middle-class blacks in this study care about more than merely managing race in response to discrimination in the public sphere; they are also concerned with nurturing a racial identity in their children. These middle-class blacks want their children to be successful members of the white world when they are grown up, but they fear that complete immersion in the white world will expose their children to racial discrimination, alienate them from the larger black community, and lead to nagging doubts about their racial identity and black authenticity. In fact, residents of all three suburban communities believe one needs to interact with other blacks in black social spaces in order to develop a black racial identity, but their suburban residence influences their access to black spaces. In majority-black Riverton and Sherwood Park, the black children live among blacks like them; therefore, they have many natural, spontaneous opportunities to interact with a black community. Thus, these parents rely on their majority-black suburb as a key agent in their children's racial socialization. In majority-white Lakeview, black families are rare. Often, a black family is the only racial minority in the subdivision. For this reason, the Lakeview parents have to take additional steps to expose their children to other blacks. In lieu of residence in a majority-black neighborhood, Lakeview parents rely on black social organizations such as Jack and Jill and black churches as key agents in their children's racial socialization. It is through their interactions in these black spaces that middle-class black children learn what it means to be black. Upholding the social world as an important site for socializing and the white world as an important work site constitutes a special pattern of assimilation that I term *strategic assimilation*. I see this form of incorporation as analogous in some ways to symbolic ethnicity theory advanced by Herbert Gans and Mary Waters. They argue whites have become so integrated into the mainstream that their ethnicity no longer dictates who they can marry, where they will live, or what occupations are available to them. In short, identifying with the ethnic component of their identity is now a symbolic gesture. Of course, the majority of blacks have not been integrated into the mainstream, and some middle-class blacks who live in white neighborhoods or work in majority-white spaces report ongoing discrimination, most notably in the public sphere. I see strategic assimilation as an intermediate step on the path to what may eventually become a symbolic racial identity.

IDENTITY AND THE SUBURBAN CONTEXT

The array of identities constructed and asserted by these middle-class blacks through their boundary-work are possible because they live in residential communities that represent exceptions to the rule in terms of where most black people live. Sherwood Park residents needn't worry about gang wars in their community or about an upturn in teenage pregnancy rates, because these things do not happen there. Riverton residents don't worry about their children's safety when they play outside. There are no drive-by shootings in Riverton. Lakeview residents don't worry (much) about whether their house will be broken into or their car will be stolen because these events are exceedingly rare. One Lakeview resident explained that she doesn't bother to lock her door when she leaves the house. There isn't any reason to. The mental stability that these communities provide distinguishes them from the black lower-middle-class neighborhoods typically studied by social scientists. These distinctions matter, because the kinds of suburban communities I report on in this book are likely to become more normative over time. We can no longer rely on studies of the black lower-middle class to understand the experiences of the black middle classes as a whole.

A Recipe for Studying the Black Middle Class

I have argued that most recent community studies of the black middle class focus on neighborhoods that are actually lower-middle-class or working-class, not middle-class. This research design is understandable; it is much more difficult for researchers to locate a black middle-class population and to convince individuals to participate in a study than it is to identify a distressed black population. For one thing, uniformly middle-class black communities are less common than poor black communities; they emerge most often in cities with large concentrations of professional blacks, such as Atlanta and Washington, D.C. These communities may be inaccessible to researchers in other regions of the country who are not in a position to travel for an extended period of time. Second, ethnographers often persuade poor or working-class respondents to participate in sociological studies with monetary inducements. But middle-class blacks are unlikely to be enticed by monetary rewards. How, then, does a researcher secure their participation? In this section, I outline the process by which I conducted this study. The methodology includes individual interviews, ethnographic observation, and undercover work as a home-seeker. I also explain why my identity as a black woman sometimes facilitated and other times hindered the data collection.

IDENTIFYING MIDDLE-CLASS BLACK SUBURBAN SITES

I collected the bulk of the data for this study in the Washington, D.C., suburbs in 1997 and 1998. Before beginning data collection, I needed to identify two suburban communities made up of stable, middle-class people. At the outset, I was interested in understanding how middle-class blacks choose among white and black neighborhoods, so I wanted to compare two suburban communities that varied in terms of their racial composition. I knew from reviewing descriptive statistics, from the U.S. census, and from reading sociological literature on suburbanization trends as well as feature articles in national newspapers that Prince George's County would be a suitable majority-black suburban site. I needed a black community with a large concentration of black professionals, a median income slightly higher than the national average, and desirable housing stock. The Prince George's County census tract referred to by the pseudonym Riverton met my criteria: at $66,144, the 1990 median family income was well above my baseline of $50,000, and the median monthly mortgage payment of $1,212 was above my $1,000 baseline. I began collecting data there in 1997.

Identifying a suitable majority-white suburban site was more difficult than I thought it would be. Journalists have written extensively about heavily black Prince George's County, but far less has been written about social life in D.C.'s predominantly white suburbs, where middle-class blacks are present in much lower numbers. There are many suburbs in the Washington, D.C., area with a low proportion of black residents. However, I needed not just *any* predominantly white suburb, but one that was comparable to Riverton in terms of median income, concentration of professionals, and quality of housing stock. I wanted racial composition to be the main difference between the two suburbs. I returned to the census to find a comparable majority-white middle-class suburb. This time, a Fairfax County, Virginia, census tract for an area that I call Lakeview met my criteria. In 1990, the median family income was $78,907 and the median monthly mortgage payment was $1,242. I verified the suitability of this suburban site with a social scientist who works as a statistician for the Census Bureau in Washington, D.C., before beginning data collection in Lakeview.

Once I had located the two suburban sites, I felt I was in a good position to explore the impact of differences in racial composition on middle-class blacks' housing decisions. However, after entering the field, I discovered an additional fault line: the stark contrast between the third site—upscale Sherwood Park—and the other Riverton subdivisions. The middle-class blacks I encountered in Riverton made me aware of Sherwood Park's elite status. Several Riverton residents who did not live in the Sherwood Park subdivision reported that they knew the community existed but didn't believe they could afford to live there. For their part, many Sherwood Park residents reported approving reactions from outsiders upon hearing that they reside in the imposing subdivision. Although my original goal was to compare two communities, I came to realize over time that the contrast between these three diverse suburban settings constituted an important methodological tool for understanding variation in the social identities of the black middle classes.

GAINING ACCESS TO THE BLACK MIDDLE CLASS

Still, identifying appropriate sites was only the first step. Conducting the study required gaining access to the residents of these middle-class suburbs. This was not easily done, as there aren't any "third places" where community members congregate to socialize, sip coffee, or have a light snack. In many pathbreaking community studies, ethnographers found their respondents by hanging out in public spaces frequented by community members. But in middle-class suburbia, residents are most often cocooned in their expansive homes, so you do not bump into them by chance. In the absence of a friendly contact person to vouch for you, it is virtually impossible to find middle-class blacks, much less convince them to participate in a study. I made headway in Riverton because a friend who lived there introduced me to a few of his neighbors, explained to them why I was in the community, and told them that I was a good person. Because he was willing to do this, identifying potential Riverton blacks to participate in the study was less stressful than my efforts in Lakeview, where I had to work harder to establish trust. I also met with the principal of the local elementary school in Riverton, a middle-age black woman who arranged for me to meet potential respondents through the Parent-Teacher Association (PTA). Through these contacts, I met many Riverton residents. On two occasions, Sherwood Park residents approached me, saying they'd heard about my study and asking why they had not been contacted for an interview.

Getting started in Lakeview, the predominantly white suburb, was much harder because of the low proportion of its population that is black, and because I did not have a contact person there to vouch for me. An obvious solution would be to interview friends of Riverton residents who live in Lakeview. But only one Riverton resident reported having a friend in Lakeview, and after first agreeing to be interviewed, this potential respondent later declined. In the early stages of the study, I tried going through the one of the two local elementary schools, writing a letter to the principal explaining my study and asking for an opportunity to address parents at the PTA meeting. She appeared to perceive my request as an unreasonable imposition and would not agree to this arrangement. I was dismayed, and I worried that I would not be able to break into the Lakeview community. Then, on a perfunctory trip to a bank in downtown D.C., the branch manager asked as she was opening my new student account what I was writing a dissertation about. I explained to her that I was studying middle-class blacks and that I was working in Riverton but hoped to interview in Lakeview. She happened to live in Lakeview, and she was one of the first blacks to move there in 1970, two years after passage of the Fair Housing Act. She not only agreed to be interviewed but suggested several of her neighbors and friends.

Having made these initial contacts in Riverdale and Lakeview, I then used snowball sampling techniques to select additional respondents. This process involves asking each respondent to identify a friend who might be willing to sit for an interview. This method works quite well for interviewers who are not well-known to the community under study. However, a problem with snowball sampling is that it produces a sample that is more representative of a group of friends than the population under study. To minimize this sampling bias, I secured neighborhood maps (plats) from the Park and Planning Commission, which I then used to identify additional residents from subdivisions and cul-de-sacs where I had already made some headway. I made it a point to meet these potential respondents at subdivision outings and meetings, such as a homeowners' association meeting and an annual block party, or to ask neighbors if they knew them.

Through these strategies, I recruited fifteen black middle-class couples from Riverton and fifteen from Lakeview. The couples were all parents, although some had children who were away at college or were young adults who no longer lived at home. I began by interviewing the spouse that I'd met or been introduced to. At the beginning of the interview, I would explain that I was talking to black couples in their community. Then, at the end of the interview, I would ask if the interviewee thought his or her spouse would be willing to participate in my study. Most spouses indicated their spouse would be interested (or convinced them to participate anyhow), and when I called again, I was able to set up an interview with him or her. However, six spouses were not interviewed. Some of them were unwilling to participate, and time constraints prevented others from participating. In two instances, spouses who had declined to be interviewed wandered in and out of the room during their spouse's interview, inserting themselves into the dialogue.

Only a handful of potential respondents refused to participate in the study; however, I did find that willing participants would sometimes forget about the interview we had set up. There were a few times when I showed up to find no one at home. After these discouraging trips, I made it a practice to call the person the evening before to remind them of our scheduled interview even if I had seen them during the week.

I also attempted to recruit black respondents at events targeted toward the larger community, such as town and PTA meetings, but I met with far less success identifying potential respondents through participant observation than through snowball sampling. One problem was that these residents did not know me, and they didn't know anyone who knew me; therefore, they were reluctant to commit to an interview. Another problem was that my gender became an unanticipated burden. I had a difficult time convincing some black male strangers that I was really conducting a study! Some of the black men in these more public settings appeared to process my script about supposedly writing a dissertation as a sophisticated ruse for getting a date with them. For example, I sat down next to a dignified sixty-year-old black man (who looked twenty years younger) at the local Riverton elementary school PTA meeting in December 1997. The students were performing a Christmas concert, and as they sang, he pointed out two young children, a spirited girl about seven and a shy boy about five, smiling approvingly as he identified them as his grandchildren. We chatted, and eventually I explained why I was there. He suggested that I should interview his son (father of the performing children), who was not seated near us. After the concert, the older man introduced me to his son, a handsome man in a dark suit and red tie, in his mid-thirties, and then wandered off to talk to other parents, leaving me alone with his son.

I told the elderly man's son that I was a graduate student at Harvard, that I was interested in talking with blacks in Riverton about their perceptions of their neighborhood, and that his father thought he would be a good candidate for the study. He listened attentively with a quizzical expression. When I completed my spiel, he immediately began to talk about his wife. I said that I was interested in interviewing *both* members of the couple. He responded, "What school did you *say* you come from?" My interview requests to black male strangers were frequently met with such queries. Occasionally they would add, "Howard? You're from Howard?" indicating they had simply misunderstood what I said. But this interaction was different; after I repeated, "Harvard," the man, still looking un-convinced, said, "Do you have a card?" I did not.

I hoped to minimize these embarrassing encounters by having business cards printed. These cards included my university's insignia as well as my student sta-tus. I also began to modify my own clothing on days when I knew I would be in the field. For instance, I decided not to wear shorts or miniskirts to public meet-ings and events.

As the study progressed, I realized that it wouldn't be sufficient to interview only the black residents of the three suburban communities. I needed to know how other members of the community felt about the identities their black neigh-bors employed. I expanded the sample to include interviews with seventeen white residents: seven from Lakeview, three from Riverton, and seven from Sherwood Park. I met white residents through participant observation, when black re-spondents referred their white neighbors to me, and when leaders of local or-ganizations gave me their contact information. Interviews with white Sherwood Park residents and most of the white Lakeview residents were completed in 1997 and 1998; however, I returned to the sites in 2002 to conduct additional inter-views with white residents in Riverton and Lakeview. Finally, I interviewed local public officials, including developers, the chair of the Prince George's County school board, the Fairfax County supervisor, childless board members of the neighborhood associations, and others.

There are always trade-offs involved in gaining access to a group. To convince residents to participate in my study, I assured them that I would disguise their actual identities to prevent their neighbors from recognizing them once the book was published. I have honored that promise, but doing so meant that I had to change some of the characteristics of individuals. For example, I replaced each person's actual occupation with a realistic substitute, one that requires the same level of education or expertise. For the same reason, I elected not to write in much detail about the interior of residents' homes.

THE INTERVIEWS

I interviewed husbands and wives separately in their homes using a loosely struc-tured interview schedule; that is, I designed a series of questions under specific topic headings such as housing decisions, neighborhood satisfaction, perceptions of racial progress, class consciousness, race relations, perceptions of workplace, race socialization, perceptions of racial discrimination, consumption patterns, friendships, parenting, community service, and social life. The interviews ranged in length from two to three hours. This process produced fifty-four individual in-terviews from black respondents, and I transcribed each of these (six spouses were either unavailable or unwilling to sit for an interview).

Because I posed a number of questions on race and race relations, I was con-cerned at the outset that people might be put off or made uncomfortable by my line of questioning. I was wrong; blacks in my sample were extraordinarily re-sponsive. This explains in part why I ended up with an incredibly rich dataset from which to draw to write this book. I attribute this to two factors. First, middle-class blacks are accustomed to being interviewed regarding their opinions. Along these same lines, a number of the blacks in this study had been to graduate school and therefore understood the process by which one carries out research in order to write a master's thesis or a dissertation. They seemed to perceive my pending graduation from Harvard as an accomplishment for blacks in general. Frequently, when I phoned to request an interview, respondents would say, "Yes, if it will help you to graduate, I'll do it." Second, my own social identity as a young, black woman was more often an advantage than not in these middle-class settings. I am southern and familiar with southern culture, and I can be very polite, reserved, and soft-spoken. These qualities, along with my status as a graduate student at Harvard University, generally helped middle-class blacks to feel comfortable with me. They were often interested in hearing about Harvard, namely, what is it like to attend the institution? What famous people have I met while there? Is Harvard as challenging as one might think?

My status as a Harvard graduate student was also useful in gaining access to white suburbanites. Whites read my enrollment at Harvard as a clear signal that I, too, was middle class, and therefore one of them. Andrew conveyed this sentiment at the beginning of his interview when he commented approvingly on my Harvard affiliation and likened it to his own alumni status with an elite university. At the same time, some whites may have been uncomfortable with me. One older white woman who has lived in Lakeview for many years responded warmly when I telephoned her for an interview after receiving her name from one of her white neighbors. But when I arrived at her home two days later and rang the bell, she looked dismayed when she realized that I was black. She gulped, "Are you Karyn?" Blanche did let me in, but the interview did not go well. I was very uncomfortable and began to feel unsafe alone in the home of a hostile white person. She was the only person who requested to terminate the interview. My interviews with whites raise interesting questions about the kind of data black researchers can generate through their interviews with whites. Blanche could not mask her surprise that I turned out to be black, and this shock dominated the interview. On the other hand, Andrew, who had already seen me around the subdivision, vowed not to give me "the flowery version" of race relations in Sherwood Park. Future research would need to explore whether the views expressed by whites like Andrew are atypical when the interviewer is black.

PARTICIPANT OBSERVATION

In addition to conducting interviews, I engaged in intensive ethnographic fieldwork in Riverton, Lakeview, and Sherwood Park. I attended homeowners' association and neighborhood association meetings, PTA meetings, church services, block parties and community-wide civic meetings. I shopped at the local stores and, occasionally, hung out at the fast food restaurants.

An unusual component of this fieldwork involved making walk-in visits to real estate offices in Prince George's County and Fairfax County. I posed as a home-seeker to gain insight into how real estate agents interact with middle-class black clients. Prior to posing as a home-seeker, I tried to secure information on the housing search by conducting interviews with real estate agents in which I disclosed the real reason I was there. I told agents that I was a graduate student and that I wanted to understand the housing market in Washington, D.C., but I didn't make much headway using this method. Agents were extraordinarily guarded. They nervously provided pat responses to my questions. After conducting two torturous interviews with real estate agents, I decided to pose as a home-seeker instead. During these visits, I explained that my fiancé and I would be moving to the area from Boston in a few months. I said that I had come down early to scout out potential homes. In order to establish our position as an upper-middle-class couple, I explained that my fiancé was busy finishing up his residency and that he would be happy with whatever choice I made.

I was both excited and anxious about doing these observations undercover. I wondered if I could sustain a fake identity as a home-seeker throughout a lengthy interaction. I wondered what would happen if none of the agents believed my fictional account. My story was apparently plausible to real estate agents; none of the agents questioned its legitimacy. Moreover, because I was actually dating a young doctor at the time of the study, I did have an insider's perspective on medical school, residency, specialty areas, and so on, and I was able to answer general questions posed by one agent about my boyfriend's trajectory in the field.

LESSONS LEARNED

Every ethnographer must learn how to deal with unanticipated problems in the field as they arise. I discuss three of the challenges I experienced during my data collection in middle-class suburbia. Two of these dilemmas are specific to middle-class populations. The other dilemma is more general, likely to arise regardless of the racial or class background of the population under study.

I mentioned in an earlier section of this appendix that I sat down next to an elderly black man at a Riverton PTA event. I remember him well, in part because he was a genuinely kind person. But I also remember him and the night of the Christmas concert because it marked the first major mistake that I made in the field. When he pointed out his grandchildren among the sea of children standing erect on the school bleachers, I commented that they were very cute and that he must be proud of them. He smiled and said, "Where are your kids?" Caught completely off guard, I responded with the truth: "I don't have kids." Clearly confused, he asked, "Then why are you here?" This exchange was very embarrassing for me. As an ethnographer, you absolutely must have a ready response for why you are in the field. And you have to be able to pitch an appropriate response, whether you are talking to a school official, like the principal, who of course knew why I was there, or a grandfather. The elderly man didn't want to know all about sociological theories, but he did want to understand why a childless woman would be present at a PTA-sponsored event.

Ethnographers studying poor communities have written extensively about the kinds of financial incentives they provide to impoverished residents to encourage them to participate in the study. I was fortunate to be studying middle-class populations, because I did not have money to pay them. Indeed, they often bought small food items for me—sodas, snacks, and occasionally, lunches. But the fact that the middle-class blacks in my study neither needed nor wanted money from me did not mean that they didn't have *any* needs. It turns out that what many residents wanted from me was expertise. When some residents found out that I was a graduate student in the Department of Sociology at Harvard, they assumed that I was an expert on just about everything. For example, Isabelle asked me to review her daughter's high school course schedule. She wanted to be sure that the college counselor had recommended courses that would prepare her for college. Bridget, a middle-age Lakeview resident, wanted me to fix her computer. My efforts to convince them that I knew very little about these disciplines were not taken seriously. Residents seemed to assume that I was simply being modest about my abilities and specialized skill set.

Studying middle-class black populations presents many challenges and rewards. Because I feel the nitty-gritty details of my experience could be helpful to other scholars who are interested in pursuing research on middle-class black populations, I have written extensively here about the problems I faced in the field and how I attempted to resolve them. But there were also many benefits to conducting this research. I certainly matured as a researcher after having negotiated the (admittedly few) interviews with difficult respondents, as well my embarrassing blunders in the field. Ethnographers warn that if you are not willing to be embarrassed, you shouldn't engage in this work. So true. It might have been easier to study the identity options of the black middle class by using a large data set, but I wouldn't have learned about the kind of internal differentiation within this group that I uncovered through qualitative methods of data collection.

In the end, I hope that the residents' unshakable confidence in my expertise (albeit as a jack-of-all-trades among some of the respondents) transfers to their reading of this book, that they see themselves in these pages, and that their willingness to open up about the intimate details of their lives contributes to a more comprehensive understanding of what it means to live out one's life as a member of America's diverse black middle class.

Notes

PREFACE

1. Leslie Innis and Joe Feagin, "*The Cosby Show*: The View from the Black Middle Class," 692.

2. See David Plotz, "The Resurrection of Marion Barry."

3. William O'Hare and William Frey, "Booming, Suburban, and Black," 30.

4. See Mary Waters, *Ethnic Options*, and Joanne Nagel, "Constructing Ethnicity: Creating and Recreating Ethnic Identity and Culture."

5. See Alejandro Portes and Min Zhou, "The New Second Generation: Segmented Assimilation and Its Variants"; Mary Waters, *Black Identities*.

6. See Joe Feagin, "The Continuing Significance of Race: Antiblack Discrimination in Public Places"; Joe Feagin and Melvin Sikes, *Living with Racism*.

7. A black executive interviewed by sociologist Elijah Anderson stated, "They're never going to envision you as being a white male, but if you can dress the same and look a certain way and drive a conservative car and whatever else, they'll say, 'This guy has a similar attitude, similar values. He's a team player.' If you don't dress with the uniform, obviously you're on the wrong team." See Anderson, "The Social Situation of the Black Executive," 17.

INTRODUCTION

1. On wealth inequality, see Melvin Oliver and Thomas Shapiro, *Black Wealth/White Wealth: A New Perspective on Racial Inequality*; Dalton Conley, *Being Black, Living in the Red*; Thomas Shapiro, *The Hidden Cost of Being African American*. On racial residential segregation, see Douglas Massey and Nancy Denton, *American Apartheid*, and Mary Pattillo-McCoy, *Black Picket Fences*.

2. Black-white gaps in educational attainment and income have declined over time, but the black-white wealth gap is still enormous. The total net worth of the

average white person is $72,000; the average black, $9,800. See Oliver and Shapiro, *Black Wealth, White Wealth;* Conley, *Being Black, Living in the Red;* and Shapiro, *Hidden Cost,* for detailed discussions of wealth disparities by race.

3. In *Detroit Divided,* Reynolds Farley, Sheldon Danziger, and Harry Holzer trace the emergence of Detroit's black middle class back to demands put forth by auto union workers in the late 1940s for higher wages and fringe benefits. They write, "When employers agreed to these demands, millions of blue-collar Americans and their families were shifted from hovering just above the poverty line into the prosperous middle class" (7). Black auto workers were included in this upwardly mobile group. To discourage auto companies from replacing white workers with black strikebreakers, the United Auto Workers union demanded equal pay for black and white workers.

4. See Pattillo-McCoy, *Black Picket Fences,* 2-3.

5. Rakesh Kochhar, Roberto Suro, and Sonya Tafoya, *The New Latino South: The Context and Consequences of Rapid Population Growth.*

6. Mary Waters and Tomás Jiménez, "Assessing Immigrant Assimilation."

7. Annette Lareau, *Unequal Childhoods,* 132-33.

8. Thomas Gieryn introduced the term *boundary-work* in "Boundary-Work and the Demarcation of Science from Non-Science," a study designed to explain how scientists distinguish "scientific" research from nonscientific intellectual pursuits.

9. This general theme, that collective identity stems from distinctions groups emphasize between themselves and others, is also raised in an earlier work by Herbert Blumer, "Race Prejudice as a Sense of Group Position." He argues that analyses of race prejudice should focus not on the predispositions of individuals but on "the process by which racial groups form images of themselves and others. This process is . . . fundamentally a *collective process.* . . . It is the *sense of social position* emerging from this collective process of characterization which provides the basis of race prejudice" (italics in original, 3-4).

10. See Michele Lamont, *Money, Morals, and Manners,* 411.

11. Lamont writes, "Future research should . . . consider differences in the boundary-work of whites and the growing number of minority upper-middle class members" (ibid., 3; see also 80).

12. Lamont's claim is based on the equalizing power of education and "the fact that a college degree remains the best predictor of high occupational status" (ibid., 11).

13. Ibid., 42.

14. Ibid., 69-75.

15. Lareau, *Unequal Childhoods,* 4.

16. William Wilson, *The Declining Significance of Race.*

17. Elijah Anderson, "The Social Situation of the Black Executive."

18. See Ann Swidler, "Culture in Action: Symbols and Strategies"; Michael Schudson, "How Culture Works"; David Laitin, *Hegemony and Culture.*

19. See Ann Swidler, *Talk of Love,* 24-25.

20. Mary Pattillo-McCoy, "Church Culture as a Strategy of Action in the Black Community."

21. Mary Pattillo, "Sweet Mothers and Gangbangers."

22. Stephen Cornell and Douglas Hartmann, *Ethnicity and Race: Making Identities in a Changing World,* 154.

23. Fredrik Barth, *Ethnic Groups and Boundaries.*

24. See Barrie Thorne, *Gender Play.* Thorne paints a vivid picture of gender relations in different settings *within* the school (e.g., lunch time vs. playground interactions), but she does not explore these patterns beyond the boundaries of the school. On the playground, boys and girls often naturally divide into separate teams on the basis of gender. In the classroom, more often than not, the teachers mix boys and girls into one group. But sometimes teachers reinforce gender boundaries, pitting the boys against the girls in math competitions or assigning classroom seating so that there is a boys' and a girls' side of the classroom. Although teachers report wanting to treat students the same, "many researchers have uncovered 'hidden curricula' of race, class, and gender in both the content and processes of schooling [which suggests] . . . schools may help reproduce class, racial, and gender inequalities that are fundamental to the larger society" (51).

25. Joe Feagin and Melvin Sikes, *Living with Racism.*

1. DEFINING THE POST-INTEGRATION BLACK MIDDLE CLASSES

1. Wilson launched the race-class debate with the publication of *The Declining Significance of Race.*

2. See Joe Feagin, "The Continuing Significance of Race"; Pattillo-McCoy, *Black Picket Fences;* Bruce Haynes, *Red Lines, Black Spaces.*

3. In *Sharing America's Neighborhoods,* Ingrid Ellen argues that stable, integrated neighborhoods are not as uncommon as previous studies have claimed. She finds that in 1990, about a third of blacks lived in neighborhoods that were 10 to 50 percent black, and about 13 percent lived in neighborhoods that were 1 to 10 percent black. Moreover, these integrated neighborhoods do not invariably tip toward black over time. More than 75 percent of neighborhoods that were integrated at the beginning of the 1980s were still integrated at the end of the decade. Of course, a neighborhood that is 50 percent black is not integrated in the same way that a neighborhood that is 10 percent black would be. Ellen's argument raises interesting questions about what we mean by the term *integration.* Historically, integration for whites often meant that one black family lived in their neighborhood. Few blacks would consider a neighborhood with a single black family "integrated."

4. Other studies report increases in the percentage of blacks indicating a preference for neighborhoods with black majorities, even if the subjects do not live in such communities at present. Although these studies report that this preference stems from fear of hostility in white neighborhoods and a concerted effort to locate a black residential space among blacks weary from their experiences with integration, majority-black communities segregated by choice may become normative if large numbers of blacks begin to act on their stated preferences. See especially Maria Krysan, "Community Undesirability in Black and White: Examining Racial Residential Preferences through Community Perceptions"; Camille Zubrinsky Charles, "Can We Live Together? Racial Preferences and

Neighborhood Outcomes"; Maria Krysan and Reynolds Farley, "The Residential Preferences of Blacks: Do They Explain Persistent Segregation?"

5. See Robert Adelman, "Neighborhood Opportunities, Race, and Class: The Black Middle Class and Residential Segregation."

6. See F. James Davis, *Who Is Black?*

7. James Blackwell, *The Black Community;* F. James Davis, *Who Is Black?;* E. Franklin Frazier, *The Negro Family in the United States;* Verna Keith and C. Herring, "Skin Tone and Stratification in the Black Community"; Bart Landry, *The New Black Middle Class.*

8. Andrew Billingsley, *Black Families in White America;* Blackwell, *The Black Community;* E. Franklin Frazier, *Black Bourgeoisie;* Stewart Tolnay, "The African American 'Great Migration' and Beyond."

9. Landry, *The New Black Middle Class;* Frazier, *The Negro Family.*

10. Frazier argues in *The Negro Family* that members of the old black elite engaged in residential segregation along class lines: "As far as possible, they sought residence in neighborhoods outside the Negro areas. In both northern and southern cities we find them living close to or within the white neighborhoods. Sometimes a small block of a street normally occupied by whites would be occupied by a small group of these [mulatto] families" (298). Willard Gatewood notes in "Aristocrats of Color South and North: The Black Elite, 1880–1920" that the old black elite carved out one or two exclusive streets within black sections of the city, designating them as elite spaces (14). And Landry points out in *The New Black Middle Class,* "Whenever possible, black elite families sought to live in white neighborhoods, if only on a single block of a street occupied by whites" (33). See also St. Clair Drake and Horace Cayton, *Black Metropolis,* 660.

11. Keith and Herring, "Skin Tone and Stratification"; Frazier, *The Negro Family;* Landry, *The New Black Middle Class.*

12. Gatewood, "Aristocrats of Color," 9.

13. Frazier, *The Negro Family,* 308.

14. Keith and Herring, "Skin Tone and Stratification."

15. Gatewood, 12.

16. Landry, *The New Black Middle Class,* 34.

17. Ibid., 25, 37–38.

18. Ibid., 38–39.

19. Frazier, *The Negro Family,* 326–27. See also Massey and Denton, *American Apartheid,* 156; W. E. B. DuBois, *Dusk of Dawn.*

20. Drake and Cayton, *Black Metropolis,* 515.

21. Frazier, *Black Bourgeoisie;* August Meier and Elliot Rudwick, *From Plantation to Ghetto.*

22. Doug McAdam, *Political Process and the Development of Black Insurgency, 1930–1970,* 92; Lawrence O. Graham, *Our Kind of People.*

23. McAdam, *Black Insurgency,* 92.

24. In "Education and Advancement: Exploring the Hopes and Dreams of Blacks and Poor Whites at the Turn of the Century," Pamela Barnhouse Walters compares the attitudes of northern immigrants, poor whites, and southern

blacks' toward education. She finds that immigrants and blacks relied on their respective communities' institutions to articulate their demands for education. Immigrants turned to their labor unions, and blacks turned to their churches. Walters argues that southern whites lacked an institutional anchor from which to voice their concerns about education, but that this latter group may have also perceived education as inessential to social mobility because the racial caste system ensured that blacks were situated at the bottom of the social hierarchy.

25. McAdam, 102.

26. Ibid.

27. Landry, *The New Black Middle Class*, 44–47.

28. Wilson, *The Declining Significance of Race*, 126.

29. Drake and Cayton, *Black Metropolis*, 513.

30. Gary Pomerantz, *Where Peachtree Meets Sweet Auburn*.

31. Frazier refers to this group as "the brown middle class" in *The Negro Family*, 317–33.

32. See Pattillo-McCoy, *Black Picket Fences;* Feagin and Sikes, *Living with Racism;* Haynes, *Red Lines, Black Spaces;* Steven Gregory, *Black Corona*.

33. Feagin, "Continuing Significance," 107.

34. For an excellent discussion of the residential outcomes of Section 8 residents, see James Rosenbaum, Nancy Fishman, Alison Brett, and Patricia Meaden, "Can the Kerner Commission's Housing Strategy Improve Employment, Education, and Social Integration for Low-Income Blacks?" As the authors explain, "The Section 8 program is a federal program that subsidizes low-income people's rents in private sector apartments, either by giving them a Section 8 certificate that allows them to rent apartments on the open market or by moving them into a new or rehabilitated building in which the owner has taken a federal loan that requires some units to be set aside for low-income tenants" (1522). The target neighborhoods vary by race and class. Some are majority white, middle-class and suburban; others are heavily black, low-income urban neighborhoods. Section 8 residents have very little say about whether they end up in the suburbs or the city. Apartments are assigned to residents based on their place on the waiting list, not their residential preference, and while they may reject an apartment, most people do not because the probability that they would be offered another apartment in their few remaining months of eligibility is very, very low.

35. Popularized by William Wilson in *The Declining Significance of Race,* the term "life chances" refers to the opportunities groups have to achieve economic mobility. Wilson argues that class position is the most important determinant of life chances. Other scholars argue that ascribed characteristics like race or gender play a central role. Still others identify resources—principally income or wealth—as the most important factors contributing to a group's life chances. In *Harlemworld,* a discussion of the varied social networks of Harlem blacks, some of whom are middle-class, John L. Jackson explores the extent to which the life chances of middle-class and poor residents overlap. But he does not examine internal distinctions drawn by members of the black middle class against one another.

36. Pattillo-McCoy, *Black Picket Fences,* 28.

37. Haynes, *Red Lines, Black Spaces,* 85, 103; Taylor, *Harlem,* 135.

38. Michael Dawson, *Behind the Mule;* Cathy Cohen, *The Boundaries of Blackness.*

39. See Shapiro, *Hidden Cost,* 87; Haynes, *Red Lines, Black Spaces,* xx; Pattillo-McCoy, *Black Picket Fences,* 14–15; Adelman, "Neighborhood Opportunities, Race and Class," 48. In his quantitative study of black middle-class neighborhoods, Adelman established a baseline for entry into the middle class at twice the poverty level and capped the middle-class category at $49,999, a figure four times the poverty level.

40. Matching Groveland to its actual counterpart in the Chicago Local Community Fact Book (144–45, 400) provides additional evidence for my argument that Groveland is a lower-middle-class rather than a middle-class community. In 1990, only 36 percent of residents earned over $50,000; the median value of homes was $65,881, and the median mortgage payment was $587.

41. See Edward Wolff, *Top Heavy;* William J. Wilson, "Rising Inequality and the Case for Coalition Politics"; William J. Wilson, "All Boats Rise. Now What?" *New York Times,* April 12, 2000.

42. Richard Stevenson, "Income Gap Widens between Rich and Poor in Five States and Narrows in One," *New York Times,* April 24, 2002.

43. On this point, see Conley, *Being Black, Living in the Red.*

44. Shapiro, *Hidden Cost.* Shapiro refers to this life-altering form of wealth as *transformative assets.*

45. Oliver and Shapiro, *Black Wealth/White Wealth,* 2.

46. Conley, *Being Black, Living in the Red,* 14.

47. See E. E. LeMasters, *Blue-Collar Aristocrats.*

48. Haynes, *Red Lines, Black Spaces,* 97, 114.

49. See Pattillo-McCoy, *Black Picket Fences;* Haynes, *Red Lines, Black Spaces;* Feagin, *Living with Racism;* Shapiro, *Hidden Cost.*

50. Pattillo-McCoy, *Black Picket Fences,* 4; Haynes, *Red Lines, Black Spaces,* xx.

51. See Pattillo-McCoy, *Black Picket Fences,* 2.

52. William J. Wilson, *The Truly Disadvantaged,* 46.

53. Paul Jargowsky, "Take the Money and Run: Economic Segregation in U.S. Metropolitan Areas"; Pattillo-McCoy, *Black Picket Fences.*

54. Douglas Massey and Nancy Denton, "Trends in the Residential Segregation of Blacks, Hispanics, and Asians," 823. See also Massey and Denton, *American Apartheid.*

55. Lincoln Quillian, "Migration Patterns and the Growth of High-Poverty Neighborhoods, 1970–1990."

56. Richard Alba, John Logan, and Brian Stults, "How Segregated Are Middle-Class African Americans?"

57. See David Dent, "The New Black Suburbs," *New York Times Magazine,* June 14, 1992.

58. On this point, see Michael Owens and David Wright, "The Diversity of Majority-Black Neighborhoods."

59. There is evidence that some white suburbs in select metropolitan areas have opened up to blacks. Scholars concerned with residential segregation report

that black-white segregation levels declined modestly from 1970 to 1990, but because these levels were so high to begin with, we will not see the immediate effect of these declines in more than a few of the nation's metropolitan areas for some time. The most dramatic decreases in black-white segregation occurred in the southern and western regions of the country. For instance, in 1970, 62 percent of suburban blacks in the Washington, D.C., metropolitan area would have had to move from their existing neighborhood in order to achieve residential integration. By 1990, this percentage had fallen to 57 percent. To be sure, these percentages are not ideal, but they do reflect an overall downward trend in residential segregation, one that scholars predict will continue. See Reynolds Farley and William Frey, "Changes in the Segregation of Whites from Blacks During the 1980s: Small Steps toward a More Integrated Society"; Adelman, "Neighborhood Opportunities, Race and Class."

60. Joel Garreau, "A Middle-Class without Precedent."

61. Dennis Gale, *Washington, D.C.: Inner-City Revitalization and Minority Suburbanization*, 114–15.

62. Ross Netherton and Nan Netherton, *Fairfax County in Virginia: A Pictorial History*, 578–79.

63. Gale, *Washington, D.C.*.

64. See Adelman, "Neighborhood Opportunities, Race and Class"; Alba, Logan, and Schults, "How Segregated"; John Logan and Richard Alba, "Locational Returns to Human Capital: Minority Access to Suburban Community Resources"; Douglas Massey, Gretchen Condran, and Nancy Denton, "The Effect of Residential Segregation on Black Social and Economic Well-Being."

65. John Logan and Mark Schneider, "Racial Segregation and Racial Change in American Suburbs, 1970–1980."

66. On this point, see Adelman, "Neighborhood Opportunities, Race and Class."

67. Journalists and marketing firms have paid far more attention to black middle-class suburban enclaves than social scientists have. After discovering that this type of suburban community, brimming over with young, college-educated, affluent blacks, had not been properly characterized as an affluent suburb, the marketing firm Claritas created an ideal type to characterize black suburban enclaves, which they labeled "Cluster 31: Black Enterprise." They found that median incomes ranging from $50,000 to $75,000 are 1.8 times more likely in Cluster 31 than in the average hypothetical suburb, that Cluster 31 people hold college degrees at 1.3 times the national average, and that Cluster 31 residents are more likely to shop in health food stores and gourmet shops. Many of these Cluster 31 communities are found in Washington, D.C. "If you knocked on doors at random in the Washington area, you would be 11 times as likely to find a Cluster 31 family as you would on average in America." See " 'Clusters': One Measure of Success," *Washington Post*, November 29, 1987.

68. Andrew Wiese, "Places of Our Own: Suburban Black Towns before 1960," 272.

69. Valerie Johnson, *Black Power in the Suburbs*, 39.

70. Ibid., 109, 115. See also Wiese, "Places of Our Own"; Gale, *Washington, D.C.*

71. Pomerantz, *Peachtree,* 162–63.
72. Johnson, *Black Power in the Suburbs,* 94.
73. See Joel Garreau, *Edge City: Life on the New Frontier.*
74. Gale (*Washington, D.C.*) reports the median sales price for a home in Prince George's County, MD, in 1984 was $82,000, compared to $118,000 in Montgomery County, MD, and $124,000 in Fairfax County, VA.
75. See Ray Oldenburg, *The Great Good Place.* Oldenburg contrasts "third places" with the home (the "first place") and the work setting (the "second place").

2. SOCIAL ORGANIZATION IN WASHINGTON'S SUBURBIA

1. On these and other urban maladies, see Monique Taylor, *Harlem: Between Heaven and Hell;* Elijah Anderson, *Streetwise;* Felipe Bourgois, *In Search of Respect.*
2. Recent community studies of urban neighborhoods point to patterns of social organization that may appear dysfunctional to an outsider but are normative within their specific urban context. In *Streetwise,* Anderson reveals the elaborate codes utilized by (mostly white) middle-class residents living in a gentrifying community to navigate potentially dangerous sidewalks and streets. Pattillo ("Sweet Mothers and Gangbangers") and Sudhir Venkatesh ("The Social Organization of Urban Street Gang Activity") find that gang members coexist openly with law-abiding citizens on the South Side of Chicago. Residents tolerate gang members primarily because they are related to them and because they can count on gang members to lend financial support to community-sponsored social activities.
3. For a fuller discussion, see Philip Clay, "The Process of Black Suburbanization"; Harold Connolly, "Black Movement into the Suburbs"; Reynolds Farley, "The Changing Distribution of Negroes within Metropolitan Areas: The Emergence of Black Suburbs"; Logan and Schneider, "Racial Segregation and Racial Change"; John Logan, Richard Alba, and Shu-Yin Leung, "Minority Access to White Suburbs: A Multiregional Comparison"; Thomas Phelan and Mark Schneider, "Race, Ethnicity and Class in American Suburbs"; Andrew Wiese, "Places of Our Own."
4. Herbert Gans, *The Levittowners,* v, xxviii.
5. Onlookers were amazed at how quickly the Levitts built homes using mass-production techniques. G. Scott Thomas writes in *The United States of Suburbia,* "Old-timers still recalled how Levitt's crews built hundreds of homes simultaneously, as trucks moved slowly down Levittown's new streets, dropping off windows, siding and toilets every sixty feet, while landscapers planted trees every twenty-eight feet." (135).
6. The Levitts were aided in their efforts to revolutionize the home construction industry by the federal government. To jumpstart housing construction after the war and to protect lenders from risks, in 1934 President Roosevelt encouraged the establishment of the Federal Housing Administration (FHA). Among its other functions, the FHA sheltered conventional banks from high-risk ventures by pledging to guarantee loans—backing home mortgages up to as much as 90 percent, for example—to builders and home-seekers. Before this fed-

eral agency came into being, conventional banks would lend money only to builders who had already lined up home buyers (see Kenneth Jackson, *Crabgrass Frontier*). Thus, a development on the grand scale of Levittown couldn't have been built, for "without FHA insurance, Levitt could not have kept the price or the down payment as low as he did" (Gans, *The Levittowners*, 285). In *Picture Windows: How the Suburbs Happened*, Rosalyn Baxandall and Elizabeth Ewen quote *Architectural Forum*, saying that the shift in bankers' lending policies inspired by the advent of FHA guarantees "is the most important change in the character of house building finance since the appearance of the amortized mortgage and the big house lenders were not slow to recognize that it yielded what their industry has conspicuously lacked: the working capital for a large scale operation."

7. See Baxandall and Ewen, *Picture Windows*, 144.

8. Ibid., 134.

9. Jackson, *Crabgrass Frontier;* Baxandall and Ewen, *Picture Windows*.

10. Baxandall and Ewen, 147.

11. Jackson, *Crabgrass Frontier*, 236.

12. Gans, *The Levittowners*, 6–9.

13. Jackson, *Crabgrass Frontier;* Gans, *The Levittowners;* Baxandall and Ewen, *Picture Windows*.

14. Bruce Lambert, "At 50, Levittown Contends with Legacy of Racial Bias," *New York Times*, December 28, 1997.

15. See Gans, *The Levittowners*, 372. Some argue that the Levitts were simply carrying out exclusionary practices sanctioned by the government and doing what all the other lenders and builders were doing at the time. Others insist that the Levitts were personally committed to racial homogeneity. Admittedly, even though restrictive covenants were declared unconstitutional in the 1948 *Shelley v. Kraemer* Supreme Court case, the FHA continued to pump money into communities stubbornly adhering to the covenants until 1950, at which point the federal agency announced that it would no longer honor applications from deliberately segregated communities. In effect, majority-white communities had been given a two-year window in which to file new applications before the FHA would acquiesce to the court's mandate. On this point, see Harrell Rodgers and Charles Bullock, *Law and Social Change: Civil Rights Laws and Their Consequences*.

16. Historians generally confirm Matt's explanation of suburban growth, though not all of them assume a celebratory tone when assessing the impact of the national highway system and the automobile industry on the dramatic expansion of suburbia. For a fuller discussion, see Jackson, *Crabgrass Frontier*.

17. Also known as Title VIII, the Fair Housing Act (FaHA) rendered a set of established discriminatory practices unlawful. After 1968, it became illegal for real estate agents to make a home "unavailable" based on the race of the applicant or to refuse to negotiate the sale of a home to blacks. Lenders and real estate agents were barred from engaging in redlining (denying loans based on geographic location or racial composition of the neighborhood) or blockbusting (fabricating claims about sweeping changes in a neighborhood's racial composition to impel whites to sell low). After 1968, it also became illegal for lenders to discriminate against blacks during any step of the financing of a home, or the

terms of a sale. In short, the FaHA was instituted to monitor the practices of real estate agents and lenders. See George Metcalf, *Fair Housing Comes of Age;* Ronald E. Wienk, "Discrimination in Urban Credit Markets"; and John Yinger, *Closed Doors, Opportunities Lost,* for a detailed history of the FaHA. There is ongoing debate about the reach of the FaHA's mandate. Some argue that the purpose of the law is simply to eradicate discrimination in the housing market. Others claim the law was meant to go one step further, that is, to actively promote integration. For a discussion of these positions, see Alexander Polikoff, "Sustainable or Inevitable Resegregation."

18. June and Randall pooled resources with eighteen other families, mostly friends from college, and bought a large plot of land in the Lakeview area in 1961. Each family built a home there, and many of the original residents still live in this small, insular community.

19. See Juliet Saltman, *A Fragile Movement: The Struggle for Neighborhood Stabilization.*

20. Sherwood Park residents explained to me that developers match the racial composition of their sales staff to the type of home-seeker they want to attract. Thus, in communities projected to be white, the sales staff will be white. In communities projected to be black, the sales staff will be black.

21. Evan McKenzie, *Privatopia,* 128.

3. PUBLIC IDENTITIES

1. Feagin, "Continuing Significance." Feagin frames racial stigma theory as the counterpoint to Wilson's well-known "declining significance of race" argument. However, Feagin's critique is not quite accurate since Wilson readily admits that racial discrimination continues in the social sphere. It is in the economic sphere, Wilson argues, that middle-class blacks have made gains so significant that their experience can be distinguished from the labor market experiences of the black poor. See Wilson, *Declining Significance of Race.*

2. Feagin, "Continuing Significance," 108.

3. For instance, some of the blacks in Feagin's "Continuing Significance" effectively employ class-based resources—a university ID, a so-called "white" phone voice, or a connection to a prominent news station—but these encounters are given short shrift in the study's overall focus compared to those that underscore the futility of class signifiers. In a much earlier study, *Black Bourgeoisie,* Frazier documents the array of signifiers the black elite adopt to demonstrate their middle-classness to others.

4. Elijah Anderson, "The Social Situation of the Black Executive."

5. See chapter 6 for a discussion of the role neighborhoods play in sustaining middle-class identity.

6. See Anderson, *Streetwise,* especially chapter 6, "The Black Male in Public"; Brooks-Gardner, "Passing By: Street Remarks, Address Rights, and the Urban Female"; Mitchell Duneier and Harvey Molotch, "Talking City Trouble: Interactional Vandalism, Social Inequality, and the 'Urban Interaction Problem.' "

7. In Feagin's "Continuing Significance," middle-class blacks report that store employees follow them around the store as they shop.

8. On the use of credentials, see Randall Collins, *The Credential Society.*

9. See Pierre Bourdieu and Jean-Claude Passeron, *Reproduction in Education, Society, and Culture;* Bourdieu, *Distinction: A Social Critique of the Judgement of Taste;* John Katsillis and Richard Rubinson, "Cultural Capital, Student Achievement, and Educational Reproduction."

10. Karen Aschaffenburg and Ineke Maas, "Cultural and Educational Careers: The Dynamics of Social Reproduction." On the difference between economic and cultural capital, see Pierre Bourdieu's "The Forms of Capital." Long before Bourdieu, Erving Goffman argued in "Symbols of Class Status" that practices and styles of interaction such as "etiquette, dress, deportment, gesture, intonation, dialect, vocabulary, small bodily movements and . . . expressed evaluations" (300) constitute important symbols of class membership.

11. See Lareau, *Home Advantage;* Jay MacLeod, *Ain't No Makin' It.*

12. Prudence Carter, *Keepin' It Real.*

13. For a recent exception, see Lareau, *Unequal Childhoods.* She reveals how middle-class black parents communicate class position to their children; however, her study is not designed to explore the processes by which these parents acquire cultural capital.

14. Aschaffenburg and Maas, "Cultural and Educational Careers"; Bourdieu, *Distinction;* Lareau, *Home Advantage;* Matthijs Kalmijn and Gerbert Kraaykamp, "Race, Cultural Capital, and Schooling."

15. Bourdieu, "Cultural Reproduction and Social Reproduction"; Bourdieu and Passeron, *Reproduction;* Gartman, "Culture as a Class Symbolization or Mass Reification?: A Critique of Bourdieu's *Distinction.*"

16. Aschaffenburg and Maas, "Cultural and Educational Careers"; Bourdieu, *Distinction;* Lareau, *Home Advantage.*

17. Lareau, *Unequal Childhoods,* 277.

18. Paul DiMaggio, "Cultural Capital and School Success"; John Mohr and Paul DiMaggio, "The Intergenerational Transmission of Cultural Capital"; Erickson, "Culture, Class, and Connections."

19. See Elijah Anderson, "The Social Situation of the Black Executive"; Laitin, *Hegemony and Culture;* Lamont, *Money, Morals, and Manners;* Schudson, "How Culture Works"; Waters, *Black Identities;* Paul Willis, *Learning to Labor;* Young, "Navigating Race: Getting Ahead in the Lives of 'Rags to Riches' Young Black Men."

20. The subdivision known as Levittown was built on Long Island in 1947. The builders, the Levitt brothers, were the first to apply the principles of scientific management to housing construction by building tract houses from prefabricated materials. Through this process, the Levitts produced up to thirty houses per day. Consequently, houses in Levittown were cheaper to build and cheaper to buy. The Levitt brothers were so successful that they later built a second Levittown in Philadelphia. Famous for their revolutionary contribution to the construction industry, the Levitts were also infamous for their commitment to residential segregation. Restrictive covenants written into the deeds to Levittown homes limited ownership to whites. The Levitts, who were Jewish, appeared to privilege profit over racial equity, reasoning, "If we sell one house to a Negro family, then 90 to 95 percent of our white customers will not buy into the community. This is their attitude, not ours. As a company, our position is simply this:

We can solve a housing problem, or we can try to solve a racial problem, but we cannot combine the two" (Bruce Lambert, "At 50, Levittown Contends with Legacy of Racial Bias," 24). See also Gans's ethnographic study of the subdivision, *The Levittowners,* and Jackson, *Crabgrass Frontier.*

21. David Sudnow, *Ways of the Hand.*

22. On scripts, see Robert Abelson, "Psychological Status of the Script Concept," and Xavier de Souza Briggs, "Doing Democracy Up Close."

23. Thomas Kochman, *Black and White Styles in Conflict,* 106.

24. See Anderson, *The Code of the Street;* Basil Bernstein, *Class, Codes, and Control;* Pattillo-McCoy, *Black Picket Fences.*

25. For some immigrant groups, what began as code-switching later became a permanent mode of behavior. A good example of this phenomenon is the experience of Irish immigrants. A despised ethnic group when they entered the United States, the Irish used ethnic and mainstream institutions to eventually overcome the stigma associated with Irish immigrants, raising their social status from "niggers turned inside out" (Noel Ignatiev, *How the Irish Became White,* 41) to mainstream white Americans (Matthew Frye Jacobson, *Whiteness of a Different Color;* David Roediger, *The Wages of Whiteness*). Eastern European Jewish immigrants faced a similar dilemma upon their arrival in the United States. Members of the American Protestant upper class carped that they "were unwashed, uncouth, unrefined, loud, and pushy" (Sacks, "How Did Jews Become White Folks?" 82). Jews' assimilation into the mainstream resided in unrestricted access to government-backed programs—the GI Bill, the FHA—social programs that catapulted them into the middle class through educational opportunities and suburban homeownership (Jacobson, *Whiteness*; Sacks, "White Folks"). Both the Irish and Jews purged themselves of the stigma associated with their social groups as the socioeconomic status of the overall group improved. According to Sacks, "money whiten[ed]" these social groups, as class eventually become more important than race (see also Davis, *Who Is Black?*).

26. It is possible that Michelle's colleague is uncomfortable being seen with any "girl" heading into a hotel, and that his concern has more to do with gendered stereotypes than race. However, the fact that he references his own race as well as Michelle's suggests that gender is not the operative term and renders such a conclusion unlikely.

27. Erving Goffman, *The Presentation of Self in Everyday Life,* 48.

28. Much of the existing research on how blacks manage social interactions in the public sphere actually focuses on working-class blacks, not middle-class blacks. These studies explore how working-class blacks construct boundaries that allow them to preserve their dignity in potentially humiliating exchanges with whites. For example, Robin Kelley shows in *Race Rebels: Culture, Politics and the Black Working Class* that working-class black bus riders expressed their sense of entitlement as consumers of a public product through a series of "discursive strategies," from accosting conductors who disrespected them, to speaking loudly from the back of the bus so that at least their voices would spill over into the segregated sections reserved for whites, to disguising their disdain for segregated travel with humor. According to Kelley, their appeal was not so much

for integration with whites as for access to the rights that should be accorded any hard-working, American citizen. He writes, "Sitting with whites, for most black riders, was never a critical issue; rather African Americans wanted more space for themselves, they wanted to receive equitable treatment, they wanted to be personally treated with respect and dignity, they wanted to be heard and possibly understood, they wanted to get to work on time, and above all, they wanted to exercise power over institutions that controlled them or on which they were dependent" (75).

Along similar lines, Wrigley ("Is Racial Oppression Intrinsic to Domestic Work?") shows in a study of black domestic workers' interactions with their white employers that these women engage in duplicitous acts of subterfuge. A preferred tactic is "the look," where workers gaze at employers in a hostile way, a strategy that trades on whites' stereotypical understanding of how black women express anger. Other studies allude to differences in the strategies employed by lower-class and middle-class blacks. Waters reports in *Black Identities* that when a West Indian woman who had lived in the United States for ten years was told by a white friend that her employer was hiring, she went down to the store for an interview. The employer was discourteous during the meeting and denied that there were any openings. When she discovered that the employer had hired two white girls after interviewing her, she confronted him, but the extent of her confrontation was to say, "I know why you didn't hire me, but it's not a problem to me, it's a problem to you" before storming off (161). Working-class blacks lack many of the cultural resources that middle-class blacks have at their disposal to resolve racial conflict in the workplace.

29. On white working-class men's ability to cross class boundaries, see Richard Sennett and Jonathan Cobb, *The Hidden Injuries of Class*. For fictional accounts of these boundary-crossing strategies, see F. Scott Fitzgerald, *The Great Gatsby;* Philip Roth, *Goodbye, Columbus*.

30. Diane Barthel, *Putting on Appearances: Gender and Advertising*, 87.

31. Anderson, *Streetwise,* 159.

32. Fred Davis, *Fashion, Culture, and Identity,* 25.

33. Philip's comment points to the relational aspect of identity construction and to the importance of social context. In many lower-middle-class and poor neighborhoods, "being black" is *not* "a negative." For example, in her study of a neighborhood on the South Side of Chicago, Pattillo-McCoy (*Black Picket Fences*) finds that lower-middle-class youth go out of their way to dress and talk "black" in an attempt to align themselves with disadvantaged members of the community.

34. Feagin and Sikes, *Living with Racism,* 135.

35. See Sharon Collins, *Black Corporate Executives: The Making and Breaking of a Black Middle Class;* George Davis and Glegg Watson, *Black Life in Corporate America: Swimming in the Mainstream;* Edward Jones, "What It's Like to Be a Black Manager."

36. Mary Jackman, *The Velvet Glove,* 130.

37. See Collins, *Black Corporate Executives;* Ellis Cose, *The Rage of a Privileged Class;* Davis and Watson, *Black Life in Corporate America*. In *Our Sepa-*

rate Ways: Black and White Women and the Personal Struggle for Professional Identity, Ella Bell and Stella Nkomo remind us of the importance of gender variation in studies of the corporate world.

38. Douglas Massey and Garvey Lundy, "Use of Black English and Racial Discrimination in Urban Housing Markets." On linguistic profiling, see John Baugh, "Racial Identification by Speech."

39. Massey and Denton, *American Apartheid,* 138.

40. On gatekeepers, see Diana Pearce, "Gatekeepers and Homeseekers: Institutional Patterns in Racial Steering."

41. See Wienk, "Discrimination"; Margery Turner, Raymond Struyk, and John Yinger, *Housing Discrimination Study.*

42. Yinger, *Closed Doors, Opportunities Lost,* 185, and Margery Turner and Stephen Ross, "How Racial Discrimination Affects the Search for Housing."

43. Lareau, *Unequal Childhoods,* 123.

4. STATUS-BASED IDENTITIES

1. Identifying status distinctions within the black middle class is not an entirely new idea. In *Black Bourgeoisie,* his classic critique of the black middle class, Frazier identified two variables shaping status differentiation: regional variation and consumption patterns. Through comparisons of middle-class blacks in southern and northern regions, Frazier argues that in southern cities like Atlanta, Charleston, and New Orleans, middle-class blacks continued to rely on standard fare—family background and skin color—to buttress their claims to membership in the black middle class after World War I, whereas in northern cities like New York, Chicago, and Detroit (Washington, D.C. also conforms to this northern model), a different set of criteria emerged—namely, education and occupation—to supersede family of origin and light skin color as prerequisites to a middle-class status. It is this latter group of middle-class newcomers, Frazier argues, who attempted to imitate white society by engaging in conspicuous consumption. For this group, "the most important thing about one's occupation is the amount of income it brings" (165–66). Before Frazier's *Black Bourgeoisie,* Drake and Cayton conducted an intensive ethnographic study of a single black community, Bronzeville, housed on Chicago's South Side. Their oft-cited *Black Metropolis* points to the internal distinctions that middle-class blacks erected against themselves while living in the overcrowded black section of Chicago. A dimension of this study that is frequently overlooked by scholars focuses on status divisions *within* the black middle class. Based on their analysis of consumption patterns and lifestyles, Drake and Cayton divide Bronzeville's black middle class into three status groupings: the "status bearers," the "strivers and strainers," and the "shadies." Status bearers were professional blacks and business owners who managed, through judicious consumption, to survive the Depression. They perceived themselves to be superior to the middle-class blacks directly below them who "accumulated money but didn't know how to spend it with taste." This second grouping, "the strainers and strivers," were obsessed with getting ahead. Through conspicuous consumption, they demonstrated that they had made it into the folds of the middle class. The bottom group, "the shadies," was composed of individ-

uals who earned substantial income from illegal or unrespectable pursuits. Their *income* qualified shadies for a space at the top of the black middle class hierarchy, but status arbiters within the black middle class appraised their lifestyles negatively and positioned them at the bottom. In Bronzeville and elsewhere, members of the black upper classes downplayed economic criteria in their status evaluations of others, emphasizing lifestyle distinctions instead.

2. Status identity is similar to class identity. Members of a status group construct and perpetuate a similar lifestyle, one that distinguishes their group from others (see Max Weber, *Economy and Society;* Randall Collins, "Situational Stratification: A Micro-Macro Theory of Inequality"). Weber coined the term "status group" in recognition of the fact that factors other than economics can shape a group's access to power. He perceived the kind of prestige that is conferred through education or culture as more consequential than the prestige derived from ownership of the means of production. Drawing on Weber, Bourdieu advances the notion that status distinctions are upheld through cultural distinctiveness (see Bourdieu, *Distinction;* Bryan Turner, *Status*).

3. Drake and Cayton, *Black Metropolis,* 517.

4. Recent exceptions include Landry's *The New Black Middle Class,* in which he distinguishes between "upper middle class" and "lower middle class" blacks on the basis of consumption patterns (although his primary focus is comparisons between the black and the white middle class), and Sandra Smith and Mignon Moore, "Intraracial Diversity and Relations among African-Americans: Closeness among Black Students at a Predominantly White University," in which the authors find lower-middle-class black students are more likely to express a preference for close interactions with other blacks than upper-middle-class black students are.

5. See Keith Johnstone, *Impro: Improvisation and the Theatre.*

6. When surveyed or interviewed, most people, black and white, call themselves "middle-class." Income seems to have little bearing on their decision. David Halle discusses this general proclivity among white, working-class men in *America's Working Man.*

7. Katherine Newman, *No Shame in My Game,* 98.

8. Quoted in Nelson Aldrich, *Old Money,* 265.

9. On the upper class, see Susan Ostrander, *Women of the Upper Class.*

10. On wealth disparities between middle-class blacks and whites, see Oliver and Shapiro, *Black Wealth/White Wealth;* Conley, *Being Black, Living in the Red;* Ngina Chiteji, "Portfolio Choices of Parents and Their Children as Young Adults: Asset Accumulation by African American Families."

11. Andrea and Gregg spent time abroad on military assignment where she grew accustomed to shopping in the commissary. She continues to carry out the bulk of her food shopping on the military base.

12. Crystal had received by mail an offer from the Olan Mills photography studio inviting her to come in to sit for a free eight-by-ten photo. Knowing that the studio's goal is to persuade you to purchase expensive *sets* of photos rather than letting you slip away with only the complimentary eight-by-ten, Crystal, laughing at the studio's temerity, threatens, "They think that I can't walk in and pick out *one* eight-by-ten glamour shot!"

13. I was somewhat unhappy, too, because I wasn't finished interviewing Jasmine.

14. See Pattillo-McCoy, *Black Picket Fences,* on the importance of tennis shoes in black popular culture; Robin Kelley, *Yo' Mama's Disfunktional!,* on ghetto culture; and Alex Kotlowitz, "False Connections," on suburban whites' futile attempts to align themselves with ghetto blacks by donning hip-hop clothing.

5. RACE- AND CLASS-BASED IDENTITIES

1. Mary Waters, *Ethnic Options.*

2. Charles Tilly, *Durable Inequality.*

3. Gunnar Myrdal, *An American Dilemma;* James McKee, *Sociology and the Race Problem.*

4. See Waters, *Black Identities.*

5. See Katherine Neckerman, P. Carter, and J. Lee, "Segmented Assimilation and Minority Cultures of Mobility."

6. Joel Garreau, *Edge City,* 167.

7. Barth, *Ethnic Groups and Boundaries,* 12 (emphasis added).

8. See Donald Horowitz, "Ethnic Identity"; Charles Hirschmann, "America's Melting Pot Reconsidered"; Milton Yinger, "Toward a Theory of Assimilation and Dissimilation."

9. On racial pessimism, see Lois Benjamin, *The Black Elite;* Derrick Bell, *Faces at the Bottom of the Well;* Andrew Hacker, *Two Nations: Black and White, Separate, Hostile, Unequal;* Cose, *The Rage of a Privileged Class.* On wealth inequality, see Oliver and Shapiro, *Black Wealth/White Wealth;* Conley, *Being Black, Living in the Red.* On residential segregation, see Massey and Denton, *American Apartheid.* On racial animosity, see Feagin, "Continuing Significance"; Feagin and Sikes, *Living with Racism.*

10. Orlando Patterson, *The Ordeal of Integration;* Thernstrom and Thernstrom, *America in Black and White.*

11. Howard Schuman, Charlotte Steeh, and Lawrence Bobo, *Racial Attitudes in America,* 12.

12. See John Gwaltney, *Drylongso: A Self-Portrait of Black America;* Robert Blauner, *Black Lives, White Lives;* Sigelman and Welch, *Black Americans' Views of Racial Inequality;* Jennifer Hochschild, *Facing Up to the Dream.*

13. Feagin, "Continuing Significance"; Hochschild, *Facing Up to the Dream;* Sigelman and Tuch, "Metastereotypes: Blacks' Perceptions of Whites' Stereotypes of Blacks"; Young, "Navigating Race."

14. See France Winddance Twine, "A White Side of Black Britain: The Concept of Racial Literacy," for a discussion of the strategies white British mothers employ to teach their biracial children how to recognize and respond to racism. The mothers discourage their children from embracing a biracial identity. They assume that a biracial identity is a distraction in racist encounters and therefore encourage the development a black racial identity instead. Twine refers to this teaching and learning transaction as "racial literacy."

15. Landry, *The New Black Middle Class,* 79. See also Earl Lewis, *In Their Own Interests: Race, Class, and Power in Twentieth-Century Norfolk, Virginia.*

16. Graham, *Our Kind of People,* 152–53. See also classic studies such as

W. E. B. DuBois, *The Philadelphia Negro;* Drake and Cayton, *Black Metropolis;* Frazier, *Black Bourgeoisie.* On memoirs, see Lorene Cary, *Black Ice;* Jill Nelson, *Volunteer Slavery: My Authentic Negro Experience;* Nathan McCall, *Makes Me Wanna Holler;* Samuel Fulwood, *Waking from the Dream.* See also Beverly Daniel Tatum, *"Why Are All the Blacks Kids Sitting Together in the Cafeteria?" and Other Conversations about Race.*

17. DuBois intended the term "double consciousness" to reflect the tension he believed black Americans experience as they negotiate two "unreconciled" identities: their status as Americans and their status as blacks. The structure of race relations in American society, he argued, created in blacks a unique "second-sight . . . this sense of always looking at one's self through the eyes of others" (*The Souls of Black Folk,* 16–17).

18. On this point, see Claire Alexander, *The Art of Being Black.*

19. Note that the socialization concerns expressed by the black parents who participated in the study reflect their middle-class position and thus differ considerably from those of poor and lower-middle-class black parents in predominantly black neighborhoods. See Anderson, *The Code of the Street;* Pattillo-McCoy, *Black Picket Fences.*

20. Robert Merton, "Insiders and Outsiders: A Chapter in the Sociology of Knowledge."

21. On ontological blackness, see Victor Anderson, *Beyond Ontological Blackness.* On feminists' construction of a common oppression, see Diana Fuss, *Essentially Speaking.*

22. See Paul Gilroy, *Small Acts.* Gilroy's "interpretive community" parallels Benedict Anderson's notion of an "imagined community" in which members feel a strong connection to one another on the basis of nationality, despite the fact that they may never actually speak to or have contact with most members of their community. Race and ethnicity theorists have appropriated Anderson's concept in order to examine membership loyalties in racial communities.

23. See Keith and Herring, "Skin Tone and Stratification," for a detailed discussion of the effect of skin tone on blacks' social mobility patterns.

24. See Drake and Cayton *Black Metropolis,* 689, and Kevin Gaines, *Uplifting the Race.*

25. Researchers disagree as to whether middle-class blacks have been able to isolate themselves from the poor or whether persistent discrimination in the housing market denies blacks this option. In *American Apartheid,* Massey and Denton argue that middle-class blacks have had far less success in this regard than their white counterparts. See Yinger, *Closed Doors, Opportunities Lost;* Pattillo-McCoy, *Black Picket Fences;* and Turner, Struyk, and Yinger, *Housing Discrimination Study,* for a detailed discussion of the impact of housing discrimination on blacks' residential options.

26. Pattillo-McCoy, *Black Picket Fences;* Kotlowitz, "False Connections," 257.

27. Orlando Patterson, "Toward a Future That Has No Past: Reflections on the Fate of Blacks in the Americas" (30, emphasis added). Also see J. Martin Favor, *Authentic Blackness.*

28. For a critique of this extraordinarily popular idea that black popular culture is representative of blacks generally, see Kelley, *Yo' Mama's Disfunktional!*

29. Katherine Newman, *Falling from Grace,* 76.

30. Drake and Cayton, *Black Metropolis.*

31. On perceptions of appropriate behavior among the white working class, see Maria Kefalas, *Working-Class Heroes.*

32. "Sapphire" is a negative depiction of black women. According to K. Sue Jewell, "The most notable characteristic of Sapphire is her sassiness which is exceeded only by her verbosity. She is also noted for telling people off, and spouting her opinion in an animated loud manner. Because of her intense expressiveness and hands-on-hip, finger-pointing style, Sapphire is viewed as comedic and is never taken seriously" (45).

33. See Hochschild, *Facing Up to the American Dream;* Mary Jackman and Robert Jackman, *Class Awareness in the United States;* Landry, *The New Black Middle Class;* Reeve Vanneman and Lynn Cannon, *The American Perception of Class;* Wilson, *The Declining Significance of Race.*

34. In *Slim's Table,* Mitchell Duneier argues persuasively that this emphasis on polarization between middle-class and poor blacks results in an unfortunate oversimplification of the black class structure. What is lost in such an analysis, he contends, is sustained attention to the values, lifestyle choices, and mechanisms of social control that characterize black working-class communities.

35. This is in marked contrast to Sherwood Park, where commercial vehicles are not allowed in driveways or on the streets unless there is a service worker present.

6. SUBURBAN IDENTITIES

1. The authors argue further that middle-class families struggle financially not because they spend excessively on extras, but because they spend a higher percentage of their wages than they can reasonably afford on expensive housing in desirable school districts.

2. Richard Moe and Carter Wilkie, *Changing Places: Rebuilding Community in the Age of Sprawl,* 12.

3. Moe and Wilkie, *Changing Places,* 9–10. The fact that tourists can already experience slavery reenactments in Colonial Williamsburg, Virginia, may have also factored into Disney's decision to abandon the project.

4. See Eugene Meyer, "Tax Rebellion in Prince George's Appears to Be Working"; *Washington Post,* "Prince George's County Council"; Michel McQueen, "Prince George's County Task Force Wants to Ease TRIM Property Tax Lid."

5. Jackson Diehl, "P.G. Officials Say TRIM Won't Aid Homeowners Soon"; Margaret Shapiro and Michel McQueen, "An Elusive Goal: After Five Years, P.G. Homeowners Still Await Benefits from Tax Revolt."

6. Jackson Diehl, "Hogan's Budget, Reflecting TRIM, Cuts Program Spending," "TRIM Brings Change to P.G. Government and Its Services"; Michel McQueen and Leon Wynter, "TRIM Bite in P.G. Services Is Largest Ever"; Leon Wynter, "TRIM Vote Forcing P.G. Schools to Take Hard Look at Education."

7. *Washington Post,* "From TRIM to Pinch and Patch"; Gwen Ifill, "Elected

P.G. Officials Stay in Background of TRIM Battle"; McQueen, "Losing Effort to Revise TRIM Cost Sixteen Times Victors' Budget."

8. McQueen and Wynter, "TRIM Bite in P.G. Services."

9. David Montgomery, "Staying Power in P.G.: TRIM Remains Untouchable amid Budget Crisis"; McQueen and Wynter, "TRIM Bite in P.G. Services."

10. See McQueen and Wynter, "TRIM Bite in P.G. Services."

11. Gary Orfield and Susan Eaton, *Dismantling Desegregation: The Quiet Reversal of* Brown v. Board of Education.

CONCLUSION

1. Oliver and Shapiro, *Black Wealth/White Wealth*, 2.

2. For a discussion of how black males negotiate public spaces, see Anderson, *Streetwise*. On the ambivalence working-class whites feel about integrating into the middle-class mainstream, see Sennett and Cobb, *The Hidden Injuries of Class*.

References

Abelson, Robert. 1981. "Psychological Status of the Script Concept." *American Psychologist* 36: 715–29.

Adelman, Robert. 2004. "Neighborhood Opportunities, Race, and Class: The Black Middle Class and Residential Segregation." *City and Community* 3: 43–63.

Alba, Richard, ed. 1989. *Ethnicity and Race in the U.S.A.* New York: Routledge.

———. 1990. *Ethnic Identity.* New Haven, Conn.: Yale University Press.

———. 1995. "Assimilation's Quiet Tide." *Public Interest* 119: 3–19.

Alba, Richard, John Logan, and Brian Stults. 2000. "How Segregated Are Middle-Class African Americans?" *Social Problems* 47: 543–58.

Aldrich, Nelson Jr. [1988] 1996. *Old Money.* New York: Allworth Press.

Alexander, Claire. 1996. *The Art of Being Black.* Oxford, Eng.: Clarendon Press.

Allen, Walter, and Reynolds Farley. 1986. "The Shifting Social and Economic Tides of Black America, 1950–1980." *Annual Review of Sociology* 12: 277–306.

Anderson, Benedict. 1991. *Imagined Communities: Reflections on the Origin and Spread of Nationalism.* London: Verso.

Anderson, Elijah. 1990. *Streetwise.* Chicago: University of Chicago Press.

———. 1999a. *The Code of the Street.* New York: W. W. Norton.

———. 1999b. "The Social Situation of the Black Executive." In *The Cultural Territories of Race: Black and White Boundaries,* edited by Michele Lamont. Chicago: University of Chicago Press.

Anderson, Victor. 1995. *Beyond Ontological Blackness.* New York: Continuum.

Armour, Jody. 1997. *Negrophobia and Reasonable Racism.* New York: New York University Press.

Aschaffenburg, Karen, and Ineke Maas. 1997. "Cultural and Educational Careers: The Dynamics of Social Reproduction." *American Sociological Review* 62: 573–87.

Baldassare, Mark. 1992. "Suburban Communities." *Annual Review of Sociology* 18: 475–94.

Barth, Fredrik, ed. 1969. *Ethnic Groups and Boundaries*. Boston: Little Brown.

Barthel, Diane. 1988. *Putting on Appearances: Gender and Advertising.* Philadelphia: Temple University Press.

Baugh, John. 2000. "Racial Identification by Speech." *American Speech* 75: 362–64.

Baumgartner, M. P. 1988. *The Moral Order of a Suburb*. New York: Oxford University Press.

Baxandall, Rosalyn, and Elizabeth Ewen. 2000. *Picture Windows: How the Suburbs Happened*. New York: Basic Books.

Bell, Derrick. 1992. *Faces at the Bottom of the Well: The Permanence of Racism.* New York: Basic Books.

Bell, Ella, and Stella Nkomo. 2001. *Our Separate Ways: Black and White Women and the Personal Struggle for Professional Identity*. Boston: Harvard Business School.

Benjamin, Lois. 1991. *The Black Elite*. Chicago: Nelson-Hall.

Bernstein, Basil. 1971. *Class, Codes, and Control*. London: Routledge and K. Paul.

Billingsley, Andrew. 1968. *Black Families in White America*. New York: Prentice Hall.

Blackwell, James. 1975. *The Black Community: Diversity and Unity*. New York: Harper & Row.

Blauner, Robert. 1989. *Black Lives, White Lives: Three Decades of Race Relations in America*. Berkeley: University of California Press.

Blumer, Herbert. 1958. "Race Prejudice as a Sense of Group Position." *Pacific Sociological Review* 1: 3–7.

Bobo, Lawrence, and Devon Johnson. 1998. "Race, Class, and Whites' Stereotypes of Blacks: The Changing Significance of Race." Unpublished manuscript.

Bourdieu, Pierre. 1977. "Cultural Reproduction and Social Reproduction." In *Power and Ideology in Education,* edited by Jerome Kardbel and A. H. Halsey. New York: Oxford University Press.

———. 1984. *Distinction: A Social Critique of the Judgement of Taste*. Cambridge, Mass.: Harvard University Press.

———. 1986. "The Forms of Capital." In *Handbook of Theory and Research for the Sociology of Education,* edited by John G. Richardson. Westport, Conn.: Greenwood Press.

Bourdieu, Pierre, and Jean-Claude Passeron. 1977. *Reproduction in Education, Society, and Culture*. Beverly Hills, Calif.: Sage.

Bourgois, Felipe. 1995. *In Search of Respect: Selling Crack in el Barrio*. Cambridge, Eng.: Cambridge University Press.

Briggs, Xavier de Souza. 1998. "Doing Democracy Up Close: Culture, Power, and Communication in Community Building." *Journal of Planning Education and Research* 18: 1–13.

Bryson, Bethany. 1996. " 'Anything but Heavy Metal': Symbolic Exclusion and Musical Dislikes." *American Sociological Review* 61: 884–99.

Burawoy, Michael, ed. 1991. *Ethnography Unbound*. Berkeley: University of California Press.

Carter, Prudence. 2005. *Keepin' It Real: School Success beyond Black and White*. New York: Oxford University Press.

Cary, Lorene. 1991. *Black Ice*. New York: Alfred A. Knopf.

Cerulo, Karen. 1997. "Identity Construction: New Issues, New Directions." *Annual Review of Sociology* 23: 385–409.

Charles, Camille Zubrinsky. 2005. "Can We Live Together? Racial Preferences and Neighborhood Outcomes." In *The Geography of Opportunity*, edited by Xavier de Souza Briggs. Washington, D.C.: Brookings Institution Press.

Chicago Fact Book Consortium. 1990. *Local Community Fact Book*. Chicago: University of Illinois.

Chiteji, Ngina. 1999. "Portfolio Choices of Parents and Their Children as Young Adults: Asset Accumulation by African American Families." *American Economic Review* 89: 377–80.

Clay, Philip. 1979. "The Process of Black Suburbanization." *Urban Affairs Quarterly* 14: 405–24.

Cohen, Cathy. 1999. *The Boundaries of Blackness: AIDS and the Breakdown of Black Politics*. Chicago: University of Chicago Press.

Collins, Randall. 1979. *The Credential Society*. New York: Academic Press.

———. 2000. "Situational Stratification: A Micro-Macro Theory of Inequality." *Sociological Theory* 18: 17–43.

Collins, Sharon. 1997. *Black Corporate Executives: The Making and Breaking of a Black Middle Class*. Philadelphia: Temple University Press.

Conley, Dalton. 1999. *Being Black, Living in the Red*. Berkeley: University of California Press.

Connolly, Harold. 1973. "Black Movement into the Suburbs: Suburbs Doubling Their Black Populations During the 1960s." *Urban Affairs Quarterly* 9: 91–111.

Cornell, Stephen, and Douglas Hartmann. 1998. *Ethnicity and Race: Making Identities in a Changing World*. Thousand Oaks, Calif.: Pine Forge Press.

Cose, Ellis. 1993. *The Rage of a Privileged Class*. New York: Harper Perennial.

Darden, Joe, and Sameh Kamel. 2000. "Black Residential Segregation in the City and Suburbs of Detroit: Does Socioeconomic Status Matter?" *Journal of Urban Affairs* 22: 1–13.

Davis, F. James. 1991. *Who Is Black?* University Park: Pennsylvania State University Press.

Davis, Fred. 1992. *Fashion, Culture, and Identity*. Chicago: University of Chicago Press.

Davis, George, and Glegg Watson. 1982. *Black Life in Corporate America: Swimming in the Mainstream*. Garden City, N.Y.: Anchor Press/Doubleday.

Dawson, Michael. 1994. *Behind the Mule: Race and Class in African American Politics*. Princeton, N.J.: Princeton University Press.

Dent, David. 1992. "The New Black Suburbs." *New York Times Magazine*, June 14.

Diehl, Jackson. 1978. "P.G. Officials Say TRIM Won't Aid Homeowners Soon." *Washington Post*, December 1.

————. 1979. "Hogan's Budget, Reflecting TRIM, Cuts Program Spending." *Washington Post*, April 1.

————. 1979. "TRIM Brings Change to P.G. Government and Its Services; Prince George's Learning Fast What TRIM Means to County." *Washington Post*, January 22.

DiMaggio, Paul. 1982. "Cultural Capital and School Success: The Impact of Status Culture Participation on the Grades of U.S. High School Students." *American Sociological Review* 47: 189–201.

DiMaggio, Paul, and Frances Ostrower. 1990. "Participation in the Arts by Black and White Americans." *Social Forces* 68(3): 753–78.

Douglas, Mary. [1970] 1996. *Natural Symbols*. New York: Routledge.

Drake, St. Clair, and Horace Cayton. [1945] 1993. *Black Metropolis*. Chicago: University of Chicago Press.

DuBois, W. E. B. [1868] 1996. *The Philadelphia Negro*. Philadelphia: University of Pennsylvania Press.

————. [1903] 1961. *The Souls of Black Folk*. Greenwich, Conn.: Fawcett.

————. [1940] 1997. *Dusk of Dawn: An Essay toward an Autobiography of a Race Concept*. New Brunswick, N.J.: Transaction Publishers.

Duneier, Mitchell. 1992. *Slim's Table*. Chicago: University of Chicago Press.

Duneier, Mitchell, and Harvey Molotch. 1999. "Talking City Trouble: Interactional Vandalism, Social Inequality, and the 'Urban Interaction Problem.'" *American Journal of Sociology* 104: 1263–95.

Ellen, Ingrid. 2000. *Sharing America's Neighborhoods: The Prospects for Stable Racial Integration*. Cambridge, Mass.: Harvard University Press.

Epstein, Cynthia. 1992. "Tinkerbells and Pinups: The Construction and Reconstruction of Gender Boundaries at Work." In *Cultivating Differences*, edited by M. Lamont and M. Fournier. Chicago: University of Chicago Press.

Erickson, Bonnie. 1996. "Culture, Class, and Connections." *American Journal of Sociology* 102: 217–31.

Farley, Reynolds. 1970. "The Changing Distribution of Negroes Within Metropolitan Areas: The Emergence of Black Suburbs." *American Journal of Sociology* 75: 512–29.

Farley, Reynolds, Sheldon Danziger, and Harry Holzer. 2000. *Detroit Divided*. New York: Russell Sage Foundation.

Farley, Reynolds, and William Frey. 1994. "Changes in the Segregation of Whites from Blacks during the 1980s: Small Steps toward a More Integrated Society." *American Sociological Review* 59: 23–45.

Farley, Reynolds, Charlotte Steeh, Maria Krysan, Tara Jackson, and Keith Reeves. 1994. "Stereotypes and Segregation: Neighborhoods in the Detroit Area." *American Journal of Sociology* 100: 750–80.

Favor, J. Martin. 1999. *Authentic Blackness: The Folk in the New Negro Renaissance*. Durham: Duke University Press.

Feagin, Joe. 1991. "The Continuing Significance of Race: Antiblack Discrimination in Public Places." *American Sociological Review* 56: 101–16.

Feagin, Joe, and Melvin Sikes. 1994. *Living with Racism: The Black Middle-Class Experience*. Boston: Beacon Press.

Fitzgerald, F. Scott. [1925] 1991. *The Great Gatsby.* New York: Simon & Schuster.

Frankenberg, Ruth. 1993. *The Social Construction of Whiteness.* Minneapolis: University of Minnesota Press.

Franklin, Raymond. 1991. *Shadows of Race and Class.* Minneapolis: University of Minnesota Press.

Frazier, E. Franklin. 1939. *The Negro Family in the United States.* Chicago: University of Chicago Press.

———. 1957. *Black Bourgeoisie.* New York: Collier Books.

Frey, William. Summer 2000. "The New Urban Demographics." *The Brookings Review* 18: 20–23.

———. 2002. "The New Suburbanization." *American Enterprise* 13: 43.

Fulwood, Samuel. 1996. *Waking from the Dream.* New York: Doubleday.

Fuss, Diana. 1989. *Essentially Speaking.* New York: Routledge.

Gaines, Kevin. 1996. *Uplifting the Race: Black Leadership, Politics, and Culture in the Twentieth Century.* Chapel Hill: University of North Carolina Press.

Gale, Dennis. 1987. *Washington, D.C.: Inner-City Revitalization and Minority Suburbanization.* Philadelphia: Temple University Press.

Gans, Herbert. 1967. *The Levittowners.* New York: Pantheon Books.

———. 1979. "Symbolic Ethnicity: The Future of Ethnic Groups and Cultures in America." *Ethnic and Racial Studies* 2: 1–20.

Garreau, Joel. 1987. "A Middle-Class without Precedent: Transcending Race Barriers and Living the American Dream." *Washington Post,* November 29.

———. 1991. *Edge City: Life on the New Frontier.* New York: Doubleday.

Gartman, David. 1991. "Culture as Class Symbolization or Mass Reification? A Critique of Bourdieu's *Distinction.*" *American Journal of Sociology* 97: 421–48.

Gatewood, Willard Jr. 1988. "Aristocrats of Color South and North: The Black Elite, 1880–1920." *Journal of Southern History* 54: 3–20.

Gieryn, Thomas. 1983. "Boundary-Work and the Demarcation of Science from Non-Science." *American Sociological Review* 48: 781–95.

Gilroy, Paul. 1993. *Small Acts.* London: Serpent's Tail.

Goffman, Erving. 1951. "Symbols of Class Status." *British Journal of Sociology* 2: 291–304.

———. 1959. *The Presentation of Self in Everyday Life.* New York: Doubleday.

———. 1963. *Stigma: Notes on the Management of a Spoiled Identity.* Englewood Cliffs, N.J.: Prentice-Hall.

Gordon, Milton. 1964. *Assimilation in American Life: The Role of Race, Religion, and National Origins.* New York: Oxford University Press.

Graham, Lawrence Otis. 1999. *Our Kind of People.* New York: Harper Collins.

Gregory, Steven. 1998. *Black Corona.* Princeton, N.J.: Princeton University Press.

Gwaltney, John. 1980. *Drylongso: A Self-Portrait of Black America.* New York: Vintage Books.

Hacker, Andrew. 1992. *Two Nations: Black and White, Separate, Hostile, Unequal.* New York: Ballantine Books.

Halle, David. 1984. *America's Working Man: Work, Home, and Politics among Blue-Collar Property Owners.* Chicago: University of Chicago Press.

Hannerz, Ulf. 1969. *Soulside.* New York: Columbia University Press.

Hartinger, John Jr. 1999. *Racial Situations: Class Predicaments of Whiteness in Detroit.* Princeton, N.J.: Princeton University Press.

Haynes, Bruce. 2001. *Red Lines, Black Spaces: The Politics of Race and Space in a Black Middle-Class Suburb.* New Haven, Conn.: Yale University Press.

Higginbotham, Elizabeth, and L. Weber. 1992. "Moving Up with Kin and Community: Upward Social Mobility for Black and White Women." *Gender and Society* 6: 416–40.

Hirschmann, Charles. 1983. "America's Melting Pot Reconsidered." *Annual Review of Sociology* 9: 397–423.

Hochschild, Jennifer. 1995. *Facing Up to the Dream.* Princeton, N.J.: Princeton University Press.

Horowitz, Donald. 1975. "Ethnic Identity." In *Ethnicity: Theory and Experience,* edited by N. Glazer and D. Moynihan. Cambridge, Mass.: Harvard University Press.

Hughes, Everett. 1945. "Dilemmas and Contradictions of Status." *American Journal of Sociology* 50: 353–59.

Ifill, Gwen. 1984. "Elected P.G. Officials Stay in Background of TRIM Battle." *Washington Post,* October 14.

Ignatiev, Noel. 1995. *How the Irish Became White.* New York: Routledge.

Inniss, Leslie, and Joe Feagin. 1995. "The Cosby Show: The View from the Black Middle Class." *Journal of Black Studies* 25: 692–711.

Jackman, Mary. 1994. *The Velvet Glove.* Berkeley: University of California Press.

Jackman, Mary, and Robert Jackman. 1983. *Class Awareness in the United States.* Berkeley: University of California Press.

Jackson, John L. 2001. *Harlemworld.* Chicago: University of Chicago Press.

Jackson, Kenneth. 1985. *Crabgrass Frontier: The Suburbanization of the United States.* New York: Oxford University Press.

Jacobson, Matthew Frye. 1998. *Whiteness of a Different Color.* Cambridge, Mass.: Harvard University Press.

Jargowsky, Paul. 1996. "Take the Money and Run: Economic Segregation in U.S. Metropolitan Areas." *American Sociological Review* 61: 984–98.

Jenkins, Richard. 1996. *Social Identity.* London: Routledge.

Jewell, K. Sue. 1993. *From Mammy to Miss America and Beyond: Cultural Images and the Shaping of U.S. Social Policy.* New York: Routledge.

Johnson, Mark. 1993. *Moral Imagination.* Chicago: University of Chicago Press.

Johnson, Valerie. 2002. *Black Power in the Suburbs.* Albany: State University of New York Press.

Johnstone, Keith. 1981. *Impro: Improvisation and the Theatre.* London: Eyre Theatre.

Jones, Edward W. July 1973. "What It's Like to Be a Black Manager." *Harvard Business Review.*

Kalmijn, Matthijs, and Gerbert Kraaykamp. 1996. "Race, Cultural Capital, and

Schooling: An Analysis of Trends in the U.S." *Sociology of Education* 69: 22–35.

Kasinitz, Philip. 1992. *Caribbean New York.* Ithaca, N.Y.: Cornell University Press.

Katsillis, John, and Richard Rubinson. 1990. "Cultural Capital, Student Achievement, and Educational Reproduction: The Case of Greece." *American Sociological Review* 55: 270–80.

Kefalas, Maria. 2003. *Working-Class Heroes: Protecting Home, Community, and Nation in a Chicago Neighborhood.* Berkeley: University of California Press.

Keith, Verna, and C. Herring. 1991. "Skin Tone and Stratification in the Black Community." *American Journal of Sociology* 97: 760–78.

Kelley, Robin. 1994. *Race Rebels: Culture, Politics and the Black Working Class.* New York: The Free Press.

———. 1997. *Yo' Mama's Disfunktional!* Boston: Beacon Press.

Kenny, Lorraine. 2000. *Daughters of Suburbia: Growing Up White, Middle Class, and Female.* New Brunswick, N.J.: Rutgers University Press.

Kirschmann, Joleen, and Kathryn Neckerman. 1991. " 'We'd Love to Hire Them But . . .': The Meaning of Race for Employers." In *The Urban Underclass,* edited by C. Jencks and P. Peterson. Washington, D.C.: Brookings Institute.

Kochhar, Rakesh, Roberto Suro, and Sonya Tafoya. 2005. *The New Latino South: The Context and Consequences of Rapid Population Growth.* Washington, D.C.: Pew Hispanic Center.

Kochman, Thomas. 1981. *Black and White Styles in Conflict.* Chicago: University of Chicago Press.

Kotlowitz, Alex. 2000. "False Connections." In *The Consumer Society,* edited by J. Schor and D. Holt. New York: The New Press.

Kronus, Sidney. 1971. *The Black Middle Class.* Columbus, Ohio: Charles E. Merrill.

Krysan, Maria. 2002. "Community Undesirability in Black and White: Examining Racial Residential Preferences through Community Perceptions." *Social Problems* 49: 521–43.

Krysan, Maria, and Reynolds Farley. 2002. "The Residential Preferences of Blacks: Do They Explain Persistent Segregation?" *Social Forces* 80: 937–80.

Lacy, Karyn. 2000. "Negotiating Black Identities: The Construction and Use of Symbolic Boundaries Among Middle-Class Black Suburbanites." PhD diss., Harvard University.

———. 2002. " 'A Part of the Neighborhood?': Negotiating Race in American Suburbs." *International Journal of Sociology and Public Policy* 22: 39–74.

Laitin, David. 1986. *Hegemony and Culture.* Chicago: University of Chicago Press.

Lambert, Bruce. 1997. "At 50, Levittown Contends with Legacy of Racial Bias." *New York Times,* December 28.

Lamont, Michele. 1992. *Money, Morals, and Manners.* Chicago: University of Chicago Press.

———. 1999a. " 'Above People Above'? Status and Worth among White and

Black Workers." In *The Cultural Territories of Race: Black and White Boundaries*, edited by Michele Lamont. Chicago: University of Chicago Press.

———, ed. 1999b. *The Cultural Territories of Race: Black and White Boundaries*. Chicago: University of Chicago Press.

———. 2000. *The Dignity of Working Men: Morality and the Boundaries of Race, Class, and Immigration*. Cambridge, Mass.: Harvard University Press and Russell Sage.

Lamont, Michele, and R. Wuthnow. 1990. "Recent Cultural Sociology in Europe and the United States." In *Frontiers of Social Theory*, edited by G. Ritzer. New York: Columbia University Press.

Landry, Bart. 1987. *The New Black Middle Class*. Berkeley: University of California Press.

Lareau, Annette. 1989. *Home Advantage*. New York: Farmer Press.

———. 2003. *Unequal Childhoods*. Berkeley: University of California Press.

LeMasters, E. E. 1975. *Blue-Collar Aristocrats: Life-Styles at a Working-Class Tavern*. Madison: University of Wisconsin Press.

Levine, Hillel, and Lawrence Harmon. 1992. *The Death of a Jewish American Community: A Tragedy of Good Intentions*. New York: The Free Press.

Lewis, Earl. 1991. *In Their Own Interests: Race, Class, and Power in Twentieth-Century Norfolk, Virginia*. Berkeley: University of California Press.

Lieberson, Stanley. 1980. *A Piece of the Pie*. Berkeley: University of California Press.

———. 1989. "Unhyphenated Whites in the United States." In *Ethnicity and Race in the U.S.A.*, edited by Richard Alba. New York: Routledge.

Logan, John, and Richard Alba. 1993. "Locational Returns to Human Capital: Minority Access to Suburban Community Resources." *Demography* 30: 243–68.

———. 1995. "Who Lives in Affluent Suburbs? Racial Differences in Eleven Metropolitan Regions." *Sociological Focus* 28: 353–64.

Logan, John, Richard Alba, and Shu-Yin Leung. 1996. "Minority Access to White Suburbs: A Multiregional Comparison." *Social Forces* 74: 851–81.

Logan, John, and Mark Schneider. 1984. "Racial Segregation and Racial Change in American Suburbs, 1970–1980." *American Journal of Sociology* 89: 874–88.

MacIntyre, Alasdair. 1984. *After Virtue: A Study in Moral Theory*. Notre Dame, Ind.: University of Notre Dame Press.

MacLeod, Jay. [1987] 1995. *Ain't No Makin' It: Aspirations and Attainment in a Low-Income Neighborhood*. Boulder, Colo.: Westview Press.

Massey, Douglas, Gretchen Condran, and Nancy Denton. 1987. "The Effect of Residential Segregation on Black Social and Economic Well-Being." *Social Forces* 66: 29–56.

Massey, Douglas, and Nancy Denton. 1987. "Trends in the Residential Segregation of Blacks, Hispanics, and Asians: 1970–1980." *American Sociological Review* 52: 802–25.

———. 1993. *American Apartheid*. Cambridge, Mass.: Harvard University Press.

Massey, Douglas, and Mary Fischer. 1999. "Does Rising Income Bring Integration? New Results for Blacks, Hispanics, and Asians in 1990." *Social Science Research* 28: 316–26.

Massey, Douglas, and Garvey Lundy. 2001. "Use of Black English and Racial Discrimination in Urban Housing Markets." *Urban Affairs Review* 36: 470–96.

McAdam, Doug. 1982. *Political Process and the Development of Black Insurgency, 1930–1970.* Chicago: University of Chicago Press.

McCall, Nathan. 1994. *Makes Me Wanna Holler.* New York: Random House.

McKee, James. 1993. *Sociology and the Race Problem.* Urbana: University of Illinois Press.

McKenzie, Evan. 1996. *Privatopia: Homeowner Associations and the Rise of Residential Private Government.* New Haven: Yale University Press.

McQueen, Michel. 1982. "Losing Effort to Revise TRIM Cost Sixteen Times Victors' Budget." *Washington Post,* December 15.

———. 1983. "Prince George's County Task Force Wants to Ease TRIM Property Tax Lid." *Washington Post,* November 1.

McQueen, Michel, and Leon Wynter. 1982. "TRIM Bite in P.G. Services Is Largest Ever." *Washington Post,* June 7.

Meier, August, and Elliot Rudwick. 1970. *From Plantation to Ghetto.* New York: Hill and Wang.

Merton, Robert. 1972. "Insiders and Outsiders: A Chapter in the Sociology of Knowledge." *American Journal of Sociology* 78 (1972): 9–47.

Metcalf, George. 1988. *Fair Housing Comes of Age.* New York: Greenwood Press.

Meyer, Eugene. 1981. "Tax Rebellion in Prince George's Appears to Be Working." *Washington Post,* May 26.

———. 1996. "Guide to Prince George's County." *Washington Post,* May 16.

Mills, C. Wright. 1951. *White Collar: The American Middle Classes.* New York: Oxford University Press.

Milner, Murray. 1994. *Status and Sacredness.* New York: Oxford University Press.

Moe, Richard, and Carter Wilkie. 1997. *Changing Places: Rebuilding Community in the Age of Sprawl.* New York: Henry Holt.

Mohr, John, and Paul DiMaggio. 1995. "The Intergenerational Transmission of Cultural Capital." *Research in Social Stratification and Mobility* 14: 167–99.

Montgomery, David. 1995. "Staying Power in P.G.: TRIM Remains Untouchable amid Budget Crisis." *Washington Post,* February 26.

Myrdal, Gunnar. [1944] 1962. *An American Dilemma: The Negro Problem and Modern Democracy.* New York: Harper and Row.

Nagel, Joane. 1994. "Constructing Ethnicity: Creating and Recreating Ethnic Identity and Culture." *Social Problems* 41: 1001–26.

———. 1995. "American Indian Ethnic Renewal: Politics and the Resurgence of Identity." *American Sociological Review* 60: 947–65.

Neckerman, Katherine, P. Carter, and J. Lee. 1999. "Segmented Assimilation and Minority Cultures of Mobility." *Ethnic and Racial Studies* 22: 945–65.

Nelson, Jill. 1993. *Volunteer Slavery: My Authentic Negro Experience.* Chicago: Noble Press.

Netherton, Ross, and Nan Netherton. 1989. *Fairfax County in Virginia: A Pictorial History.* Norfolk, Va.: Donning Company Publishers.

Newman, Katherine. 1988. *Falling from Grace.* New York: The Free Press.

———. 1993. *Declining Fortunes.* New York: Basic Books.

———. 1999. *No Shame in My Game.* New York: Vintage Books.

Norris, Michele. 1991. "A Shift to Middle Class: Black Influx Boosting Economy." *Washington Post,* March 3.

———. 1991. "Glendening Dares to Tread on Sanctity of Property Taxes." *Washington Post,* April 1.

Ogbu, John. 1990. "Minority Status and Literacy in Comparative Perspective." *Daedalus* 119: 141–68.

O'Hare, William, and William Frey. 1992. "Booming, Suburban, and Black." *American Demographics* 14: 30–38.

Oldenburg, Ray. [1989] 1997. *The Great Good Place: Cafés, Coffee Shops, Community Centers, Beauty Parlors, General Stores, Bars, and Hangouts and How They Get You through the Day.* New York: Marlowe.

Oliver, Melvin, and Thomas Shapiro. 1995. *Black Wealth/White Wealth: A New Perspective on Racial Inequality.* New York: Routledge.

Orfield, Gary, and Susan Eaton. 1996. *Dismantling Desegregation: The Quiet Reversal of Brown v. Board of Education.* New York: The New Press.

Ostrander, Susan. 1984. *Women of the Upper Class.* Philadelphia: Temple University Press.

Owens, Michael, and David Wright. 1998. "The Diversity of Majority-Black Neighborhoods." *Rockefeller Institute Bulletin* 8: 1–20.

Park, Robert. [1926] 1950. *Race and Culture.* Glencoe, Ill.: Free Press.

Parkin, Frank. 1979. *Marxism and Class Theory: A Bourgeois Critique.* New York: Columbia University Press.

Patterson, Orlando. 1972. "Toward a Future That Has No Past: Reflections on the Fate of Blacks in the Americas." *Public Interest* 27: 25–62.

———. 1997. *The Ordeal of Integration.* Washington, D.C.: Civitas.

Pattillo, Mary. 1998. "Sweet Mothers and Gangbangers: Managing Crime in a Black Middle-Class Neighborhood." *Social Forces* 76: 747–74.

Pattillo-McCoy, Mary. 1998. "Church Culture as a Strategy of Action in the Black Community." *American Sociological Review* 63: 767–84.

———. 1999. *Black Picket Fences.* Chicago: University of Chicago Press.

Pearce, Diana. 1979. "Gatekeepers and Homeseekers: Institutional Patterns in Racial Steering." *Social Problems* 26: 325–42.

Peterson, Richard, and A. Simkus. 1992. "How Musical Tastes Mark Occupational Status Groups." In *Cultivating Differences,* edited by M. Lamont and M. Fournier. Chicago: University of Chicago Press.

Pettigrew, Thomas. 1981. "Race and Class in the 1980s: An Interactive View." *Daedalus* 110: 233–55.

Phelan, Thomas, and Mark Schneider. 1996. "Race, Ethnicity, and Class in American Suburbs." *Urban Affairs Review* 31: 659–80.

Plotz, David. 1993. "The Resurrection of Marion Barry." *Washington City Paper* 13: 26–34.

Polikoff, Alexander. 1986. "Sustainable Integration or Inevitable Resegregation." In *Housing Desegregation and Federal Policy,* edited by John Goering. Chapel Hill: University of North Carolina Press.

Pomerantz, Gary. 1996. *Where Peachtree Meets Sweet Auburn.* New York: Penguin Books.

Portes, Alejandro, and Min Zhou. 1993. "The New Second Generation: Segmented Assimilation and Its Variants." *Annals of the American Academy of Political and Social Science* 530: 74–96.

Powdermaker, Hortense. 1939. *After Freedom: A Cultural Study of the Deep South.* New York: Viking Press.

Quillian, Lincoln. 1999. "Migration Patterns and the Growth of High-Poverty Neighborhoods, 1970–1990." *American Journal of Sociology* 105: 1–37.

Rodgers, Harrell, and Charles Bullock. 1972. *Law and Social Change: Civil Rights Laws and Their Consequences.* New York: McGraw-Hill.

Roediger, David. 1991. *The Wages of Whiteness.* New York: Verso.

Rosenbaum, James, Nancy Fishman, Alison Brett, and Patricia Meaden. 1993. "Can the Kerner Commission's Housing Strategy Improve Employment, Education, and Social Integration for Low-Income Blacks?" *North Carolina Law Review* 71: 1519–56.

Roth, Philip. [1959] 1987. *Goodbye, Columbus.* New York: Vintage Books.

Rubin, Lillian. 1994. *Families on the Fault Line.* New York: HarperCollins.

Sacks, Karen. [1994] 1996. "How Did Jews Become White Folks?" In *Race,* edited by Stephen Gregory and Roger Sanjek. New Brunswick, N.J.: Rutgers University Press.

Saltman, Juliet. 1990. *A Fragile Movement: The Struggle for Neighborhood Stabilization.* New York: Greenwood Press.

Schneider, Mark, and Thomas Phelan. 1993. "Black Suburbanization in the 1980s." *Demography* 30: 269–79.

Schudson, Michael. 1989. "How Culture Works." *Theory and Society* 18: 153–80.

Schuman, Howard, Charlotte Steeh, and Lawrence Bobo. 1985. *Racial Attitudes in America.* Cambridge, Mass.: Harvard University Press.

Sennett, Richard, and Jonathan Cobb. 1972. *The Hidden Injuries of Class.* New York: Vintage Books.

Shapiro, Margaret, and Michel McQueen. 1983. "An Elusive Goal: After Five Years, P.G. Homeowners Still Await Benefits from Tax Revolt." *Washington Post,* August 16.

Shapiro, Thomas. 2004. *The Hidden Cost of Being African American.* New York: Oxford University Press.

Sigelman, Lee, and Stephen Tuch. 1997. "Metastereotypes: Blacks' Perceptions of Whites' Stereotypes of Blacks. *Public Opinion Quarterly* 61: 87–101.

Sigelman, Lee, and Susan Welch. 1991. *Black Americans' Views of Racial Inequality.* New York: Cambridge University Press.

Simpson, Andrea. 1998. *The Tie That Binds: Identity and Political Attitudes in the Post–Civil Rights Generation.* New York: New York University Press.

Smith, Sandra, and Mignon Moore. 2000. "Intraracial Diversity and Relations among African-Americans: Closeness among Black Students at a Predominantly White University." *American Journal of Sociology* 106: 1–39.

Stack, Carol. 1996. *Call to Home: African Americans Reclaim the Rural South.* New York: Basic Books.

Storrs, Debbie. 1999. "Whiteness as Stigma: Essentialist Identity Work by Mixed-Race Women." *Symbolic Interaction* 22: 187–212.

Strauss, Anselm, and J. Corbin. 1998. *Basics of Qualitative Research.* Thousand Oaks, Calif.: Sage.

Sudnow, David. 1978. *Ways of the Hand: The Organization of Improvised Conduct.* New York: Harper & Row.

Swidler, Ann. 1986. "Culture in Action: Symbols and Strategies." *American Sociological Review* 51: 273–86.

———. 2001. *Talk of Love: How Culture Matters.* Chicago: University of Chicago Press.

Tatum, Beverly Daniel. 1997. *"Why Are All the Black Kids Sitting Together in the Cafeteria?" and Other Conversations about Race.* New York: Basic Books.

Taylor, Charles. 1989. *Sources of the Self.* Cambridge, Mass.: Harvard University Press.

Taylor, Monique. 2002. *Harlem: Between Heaven and Hell.* Minneapolis: University of Minnesota Press.

Thernstrom, Stephan, and Abigail Thernstrom. 1997. *America in Black and White.* New York: Simon and Schuster.

Thomas, G. Scott. 1998. *The United States of Suburbia: How the Suburbs Took Control of American and What They Plan to Do with It.* Amherst, N.Y.: Prometheus Books.

Thorne, Barrie. 1993. *Gender Play: Girls and Boys in School.* New Brunswick, N.J.: Rutgers University Press.

Tilly, Charles. 1998. *Durable Inequality.* Berkeley: University of California Press.

Tolnay, Stewart. 2003. "The African American 'Great Migration' and Beyond." *Annual Review of Sociology* 29: 209–32.

Turner, Bryan. 1988. *Status.* Philadelphia: Open University Press.

Turner, Margery Austin, and Stephen L. Ross. 2005. "How Racial Discrimination Affects the Housing Search." In *The Geography of Opportunity: Race and Housing Choice in Metropolitan America.* Edited by Xavier de Souza Briggs. Washington, D.C.: Brookings Institute.

Turner, Margery, R. Struyk, and J. Yinger. 1991. *Housing Discrimination Study.* Washington, D.C.: U.S. Dept. of Housing and Urban Development.

Vanneman, Reeve, and Lynn Cannon. 1987. *The American Perception of Class.* Philadelphia: Temple University Press.

Venkatesh, Sudhir. 1997. "The Social Organization of Urban Street Gang Activity." *American Journal of Sociology* 103: 82–111.

Walters, Pamela Barnhouse. 1999. "Education and Advancement: Exploring the Hopes and Dreams of Blacks and Poor Whites at the Turn of the Century." In *The Cultural Territories of Race: Black and White Boundaries,* edited by Michele Lamont. Chicago: University of Chicago Press.

Warren, Elizabeth, and Amelia Warren Tyagi. 2003. *The Two-Income Trap:*

Why Middle-Class Mothers and Fathers Are Going Broke. New York: Basic Books.

Washington Post. 1982. "Prince George's County Council." October 27.

Washington Post. 1983. "From TRIM to Pinch and Patch." September 8.

Waters, Mary. 1990. *Ethnic Options.* Berkeley: University of California Press.

———. 1999. *Black Identities.* Cambridge, Mass.: Harvard University Press and Russell Sage.

Waters, Mary, and Tomás Jiménez. 2005. "Assessing Immigrant Assimilation: Empirical and Theoretical Challenges." *Annual Review of Sociology* 31: 105–25.

Weber, Max. [1920] 1968. *Economy and Society.* Edited by G. Roth and C. Wittich. Berkeley: University of California Press.

Wellman, Barry. 1999. *Networks in the Global Village.* Boulder, Colo.: Westview Press.

Wienk, Ronald E. 1993. "Discrimination in Urban Credit Markets." *Housing Policy Debate* 3(2): 217–40.

Wiese, Andrew. "Places of Our Own: Suburban Black Towns before 1960." *Journal of Urban History* 19: 30–54.

Williams, Patricia. 1991. *Alchemy of Race and Rights.* Cambridge, Mass.: Harvard University Press.

Willie, Sarah. 2003. *Acting Black: College, Identity, and the Performance of Race.* New York: Routledge.

Willis, Paul. [1977] 1981. *Learning to Labor.* New York: Columbia University Press.

Wilson, Frank. 1995. "Rising Tide or Ebb Tide? Recent Changes in the Black Middle Class in the U.S., 1980–1990." *Research in Race and Ethnic Relations* 8: 21–55.

Wilson, William J. 2000. "All Boats Rise. Now What?" *New York Times*, April 12.

———. 1979. *The Declining Significance of Race.* Chicago: University of Chicago Press.

———. 1987. *The Truly Disadvantaged.* Chicago: University of Chicago Press.

———. 1996. *When Work Disappears.* New York: Knopf.

———. 2000. "Rising Inequality and the Case for Coalition Politics." *Annals of the American Academy of Political and Social Science* 568: 78–99.

Winddance Twine, France. 1996. "Brown-Skinned White Girls: Class, Culture and the Construction of White Identity in Suburban Communities." *Gender, Place, and Culture* 3: 205–24.

———. 2004. "A White Side of Black Britain: The Concept of Racial Literacy." *Ethnic and Racial Studies* 27: 878–907.

Wolff, Edward. [1996] 2002. *Top Heavy: The Increasing Inequality of Wealth in American and What Can Be Done about It.* New York: New Press.

Woodward, C. Vann. 1974. *The Strange Career of Jim Crow.* New York: Oxford University Press.

Wrigley, Julia. 1999. "Is Racial Oppression Intrinsic to Domestic Work?" In *The Cultural Territories of Race,* edited by Michele Lamont. Chicago: University of Chicago Press.

Wynter, Leon. 1982. "TRIM Vote Forcing P.G. Schools to Take Hard Look at Education." *Washington Post,* November 8.

Yin, Sandra. 2001. "Southern Comfort." *Forecast* 21: 1–4.

Yinger, John. 1995. *Closed Doors, Opportunities Lost: The Continuing Costs of Housing Discrimination.* New York: Russell Sage.

Yinger, Milton. 1981. "Toward a Theory of Assimilation and Dissimilation." *Ethnic and Racial Studies* 4: 249–64.

Young, Alford. 1999. "Navigating Race: Getting Ahead in the Lives of 'Rags to Riches' Young Black Men." In *The Cultural Territories of Race: Black and White Boundaries,* edited by Michele Lamont. Chicago: University of Chicago Press.

Index

Abelson, Robert, 88
Adelman, Robert, 22, 240n39
affirmative action, 90
Alana (Lakeview resident), 126; on chil-
    dren's racial identity, 170, 171, 172;
    on class boundaries, 181, 182; inter-
    actions with whites, 83–84; on pub-
    lic schools, 216; on welfare recipi-
    ents, 118–19; on workplace
    discrimination, 99
Alba, Richard, 44
alliance formation, 19. *See also* cross-
    racial alliances
Amara (Sherwood Park child), 167
Amber (Riverton child), 142–43
American Apartheid (Massey and Den-
    ton), 100, 251n25
American Missionary Association, 28
ancestry, black class structure and, 23–
    26, 24–26
Anderson, Benedict, 251n22
Anderson, Elijah: on class boundaries,
    177; middle-class black identity as
    formulated by, 13; on poor black
    parents, 7; on middle-class black
    status indicators, 38–39, 93, 235n7;
    on workplace cultural resources,
    72–73
Andrea (Sherwood Park resident), 1–2,
    104, 134, 138, 188, 249n11
Andrew (white Sherwood Park resident),
    67–68, 189, 194–95, 232
apartment rental, 126, 133–34, 239n34
Architectural Forum, 243n6

assimilation: segmented, 150–51; struc-
    tural, xiii–xiv. *See also* integration
assimilation, strategic: authentic black-
    ness and, 153–57; black/white
    worlds and, 157–58, 158 table 4;
    class-based identities and, 152–53,
    158; defined, 151, 153; race-based
    identities and, 151–52, 157–58, 226;
    racial dualism and, 172–73; regional
    diversity in, 159
Atlanta (GA), xiii, 44, 156
Audrey (Lakeview resident): on class
    boundaries, 180–81; on housing dis-
    crimination, 103, 104, 106–7, 111;
    on Lakeview, 59; "middle class" as
    defined by, 34; on welfare recipients,
    117–18, 119
authenticity, black, 153–57, 225
automobile industry, 243n16

bank loans, 242–43n6, 243–44n17
Barth, Fredrik, 9–10, 159, 165, 183
Baumgartner, M. P., 186
Baxandall, Rosalyn, 243n6
Bell, Ella, 247–48n37
biracial identity, 250n14
Black Bourgeoisie (Frazier), 6, 244n2,
    248n1
black communities: black preferences for,
    237–38n4; class boundaries in, 12;
    exclusionary boundary-work with,
    174–77; ideological vs. geographical,
    158 table 4; influence of suburban
    developers on, 17–18; middle-class

Text:	10/13 Sabon
Display:	Akzidenz Grotesk Condensed
Compositor:	Binghamton Valley Composition
Indexer:	Kevin Millham
Illustrator:	Bill Nelson
Printer and binder:	Maple-Vail Manufacturing Group